TAMERLANE

HAROLD LAMB

TIMUR. PAINTED DURING THE LIFE OF THE
GREAT AMIR, WHEN HE WAS ABOUT FIFTY
YEARS OF AGE. (*Martin*)

A STAR BOOK

TAMERLANE

The Earth Shaker

By
HAROLD LAMB

ILLUSTRATED

GARDEN CITY PUBLISHING COMPANY
GARDEN CITY, NEW YORK

DS
23
L3

Stechert .67 Oct '37 (carnegie)

14820

TAMERLANE

PRINTED IN THE UNITED STATES OF AMERICA

TO
MY FATHER

CONTENTS

Foreword

Part One

Part Two

viii CONTENTS

CONTENTS

TAMERLANE

"This is the resting place of the illustrious and merciful monarch, the most great Sultan, the most mighty Warrior, Lord Timur, conqueror of the Earth."

INSCRIPTION OVER THE DOOR OF THE ANTECHAMBER OF TAMERLANE'S TOMB IN SAMARKAND.

TAMERLANE

Foreword

THE ATTEMPT

FIVE HUNDRED AND FIFTY YEARS AGO a man tried to make himself master of the world. In everything he undertook he was successful. We call him Tamerlane.

In the beginning he was a gentleman of little consequence—master of no more than some cattle and land in that breeding ground of conquerors, Central Asia. Not the son of a king, as Alexander was, or the heir of a chieftain, like Genghis Khan. The victorious Alexander had at the outset his people, the Macedonians, and Genghis Khan had his Mongols. But Tamerlane gathered together a people.

One after the other, he overcame the armies of more than half the world. He tore down cities, and rebuilt them in the way he wished. Over his roads the caravan trade of two continents passed. Under his hands he gathered the wealth of empires, and spent it as he fancied. Out of mountain summits he made pleasure palaces—in a month. More, perhaps, than any human being within a life he attempted "To grasp this sorry Scheme of Things entire . . . and then, Remould it nearer to the heart's desire."

Tamerlane he was, and only as Tamerlane is he known to us to-day. In our general histories his empire

is called only Tamerlane's—although our ancestors of
five centuries ago spoke of it as Tatary. Vaguely they
knew him as a dominant and merciless figure, moving
beyond the gates of Europe among golden tents and
towers built of human skulls lighted at night by spirit
beacons.

Asia knew him well—both to its pride and its sorrow.
And there his enemies said that he was a great gray
wolf eating the earth; while his followers called him
lion and conqueror.

The blind Milton, pondering the legends of Tamerlane, seems to have drawn from them the somber colors
with which he painted the magnificence of his Satan.

And the fantasies of the poets have been followed by
the silence of the historians. Tamerlane could not
easily be classified. He was part of no dynasty—he
founded one; he was not, like Attila, one of the bar-
barians who harried Rome—out there in the limbo of
things he built a Rome of his own in the desert. He
made a throne for himself, but he spent most of his
years in the saddle of a horse. And when he built
he used no previous pattern of architecture; he made a
new one according to his own inclination, out of cliffs
and mountain peaks and a solitary dome that he saw
in Damascus before he burned that city. This swelling
dome of Tamerlane's fancy has become the *motif* of
Russian design, and is the crown of the Taj Mahal.
And the Taj Mahal was built by one of the Moghuls—
Tamerlane's great grandchildren.

History has dealt fully with the Europe of his day.
We know how Venice was dominated by the Council
of Ten, and how Rienzi became the Mussolini of that
time, a generation after the death of Dante. Petrarch
was writing then, and in France the Hundred Years'

War was dragging through its sterile course, while Orleanist and Burgundian wrangled with the butchers in Paris, under the indifferent eyes of the half-mad Charles the Sixth. Europe was young then, rousing from the darkness of the middle ages. Not yet had the fire of the Renaissance given it brilliance.

And Europe looked to the east for the luxuries of civilization—for linen and buckram and spice, for silk and iron and steel and china-ware. Silver and gold and precious stones came out of the east. By this over-land trade Venice and Genoa had grown great; Cordova and Seville in Spain had been built by the Arabs, and the palaces of Granada. Constantinople was half oriental.

There is to-day near a junction of the Trans-Siberian railway a stone obelisk bearing on one side the word Europa and on the other Asia. In Tamerlane's day this stone would have been placed some fifty degrees of longitude farther west, about in the suburbs of Venice. Europe proper would have been no more than a province of Asia. A province of barons and serfs where the cities as a rule were no more than hamlets and life—so says the chronicler—an affair of murmuring and misery.

We know the setting of the European scene of that century, but not the man who rose to dominate the world. To those Europeans Tamerlane's magnificence seemed unearthly and his power demoniac. When he appeared at their threshold, their kings sent letters and envoys to "Tamburlan the Great, Lord of Tatary."

Henry IV of England, who had fought beyond the border with the Prussian Knights, congratulated the unknown conqueror upon his victories; Charles VI, King of France, sent praise to "The most victorious and serene Prince, Themur." And the shrewd Genoese raised his standard outside Constantinople, while the Greek Emperor Manuel appealed to him for aid. The Lord Don Henry, by grace of God King of Castile, dispatched to Tamerlane as envoy the good knight Ruy de Gonzales Clavijo. And Clavijo, following the conqueror to Samarkand, returned to report in his own way who Tamerlane was.

"Tamerlane, Lord of Samarkand, having conquered all the land of the Mongols, and India; also having conquered the Land of the Sun, which is a great lord-ship; also having conquered and reduced to obedience the land of Kharesm; also having reduced all Persia and Media, with the empire of Tabriz and the City of the Sultan; also having conquered the Land of Silk, with the land of the Gates; and also having conquered Armenia the Less, and Erzerum, and the land of the Kurds—having conquered in battle the lord of India and taken a great part of his territory: also having destroyed the city of Damascus, and reduced the cities of Aleppo, of Babylon and Bagdad; and having overrun many other lands and lordships and won many battles, and achieved many conquests, he came against the Turk Bayazid (who is one of the greatest lords of the world) and gave him battle, conquering him and taking him prisoner."

Thus said Clavijo, who stood before Tamerlane and saw at his court of Samarkand princesses from the royal families of most of the world, and ambassadors from Egypt and China. He himself as envoy of the Franks was treated courteously because "even the smallest fish have their place in the sea."

In the European pageantry of kings, Tamerlane has been given no place; in the pages of history there is only a fleeting impression of the terror he aroused. But to the men of Asia he is still *The* Lord.

After five centuries it is clear to us that he was the last of the great conquerors. Napoleon and Bismarck are secure in their niches; we know the details of their lives. But the one died a failure, and the other triumphed in the political leadership of a single empire. Tamerlane created an empire, and was successful in every campaign he undertook; he died on the march toward the last power strong enough to oppose him.

To understand what he attempted we must look at the man as he lived. To do this it is necessary to put aside the histories of Europe, and close our eyes to modern civilization, with its prejudices. And to look at Tamerlane through the eyes of the men who rode at his side.

As Clavijo did, we must penetrate the veil of terror and go beyond the towers of human skulls, past Constantinople, and over the sea into Asia—along the highway of the Land of the Sun, on the road to Samarkand. The time is the year of Our Lord 1335.

The place is a river.

Part One

CHAPTER I

BEYOND THE RIVER

"I<small>T IS</small>," the good knight Clavijo said, "one of the four rivers that flow out of Paradise. And the country is very bright, gay and beautiful."

A cloudless sky overhead—blue ridges of mountains in the distance, rising to the snow peak that was called the Majesty of Solomon. The rolling foothills were covered with meadows, and the streams raced down still cold from the chill of the higher ranges. In these uplands sheep grazed, watched by the out-shepherds on shaggy ponies. Cattle clustered lower down in the lush grass of the glens near the villages.

The river twisted among masses of limestone. More sedately it flowed out into a long valley dark with mulberry trees and the tangle of vineyards. Channels led from it into fields of rice and melons and rolling barley—irrigation ditches where creaking wheels raised the water slowly.

They called the river the Amu. And it had been from time immemorable the border between Iran and Turan—between south and north. To the south lay Khorassan, the Land of the Sun where the Iranians spoke Persian and cultivated the soil. They were wearers of turbans, gentlefolk and beggars of elder Asia.

Beyond, to the north, lay Turan, out of the depths of which the nomads had come, the cattle breeding,

horse raising races—the helmeted men. Except for
the river, there was no frontier. The land to the north
of the river was called *Ma-vara'n-nahr*, Beyond the
River.

Hither, the traveler crossed the river, to go to
Samarkand. He threaded through gullies and a dense
oak forest and entered the maw of a gorge where ridged
sandstone walls rose six hundred feet overhead and
echoes mocked him. In the gloom of this red defile—
they called it the Iron Gate—in a place where no more
than two laden camels could pass, dark-faced men
leaned on their spears and looked at the travelers.

They were large men, with thin mustaches that fell
to their wide chins; they spoke slowly, drawling their
words; and they wore chain armor, their helmets
crested with horsetails, and they were the guards of
Tatary.

The first caravan *sarai* beyond the Iron Gate was a
fertile spot with a small river of its own, shut in by
hills. They had named it the Green City. Around
it ran a moat filled with water, and through the mesh
of blossoming fig and apricot trees uprose the white
domes of tombs, and spearlike minarets that served
also for watch towers.

In the Green City Tamerlane was born, and he loved
it. His home was a house of wood and unburned clay,
with a walled courtyard and a garden within the wall.
It had a flat roof with a parapet, where a boy could lie
unseen and listen at dusk to the muezzin's long call
to prayer, while the sheep and the cattle were driven
in from the fields.

Here, too, came bearded men in flaming silk robes
who spread their sleeping rugs and talked of caravans
and happenings, and always of war. For the shadow
of war lay over the valley of the Green City.

"*Erein mor nigen bui*"—Tamerlane heard this phrase often. "A man's path is only one."

He did not bother his head about it much—or the gravely intoned verses from the Koran. The words of the elder men were law, but the boys liked to watch their weapons, and speculate upon the cutting edge of a sheathed tulwar, or the meaning of a broken spear shaft.

These boys grew up among horses, and matched their steeds in the clover meadows across the Samarkand road. With their bows they hunted quail and foxes, and their trophies they kept in a castle of their own among rocks beneath the overhang of a cliff. Here they played at siege, while their dogs slept and the horses grazed. Tamerlane was the leader—he had no more than three or four companions—in this game of mimic war.

He was gravely purposeful in play, and he never laughed. Although his horses were not as good as some of the others, he was the best rider of his troupe. And when they were old enough to be given hunting swords, he soon established his mastery with the weapons.

Perhaps this seriousness was bred of his near-solitude. His mother died while he was young, and his father, a chieftain of the Barlas Tatars spent most of his hours in talk with the green turbaned holy men who had visited the shrines of Islam and gained sanctity thereby. The son had his falcons, his dogs and his companions. But there were only two servitors in the house, and the horses did not fill half the stable. The father was not a reigning chieftain; he came of a line of men distinguished in war, but he was poor.

The boy rode afield and sat much in his eyrie, looking at the Samarkand road. Down this highway rode cavalcades of wealthy Persians, with armed guards about their veiled women—the Tatar women did not veil. Lean Arab traders escorted horse trains, with loads of brocades from Cathay and raw silk and rugs from the northern looms. Moving through the yellow dust came also slave caravans, and beggars with staff and bowl, and holy men looking for disciples.

At times there appeared a Jew with his mules or a slender Hindu voicing tales of Afghan robbers. At the hour of dusk they raised their tents among the animals and the cook fires that smelled of dung and wormwood. And, kneeling and sitting back on his heels outside their circle, Tamerlane listened to their talk of prices and the world of Samarkand. When his father scolded him for sitting with the caravan men, he made answer.

"A man's path is only one."

CHAPTER II

THE HELMETED MEN

THE VALLEY and all in it was the heritage of the Barlas clan. It could not be said they owned it. The right of grazing and cultivating land, with its fat cattle, and vineyards and pastures was theirs so long as they could keep it. The Khan beyond the mountains had given it to their ancestors long since, and they held it as the clans of Scotland held their lands, by virtue of their swords and the craft and dignity of their chieftains. They were Tatars, long of limb and big of bone. Bearded, sun-scorched, they walked—when it was necessary to walk at all—with a swagger and without turning aside for any one, unless a Tatar greater than they.

They all kept strings of horses, rangy and long enduring, accustomed to the hills. Only a few were fortunate enough to own mounts of a swift-footed racing breed, or ponies trained on the polo field. Their reins were heavy with silver work and they had a liking for embroidered silk to cover the saddles. The poorest of these Tatars [1] would not have thought of going from his tent to the mosque without mounting his horse.

They held to their tents by choice, and by custom, and they said, "A coward builds a tower to hide in." But their tents were domes of white felt or carpeted

[1] Tamerlane's clansmen were called many things, including devils and mighty men of war. By common consent they are most often called Tatars, and the earliest of their chroniclers describes them so. They were one of the clans of high Asia that were named Scythians in the elder days, and sometimes Turks. With the Mongol Horde they had come from the northern plains to this fertile mountain land.

24

pavilions, and many of them had a residence of some kind in the city, where guests could be entertained or their women sheltered at need. A century ago the Tatars had been nomads in truth, searching the desert for pasturage. War had made their ancestors masters of most of Asia, and these men were children of war. They knew the truth of the saying:

"The sand of the desert is lightly blown away by a breath; still more lightly is the fortune of man destroyed."

Hugely they feasted, weeping over the wine cup, but they laughed in battle. Few of them did not have upon them the white scars of wounds. And few of them died under a roof. As a matter of course they went about in light armor—linked steel mail under flowing surcoats of striped silk. The instinct of the desert warfare was still in them.

Hunting was their passion, in the intervals of quiet, and they would part with their sheep and cattle for the trained falcons that the hillmen brought down to sell to them. A good hawk added to a man's dignity, but a golden eagle that could be flown at stag gave honor to a whole family. Some had hunting leopards that were carried blindfold upon the crupper of a saddle and loosed to stalk deer while the riders watched.

With the long, heavy bow they were expert, bringing down birds with double headed arrows, and going on foot against tigers. When they knelt on the carpet to eat, they dipped their fingers into a common pot, and their dogs sat behind them, while the hawks screamed from the perches. Game was their favorite dish, and horseflesh, and they had a weakness for the fare of the Arabs, the haunch of a camel.

They admired the chivalry of the Arabs, and like these nomads of the dry lands they were restless unless they were in the saddle, to raid or hunt or to join the standards of war. They spent most of their time away at the court of the King Maker.

The pride of the Barlas men was the pride of a military caste. Theirs was the aristocracy of the sword. To intermarry with Iranian merchants and farmers was to lose their race. As a consequence, being poor men of business, they were on the road to ruin.

They were unreasonably generous and equally unreasonably headstrong and cruel. Property they gave away or pawned, to pay for their banquets. Hospitality was their obligation, and their courtyards were packed with wayfarers, while their sheep progressed steadily into the pot.

Other men than the Barlas Tatars fared better in the valley of the Green City. Iranian peasants moved patiently between their irrigation ditches; Sarts, city dwellers, sat in the stalls of the market place; Persian nobles gambled and built pleasure gardens, and listened to the readers of the Koran. These wearers of the turban followed the law of the Koran, while the helmeted men still adhered to the law of Genghis Khan.

And the lot of the Barlas clan was all the worse because it had no chieftain. Taragai, once head of the clan, was a mild man full of his dignity. He had listened to the expounders of the law of Islam, and had withdrawn to a monastery to meditate—Taragai the father of Tamerlane. No one lived in the white clay palace outside the Green City.

"The world," Taragai told his son, "is no better than a golden vase filled with scorpions and serpents. I am tired of it."

Like many other fathers, he lectured to his son upon the glory and worth of his ancestors, who had been masters of the mountain ranges far in the north, above the Gobi desert. These were rare tales of pagan days, and Taragai in spite of his renunciation of the world seemed to enjoy the telling. He described hosts of riders living with their cattle, migrating with the snows, lying in wait along the caravan routes, and marching behind their horned standard to harry Cathay—tribal hunts that lasted for two or three moons, over five hundred miles of prairie. He told of the sacrifice of white horses at a chieftain's grave, and how the horses went through the gate of the sky— where the northern lights flamed—to serve the spirits in the world beyond the sky.

He named princesses of Cathay who were sent as brides to the desert Khans, with wagon loads of silk and carved ivory, and he described how victorious Khans drank mare's milk from the skull of their enemies plated with gold.

"So it was, my son," he explained often, "until the day when Genghis Khan led his Mongols to the conquest of the world. It was written that this should be. And when the dark angel stood over Genghis Khan and he died, he divided the world into four empires among his sons and the son of his eldest who died before him.

"To his son Chagatai he gave the empire of this part, where we dwell. But the children of Chagatai gave themselves to wine and hunting. In time they withdrew to the mountains of the north. And there, now, the Khan, the *tura*, feasts and hunts, leaving the government of Samarkand and all Beyond the River to the lord who is called the King Maker. The rest thou knowest.

"But, O my son," he ended, sadly shaking his head, "I would not have thee depart from the path of the law of God, whose messenger is Muhammad (upon

the uncle of Timur, who was seldom at the Green City. The Hadji, who had made the pilgrimage to Mecca, had no interest at all in Timur. He was suspicious and impetuous and gloomy, and under him the fortunes of the clan went from bad to worse.

Most of the nobles and warriors drifted away to serve the King Maker. And there also Timur went, at his father's advice.

CHAPTER III

THE KING MAKER OF SALI SARAI

A T THIS TIME TIMUR—we cannot very well call him Tamerlane—was a young gentleman of leisure. And leisure with Timur meant activity. He was powerful in body, a fine physique, wide-shouldered, long-limbed. His head was large and splendidly poised—a high forehead and full dark eyes that moved slowly and looked directly at a man. He had the broad cheek bones and wide sensitive mouth of his race, evidences of the vitality in him. The energy in him was little less than ferocious. A youth of few words, a deep and penetrating voice. He had no love of foolery and in all his life he never appreciated a jest.

We are given a glimpse of him riding down a deer with his companions over the open plain in winter. Timur was in the lead when his horse came to a gully that was both wide and deep. Timur tried to turn the horse, and, failing, kneed him forward to the jump. His mount did not quite clear the gully, and slipped back with his hind feet, while the young Tatar kicked himself loose from the stirrups and swung to safety. The horse fell and was disabled—Timur going around the gully to his companions and mounting a led horse.

Light began to fail, and the riders turned back. Darkness and a heavy rain soon lost them in the open steppe. They were suffering from cold when they passed some black mounds that looked like tents. "They are sand hills," said Timur's companions. The son of Taragai threw his reins on the horse's neck and

gripped the mane. The pony stretched his neck and
neighed, so Timur turned toward the mounds, and
presently a light was seen, and the shapes in the rain
disclosed themselves as black felt tents.

At once the young Tatars were assailed by the dogs
and men who believed them to be raiders as a matter
of course.

"Nay, ye people of the tents," Timur cried, "I am
the son of Taragai."

Weapons were put away and hospitality extended—
broth heated up in the pot over the fire, and quilts
spread in a dry spot for the guests. The fleas in the
quilts banished slumber, and Timur abandoned the
coverlets, to stir up the fire and tell stories, his hosts
coming forth to listen until daylight and the end of the
storm. Years later Timur sent reward to the family
of the black tents.

In this early world of Islam hospitality was an obligation to be accepted as such and returned only in kind.
The Tatars were great wanderers, and Timur had the
freedom of every tent and courtyard from Samarkand
to the Land of the Sun. With his handful of companions he might travel a thousand miles in a fort-
night, through the mountain tracks or down along the
desert's edge—carrying nothing more with him than
his sword and a light hunting bow. The Arabs of the
caravan camps talked to him, being honored by the
presence of a chieftain's son; hillmen, washing river
gravel for particles of gold, told him their legends
and gossip of their horses and women of other clans;
he played chess with the barons of the clans in their
citadels.

"The King Maker of Sali Sarai has asked for thee,"
they said.

Timur had taken thought for the remnants of his

father's possessions. The sheep he divided up into flocks, giving them to the care of herders whose pay was a fourth of the milk, the butter and the wool. The goats, horses and camels were cared for in the same way. No other property is mentioned.

With him Timur took the best of the string of horses, and a boy—Abdullah, born in his own house— to serve him. And with this escort he rode south through the foothills toward the great river Amu. So might a youthful esquire-at-arms have traveled to the court of his king, in Norman England—except that no squire of Christiandom rode clad in soft shagreen boots and a high crowned white felt hat, bordered with sable, and a coat-robe of dressed horsehide with wide flaps over the shoulders, girdled with a heavy leather belt ornamented with silver work and turquoise. And few youths of England were so utterly alone as Timur, his mother dead, his father in a monastery and his kinsmen more than ready to become his enemies. An adventurer, he joined the camp of warriors without a king.

"Instead of religion," Kazgan the King Maker told him, bluntly, "brothers." [1]

There were many eyes to watch him—to judge his horsemanship, the way he handled his sword in the bouts that would have hazarded his life if he had not been sure of his blade. Taragai had been a chieftain, and Timur was his only son.

And in Sali Sarai, where two thousand Tatars— lords, youths and warriors—encamped in the forests, no one thought of teaching Timur anything. He had to find out for himself, and find out he did.

---

[1] *"Din ayiri, Kardash"*—"Religious faith aside, brothers." They spoke Turki, but their written language was the Mongol-Uighur of Central Asia, now vanished. Most of them including Timur knew a good deal of Arabic —the Latin of Asia.

One of the horse guards galloped in with the tidings that raiders had come over the border and were driving off horses. Kazgan the Amir called Timur to him and ordered the scion of the house of Barlas to go with a company of the younger men and bring back the horses. Timur rose at once—he had been sitting with the Amir's men—and set out. It was a task that delighted him, a mounting of horses and a swift dash for half a day along the tracks of the invaders.

They proved to be Persians from the west, and they had gathered up plunder on the way, putting it into packs on the captured horses. At sight of the Tatars they divided into two parties, one remaining with the pack animals, the other advancing toward the pursuers. Timur's companions advised him to attack the baggage train.

"Nay," he said, "if we overcome the fighting men, the others will flee."

The raiders stood their ground long enough to exchange a few sword cuts with the helmeted men, but they knew themselves outmatched and scattered. Timur escorted back the horses and gear to their owners, and Kazgan praised him, rewarding the young Barlas warrior with his own bow case.

Thereafter Kazgan the King Maker liked the son of Taragai and began to show him favor.

"Thou art of the family of the Gurigan, the Splendid," he said, "but thou art *not* a *tura*, a descendant of the family of Genghis Khan. Before thy life, the ancestor of thy house Kayouli made an agreement with Kabul Khan, the ancestor of the house of Genghis. The agreement was that the offspring of Kayouli should be leaders and commanders of the army, while the house of Kabul should rule as Khans.

It was so said between them, and it was written on steel and the steel is kept in the archives of the great Khans. Thy father has said this to me and it is true."

And he added thoughtfully. "Surely my path has been only one. I have drawn my reins to the path of war, and I have not turned aside from the struggle. Now men follow me, and my name is glorious. That is the one path, and there is no other."

This Timur knew. He knew also that Chagatai the son of Genghis Khan had ruled all that portion of the earth including the lands of the Afghans to the south and the vaster mountain ranges behind the Majesty of Solomon. In the hundred years since then the children of Chagatai's line had loosened their grip on their heritage; individual Tatar clans had become virtually rulers of their own provinces and the Khans had retired to the north to hunt and drink, until now they only appeared near the Green City to pillage and carry off what struck their fancy under pretext of putting down a revolt.

Kazgan had been the amir, the commander, of such a Khan, and had made Samarkand his residence, until he tired of watching disastrous raids and had dared rebel against the Khan. Long and bitter fighting followed, ending in the death of the Khan, and leaving Kazgan lord in reality of Samarkand and the provinces of the Barlas and other Tatar clans. To fulfill the law of Genghis Khan, and to satisfy these warriors who now looked to him for leadership, he had called a council and elected a descendant of the royal line Khan of Samarkand—a puppet king, fed and protected by Kazgan and good-naturedly indifferent to other matters. Thus was Kazgan called the King Maker.

Like Timur, he was of a small family, not a *tura* of the royal blood of Genghis Khan. Audacious, he had made alliances; just and upright, he had enforced the respect of the restless Tatars. He was blind in one eye from an arrow wound. After the great stroke of his rebellion, he devoted himself to hunting and only lifted the standard of war at need. He could not feel certain of the support of the Tatar clans, and he saw in Timur a chieftain's son who could aid him greatly.

Other amirs of the King Maker's court had interests of their own. They gave tribute and the outward show of loyalty to Kazgan's puppet on the throne of Samarkand, but they had all shared in Kazgan's successful revolt. Some of them could muster ten thousand riders to their standards, and only Kazgan's sagacity kept the reins of power in his hands.

He noticed that Timur was a favorite of the *bahaturs,* the men among the Tatars who had won a name for valor. They were the berserks of the clans who went to battle as if to a feast, and Taragai's son took his place among them as if by right. He went off with them on raids and they returned, to sit on Kazgan's carpet and tell tales of his recklessness and daring.

It seemed that there was in Timur a spark of sheer eagerness that made him love a risk for the sake of its danger. But, more than that, in a crisis Timur remained quiet and thoughtful. "A breeder of action," the *bahaturs* said. His overflowing physical energy made light work of long rides and sleepless nights. Timur had the qualifications of leadership, and he liked to lead. And he was overconfident—too full of his own strength. He asked Kazgan for the headship of the scattered Barlas clan.

"Wilt thou not wait?" the King Maker, who did not at all approve the suggestion, made answer. "It will be thine, some time or other."

After a while it occurred to Kazgan to give Timur a wife. And he chose one of his granddaughters, who was also of the reigning family of another clan.

CHAPTER IV

THE LORD'S LADY

THE CHRONICLE tells us of Timur's bride that her beauty was like the young moon, and her body graceful as the young cypress. She must have been about fifteen years of age, because she had been allowed to ride to the hunts with her father. Her name was, hereafter, Aljai Khatun Agha—the Lord's Lady Aljai.

At that time the women of the Tatars went unveiled. They knew nothing as yet of the seclusion of *harim*, sanctuary. In the saddle, from an early age, they accompanied their lords through the varying fortunes of journey and campaign and pilgrimage. Being children of conquerors they had their share of pride, and the vitality that comes from life in open country. Their great-grandmothers had had the care of all the family property, including the milking of camels and the making of boots.

The Tatar women of Timur's day had property of their own—marriage portions and gifts of their lords. Wives of the greater nobles were mistresses of separate establishments, having quarters to themselves in the palaces and individual groups of pavilions on the march. Unlike their sisters of Europe they did not occupy themselves with the embroidery frame or the tapestry or rug loom. They were companions of warriors, their duty the care of their young children; they took their place at the banquets of rejoicing, and, if their lord's enemies prevailed over him, they were part of the spoils of defeat.

Princess Aljai came down from her home on the

northern border escorted by her kinsmen and slaves.
She presented herself before the King Maker, and
there for the first time she saw the face of the man
who was to be her master—the lean and bearded face
of Timur who had come in from an excursion with the
bahaturs to be present at his wedding.

"Thy fate is written upon thy forehead," the learned
men had said to her, "and alter it thou canst not."

For the King Maker and his lords the wedding was
simply an occasion for feasting, but for this daughter
of the powerful Jalair clan it was the first day of her
destiny. She was not present when the agreement was
read before the Muhammadan judges and the names
of witnesses written down, as the Koran ordained.

Her preparations were otherwise. She bathed in
rose water, and her long, dark tresses were washed
first in oil of sesame then in hot milk until they
gleamed as softly as silk. Then she was dressed in a
gown of pomegranate red, embroidered with gold
flowers. The gown was sleeveless, like the over-robe
of white silk stiffened with cloth-of-silver—the robe
that, trailing behind her, was borne in the hands of her
women.

Over her slender shoulders fell the mass of black
hair. Black jade pendants hung from her ears, and
her head was made splendid by a cap of gold cloth, silk
flowers covering its crown, and heron's plumes sweeping back upon her hair.

So clad, Aljai advanced among the carpets where
sat the Tatars—for the moment the girl drew their
eyes. And again when she changed her dress and came
back in different colors. Even her clear olive skin was
tinted white with rice powder or white lead. A blue-
black line was drawn over and between her eyebrows
with woad juice.

While the men mixed spirits with their wine to get drunk the quicker and Aljai walked between them, impassive of face, erect and frightened, the King Maker scattered fistfuls of pearls among the throng, and at his summons the *nakars* thundered—the bronze-bound saddle drums that were the summons to rejoicing or war.

"Upon the twain," cried Zain ad-Din, "be the peace of God, the one God!"

It was then the hour for gifts, not to the bride but to the assembled Tatars. Kazgan rose and went from group to group, his slaves carrying *khalats*, court coats. To some were given scimitars, to others girdles of price. For Kazgan, a Tatar of the old stock, was no niggard. And, besides, he knew the advantage to himself of mutual good-will.

While the nobles and warriors lay, contented and more than a little drowsy, on the carpets in the sun-flecked shade of the oak and willow groves, story tellers came and squatted among them. Guitars strummed plaintively, and mellow voices recited well remembered tales—the listeners marking with appreciative ear the familiar inflections and gestures. They knew the stories as well as the tellers and would have felt cheated if a phrase had been altered or left out of the interminable, droning narratives. From time to time, remembering their manners, they gulped loudly, to show their appreciation of the feast.

Daylight faded and slaves appeared bearing torches. Lanterns were hung along the bank of the river and under the trees. Fresh leather platters of food were laid among the guests who exclaimed gutturally at the sight of smoking quarters of young lamb, and haunches of horses and barley cakes soaked in honey.

Once more Aljai passed among them, this time not

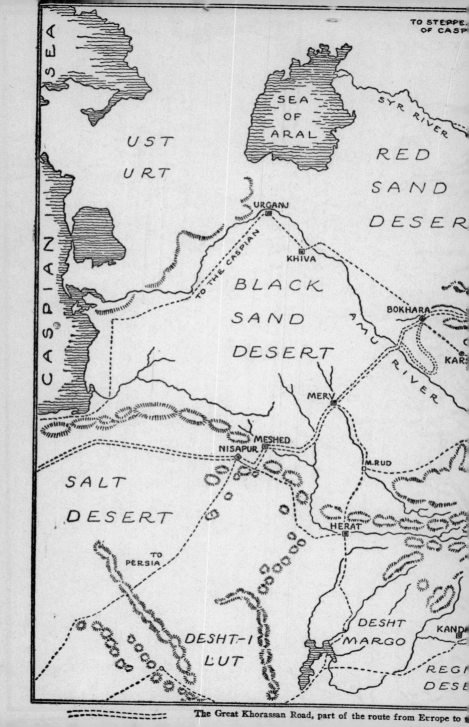

The Great Khorassan Road, part of the route from Errope to

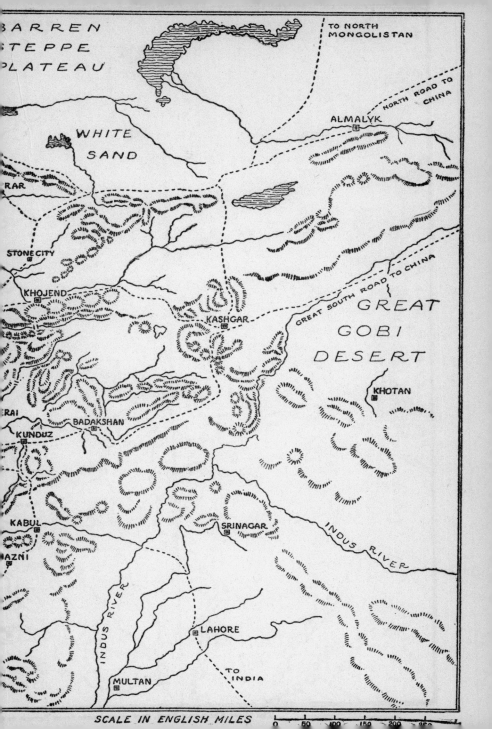

to return. Timur led a white Arab charger over the carpets, a smooth paced horse of racing blood, silk caparisoning hanging over its saddle down to the ground. Upon the charger he lifted Aljai, and led her away to his own pavilion.

Here, apart from the guests, her women had come to help her out of her head-dress and train. With them they had brought the chests of her belongings. They smiled when they felt her trembling under their hands when they took from the girl her outer robe, leaving her standing in her slippers and in the sleeveless gown and the heavy veil of her long hair.

They salaamed to the young lord who came into the pavilion silently. He had eyes only for Aljai, and the serving women withdrew. Timur's few followers, who had assembled at the tent entrance to salute their mistress, now closed the curtain and went off to their quarters.

That night Aljai, lying in the young warrior's arms, heard above the distant rush of the river and the murmur of voices the harsh thunder of the drums.

She was the first of Timur's possessions. She did not live long, but while she lived no other woman shared her place at Timur's side.

There is no doubt that from his twentieth to his twenty-fourth year Messire Timur found life very good indeed. He made a home for Aljai out of a wing of the tenantless white clay palace of the Green City. He adorned the dwelling after his own taste, with the carpets, the silver and tapestry work that was the fruit of his soldiering. His father gave him the family cattle and pasture rights.

Amir Kazgan appointed him *Ming-bashi*, commander of a thousand—colonel of a regiment, we would say. And Timur rejoiced in his thousand, feeding them well, and never sitting down to a meal without some of them at his side. In his girdle he carried a list of their names. Kazgan, a judge of warriors, allowed Timur and his thousand to lead the advance of the army.

Often along the Samarkand road Timur would ride to his home a day ahead of the main body, the white dust rising about his horses in the moonlight, to greet Aljai and to make ready a feast for the lords that came behind him. He relished the splendor of these banquets in the water garden of the Green City. When Aljai bore him a son, Timur named the boy Jahangir—the World Gripper—and summoned all the amirs of the King Maker to a festival. They rode in to honor Timur—except his uncle Hadji Barlas, and Amir Bayazid Jalair, ruler of his wife's clan.

"Truly," said the guests, "Timur is a son of the Gurigan, the Splendid."

And the wild hill clans that had served Aljai's fathers made up songs about the master and the mistress of the Green City.

Aided by Timur's daring, Kazgan gained new victories in the western desert and the southern valleys, bringing back to Sali Sarai the Malik of Herat as captive. He had profited much from the unselfish service of the young Barlas warrior, and together they might have continued to grow in power, when a new dissension broke out among Kazgan's amirs.

They demanded that the captive Malik be put to death and his personal property divided among them. Kazgan had given his word to the Malik that he should come to no harm, and when the amirs grew more insistent—the Malik was an old foeman and wealthy—Kazgan secretly warned his prisoner, and freed him when they were hunting south of the river on the way to Herat. It is not clear whether Timur was sent, as one account has it, to escort the Malik back to Herat.

In any case he was absent when his protector Kazgan was put to death. The King Maker was indulging his fondness for hunting, and was still south of the river unarmed with a few followers, when two chieftains who cherished a grievance against him attacked Kazgan and shot him down with arrows.

Timur heard of it and rode up in time to carry the body back across the river, and bury it in the forest of Sali Sarai.

Then, before trying to protect his own possessions, he swam his horse again south over the Amu river to join the officers of the King Maker who were pursuing the murderers into the mountains. One of the oldest of the traditions of the Tatars was that a man should not sleep under the same sky with the slayer of his kin. The two chieftains who had struck down Kazgan did not live long.

Hunted from ravine to heights, changing horses at each village, they could not shake off the Tatars who followed their tracks and cut off the avenues of escape. The murderers were caught on the upper slopes of the mountains and their lives ended in a swift flashing of swords. This done, Timur hastened back to his own valley. He found a new order of things.

When a ruler died in mid-Asia, his son might take the throne only if the late chieftain had left a well founded dominion and the son were able enough to hold it for himself; otherwise, at best, there would be a council of the great vassals and a new ruler chosen. At the worst—more often than not—there would be a general struggle for the throne and the strongest would seize it. They had a proverb, these helmeted men—

"Only a hand that can grasp a sword may hold a scepter."

Kazgan's son made a brief attempt to take the reins of authority in hand at Samarkand, but soon fled, preferring life to dignity. Then Hadji Barlas and the Jalair prince appeared at Samarkand and claimed the overlordship of the Tatars.

Meanwhile the other amirs retired to their various citadels and mustered their warriors to the standards, preparing to defend their own possessions and raid their neighbors. It was the old weakness of the Tatars—clan struggling with clan for mastery. With one accord they would have followed a leader strong enough to whip them into place. But Kazgan had fallen in his blood, and Hadji Barlas and Bayazid Jalair were not the men to bridle these unruly spirits.

In such a time of trouble Taragai, the father of Timur, died in his monastery. Most of the Barlas men had followed the Hadji to Samarkand. Timur was left solitary in the Green City with a few hundred warriors.

And then, having watched events from behind his mountains, the great Khan of the north appeared upon the scene. He came, remembering the rebellion of a generation ago, with a powerful host—as vultures flock together upon a fallen horse.

CHAPTER V

TIMUR, DIPLOMAT

At the coming of the Khan, the Tatar amirs drew back before the common peril. Except that Bayazid Jalair, whose city of Khojend was the northern gateway of all their lands and in the path of the invaders, hastened back to his people and offered gifts and submission to the Khan.

Hadji Barlas proved as irresolute as he had been impulsive before. He summoned all the fighting men of the clan from around the Green City and Karshi—upon the death of Taragai he claimed undisputed leadership of the clan. Then he changed his mind about fighting and sent to Timur word that he would withdraw with the people and cattle towards Herat in the south.

But Timur was not willing to leave the Green City masterless in the path of the northerners. "Go whither thou wilt," he said to his uncle. "I will ride to the court of the Khan."

He knew that the Khan of the north, lord of the Jat Mongols—the Border Mongols—had come down into the fertile lands of Samarkand to reassert his old rights, but with an inclination to plunder. And Timur meant, somehow, to keep the marauders out of his valley. Aljai and her infant son he sent to the court of her brother who was advancing from the mountains of Kabul. He might have gone with her and found safety in this way. To resist with his few hundreds the army of the Jat Mongols twelve thousand strong would have been idle folly. His father and the King Maker had both warned him not to yield to this Khan of the north, who might be expected to put the Tatar princes to death and install his own officers in their place. But after all the Khan was Timur's titular prince—the ruler of his ancestors.

There seemed to be nothing that Timur could do. His clan, the chronicler says, was like an eagle without wings. Fear and uncertainty reigned in the Green City. For days warriors fled down the Samarkand road with the best of their horses and their women. Others, who had determined to stay with their possessions, observed that Timur was tranquil and hurried to him to pledge allegiance and so make claim upon his protection.

"The friends of an hour of need are not true friends," he said. He would have none of that. A motley and numerous following would only have afforded the Khan an excellent reason for attacking him.

Instead, he made certain preparations. With all due honor he placed the body of his father in the burial ground of the holy men at the Green City. He went then to his spiritual counselor the wise Zain ad-Din, and talked with him through the night. What passed between them we do not know, but Timur began to gather together the best of his movable possessions— horses of a racing breed, silver ornamented saddles, and above all gold and jewels of all kinds. Probably Zain ad-Din opened to him the coffers of the Church, because the northern Khan was the lineal foe of the law and the leaders of Islam.

At once the Jat Mongols appeared. Scouts on shaggy hill ponies rode down the Samarkand road, long tufted lances gleaming on their shoulders, their led ponies already well loaded with loot. Bands of riders followed, moving through the fields of ripe wheat, grazing their horses as they advanced. The officer commanding the scouts made for the white palace, and was astonished when Timur, youthful and undisturbed, greeted him as a guest.

Timur gave a feast for the Jat officer, slaughtering sheep and cattle with a lavish hand. And the officer, reduced to the status of a guest, could only eye longingly the assembled possessions of his young host. He could not allow his men to loot but he demanded extravagant gifts, and Timur satisfied even his avarice.

Then Timur announced his intention of going to the Khan. With him he took a cavalcade of his own followers in court dress, and all his remaining wealth. Near Samarkand he encountered two other Jat officers with the advance guard of the army. They were both insolent and eager for gold, and Timur gave them more than even their greed had hoped for.

Beyond Samarkand he came to the *ordu* or royal encampment of the Khan, Tugluk.

Between horse herds and lines of tethered camels white felt tents covered the plain. The wind stirred the long horsetails of the standards and raised a dust of dried sheep's droppings. Here the warriors were robed in barbaric splendor, in the flowered satins of China, their high boots resplendent with gold embroidery, and their wooden saddles covered with the softest shagreen. The long lance and the nomad's bow were their favorite weapons—deadly weapons in their hands.

Tugluk sat on a white felt by his standard—a broad-faced Mongol with high cheek bones and little, shifting eyes, and a thin beard. A suspicious soul, a magnificent plunderer, and a dour fighter. Timur, dismounting in front of the half circle of Jat nobles, found himself

before the likeness of his own ancestors. In due form
he went through the *karnash*, the greeting to his prince.

"O Father, my Khan, Lord of the *Ordu*," he said,
"I am Timur chieftain of the Barlas men and of the
Green City."

The Khan was struck by his fearlessness, by the rich-
ness of his silver inlaid mail. Timur boasted when he
announced himself leader of the Barlas warriors—who
were mostly fleeing with Hadji Barlas. But it was
no time for half-titles. And his gifts to the Khan
were magnificent. It was apparent even to the avaricious nomads that he kept nothing for himself, and
the Khan conceived a liking for him.

"I would have had more to lay before thee, O my
Father," Timur asserted boldly, "but three dogs, thy
officers, have fed their greed with my goods."

This was pure inspiration, and Tugluk Khan began
to ponder how much wealth had escaped him. He
ended by sending couriers in haste to the three offending officers with orders to restore what they had taken
from Timur. True, Tugluk bade them send the gifts
to Hadji Barlas, but this was because he wanted to
claim everything himself from the Hadji—he could
not very well take more from Timur.

"They are dogs," he assented, "but they are my
dogs, and by Allah their greed is like a hair upon my
eyeball or a splinter in my flesh."

Had Machiavelli known these children of the
steppes, he might well have written another book.
Deception was an accomplishment with them, and intrigue a fine art. They were a fighting race, but so
long accustomed to warfare that they only took up
weapons as a last resource. Timur made more than
a few friends in the encampment of Tugluk.

"The princes of Samarkand," said the Jats. "are

scattered like quail under the shadow of a hawk. Only Timur is here, and he is a man of sense. We should conciliate him and rule through him."

They did nothing for the moment because the three officers, suspecting that the Khan would strip them of their property by way of punishment, banded together and made off towards their own lands pillaging as they went. Arriving at the northern border they proceeded to raise armies and stir up strife in the absence of the Khan. Tugluk hesitated and asked advice of Timur, who seemed to be full of resource.

"Go to thy lands," Timur urged him, with all gravity. "There thou wilt find only one peril. Here, thou wilt find two—one before thee and one behind."

The Khan withdrew to his own country to punish the rebels. Before doing so he appointed Timur *Tuman-bashi*—Commander of Ten Thousand—giving him a written authority and a seal. This was the dignity held by Timur's fathers in the old régime of the Mongols.

Timur had saved his valley and its cities from devastation, and he had now the Khan's appointment as head of his own clan. And, with the lifting of the mutual peril, the Tatar princes returned to their feuds with alacrity. The next three years are a vista of kaleidoscopic changes.

Hadji Barlas and the Jalair chieftain again joined forces and decided to eliminate Timur by killing him. They invited the young warrior to their pavilions. But when he found armed men sitting with the princes he scented treachery. Pretending that he was troubled with a sudden nose bleed he went on through the inner compartments until he reached his own followers. They went at once to the horses and made off. Bayazid

Jalair afterwards felt ashamed of the plot and expressed regret to Timur. But the Hadji was a dour soul. He marched upon the Green City to take possession of the valley.

Timur was in no mood to give it up, especially now when he had the Khan's grant in his pocket and several thousand men at his back. He mustered his followers and the armies of nephew and uncle skirmished briefly on the Samarkand road—Hadji Barlas withdrawing suddenly toward the great city. Elated, Timur followed him up. But the next day nearly all his followers deserted him to go over to the Hadji, who had prevailed upon them to join the main body of the clan.

Timur then rode off to ally himself with Amir Hussayn, the brother of Aljai, who had come over with his mountain clans and Afghans from the region of Kabul. This fighting between the clans went on [1] until Tugluk appeared again, "Like a stone dropping among birds."

This time his mood was sterner. He had decided to reconquer everything, and he put to death Bayazid Jalair at once. Hadji Barlas fled again with his men to the south but lost his life soon after at the hands of thieves. Amir Hussayn dared meet the Jat horde in the field and was soundly trounced and forced to flee for his life. Timur stood his ground at the Green City.

Tugluk Khan sated with victory left his son Ilias as ruler of the Tatar countries, with the Jat general Bikijuk to see that he was obeyed. The Khan named

[1] This warfare in the heart of Central Asia is an old story, and is very much the same to-day. On a modern map, the lands of the Tatar princes would include Afghanistan above Kabul and the northeast portion of Persia, all of Bokhara and Transcaucasia and most of Russian Turkestan. At least a hundred thousand men were under arms, but to give details of the strife would require a whole book. Only the thread of Timur's adventures is followed here. Between 1360 and 1369 he was occupied incessantly in the civil wars of the Tatars.

Timur prince of Samarkand, under the two Jats. This was dignity enough, and a shrewd brain might have found in it opportunity to gain goods and power.

Timur protested being placed under the authority of the northerners, but the Khan reminded him of the agreement between their ancestors—that the family of Genghis Khan should rule, and the family of the Gurigan should serve. "Thus it was said between thy forefather Kayouli and my ancestor Kabul Khan." An agreement made by one of his family Timur held to be binding upon himself. Angered, he tried to make the best of things in the Green City.

But the Jat general Bikijuk proceeded to ravage all of Samarkand and Prince Ilias was more than satisfied with plunder. Timur heard that the girl children of Samarkand had been sent off as slaves, with the venerable *sayyids* as captives. Zain ad-Din, the spokesman of the Church, cried out in wrath, and Timur sent a missive to the Khan complaining of the marauders. This having no effect, he assembled his followers and rode north, setting free by force many of the captives. It was reported to the Khan that Timur had rebelled, and Tugluk gave an order for his death.

Word of this reached Timur. Weary of wrangling and heartsick over the ruin of his country, he consigned diplomacy to the devil, and mounted his horse to go into the desert.

It was a happy choice. As with Bruce of Scotland, outlawry suited him better than conspiracy.

CHAPTER VI

THE WANDERER

WESTWARD stretched the desert floor, red and barren and bare. Red clay, gashed and cracked by the baking of the sun, glared underfoot. Hot puffs of wind stirred the surface sand and lifted it in a haze of dust. This haze wavered about the crests of rotting sandstone like the spray of a dry sea. Only in the early morning and late afternoon could objects be seen clearly because in the middle of the day this haze and the shimmering furnace of the sky overhead made sight a torment.

But it was not the true desert, because empty river-beds twisted among outcroppings of gray granite, toward the wide river Amu. The yellow water of the river—that had made a paradise of Sali Sarai four thousand feet above this plain—bred a sterile kind of growth about it. Near it the clay banks were covered with reeds and a scum of saxaul, sometimes half buried in sand, sometimes projecting upward grotesquely with its gnarled roots exposed.

Besides the river, there were wells with water good enough for the animals but unfit for humans. Wherever the water was sweet the camps of the desert dwellers could be found—nomad Turkomans guarding their sheep with an eye out for a passing caravan that might be weakly guarded enough to raid. And men who had fled from blood-guilt to the barren land.

Across the Red Sands, as they called this clay steppe —Timur made his way. He had brought Aljai with

50

him, and a score of followers who had chosen to make trial of adversity with him. They had pack horses with spare armor, some weapons and odds and ends of jewels by way of wealth. They had ample water skins and they traveled swiftly, being strong enough to guard the horses that grazed nightly on the dry grass of the hillocks. They went from one well to another until they found Aljai's brother, Amir Hussayn. He also was a fugitive, a lean and obstinate man, courageous enough and avaricious. At Kabul he had been the prince of a reigning house, and his chief desire was to regain what he had lost.

Secretly Hussayn thought himself superior to Timur —he was a little older—but he appreciated the magnificent fighting ability of the Tatar. Timur on the other hand could not understand Hussayn's greed, but he was glad of an ally.

Aljai was the bond between them. She was a true grandchild of the King Maker; she could laugh at adversity, even while her quick brain pondered its problems. She never complained of their hardships, and her high spirits banished Timur's moodiness.

The four of them—Hussayn had brought with him one of his wives, Dilshad Agha, a notable beauty—discussed the situation while they camped at the well where they had met. They had now sixty men well mounted, and they decided to go on to the west, where they would find the trade roads and large cities below the Sea of Kharesm, now called the Sea of Aral.

Timur led them to Khiva, where the governor recognized his unexpected guests. He seemed more than willing to pillage them and sell them to the Jat Mongols. It was no tarrying place for the fugitives and they set out into the plain. They were pursued by several hundred horsemen and the governor himself.

Riding off to the summit of a ridge, Timur and Hussayn turned on the Khivans in spite of the odds against them, and their headlong charge down the slope surprised the assailants.

There followed one of the bitter struggles between horsemen in which the Tatars were at home. They thrust their small round shields high on their left arms. Their powerful, double curved bows sped the heavy, steel tipped arrows with force enough to smash through chain mail. And these warriors could wield a bow with either hand, and shoot to the back as well as the front.

They carried their bows ready strung in open sheaths at one hip, the arrow case also open at the other. The bows were often strengthened with iron and horn, and had the range and impact of the English long-bow of the time. With such weapons under their finger tips the Tatars were almost as formidable as modern cavalry armed with the revolvers of three generations ago. Drawing the bow with one hand, the arrow with the other, in a single motion, they could shoot as quickly, and did not need to stop to reload a cylinder. In fact the open sheaths are similar to the modern belt holster, the iron forearm pieces to the leather cuff of the range rider of to-day.

The small shield bound to the biceps, and the short bow enabled them to shoot around the head of a horse with ease.

They guided their quick footed ponies in and out among the Khivans, weaving through their more numerous foemen, bending over their saddle horns, yelling as they rode. They rushed in groups of twelve, scattered among the Khivans and retreated as swiftly as they had come. Only at need did they draw their scimitars or short battle maces. With edged steel they were ferocious, but the bow was their favorite weapon.

Saddles emptied rapidly on both sides. The various leaders kept out of the heart of the struggle, knowing that they would be surrounded and cut down at all cost if they ventured in. Riders unhorsed had to look out for themselves, and get another mount if they could. But one of the Tatars, Elchi Bahatur, stood his ground on foot with such recklessness that Timur rode up and snatched away his bow, cutting the cord so that he would be forced to go and look for safety.

At this moment Amir Hussayn charged through the Khivans toward the governor. He cut down the standard bearer but was hemmed in by foemen, and was circling desperately when Timur saw him, and went to aid him. Timur's sudden onset made the Khivans turn to meet him, and Hussayn slipped out from among them unhurt, while the young Tatar reined back his horse, defending himself with his sword on either hand, until several of his men came up and the Khivan riders scattered.

It was the moment for a charge and Timur shouted to his warriors. Hussayn's horse was struck by an arrow and threw its master. Dilshad Agha, the amir's wife, saw him fall and galloped up, dismounting to offer him her horse. Again in the saddle, Hussayn joined the Tatars.

Timur made for the Khiva governor and shot an arrow at him. The shaft smashed into the man's cheek and knocked him to the ground. Bending down from the saddle, Timur picked up a short spear without drawing rein, and drove it through the Khivan's body. At the death of their leader the assailants scattered, the Tatars following them up with arrows until their arrow cases were empty. Then Timur mounted Dilshad Agha on the same horse with Aljai, and drew back to the ridge with the women and the survivors of the conflict.

Only seven men remained alive upon the ridge, and most of these were slightly hurt. The Khivans dismounted in the plain and consulted for a while. It was near sunset and Timur decided to strike off into the desert, the Khivans following but missing them in the darkness.

"Nay," Timur laughed at his companions, "we have not yet come to the end of our road."

Blindly they wandered through the night and came upon a well by sheer good fortune, finding there also three of their men, soldiers from Balkh who had escaped on foot. While the rest slept, refreshed— the water of the well proved to be sweet—Timur and Hussayn discussed the situation and agreed to separate to avoid the chance of recognition again.

In the first daylight they found that the three Balkhis were gone, with three of the seven horses. They divided the remaining mounts, agreeing to meet again, if possible, far to the south in Hussayn's homeland. Timur watched Hussayn ride away, and then loaded what remained of his baggage on one pony, giving the better horse to Aljai. He had kept only one man with him, and Aljai smiled, seeing him trudging through the sand who had never gone from his house unless in the saddle.

"Surely," she cried, "our fate cannot be worse than this—that we should be obliged to walk."

They had no food but they noticed goat herders in the distance and turned off to buy several goats, roasting the quarters of one at once, rejoicing in the food. The others they dressed on stones and added to the packs. Timur asked the herders if there was any trail out of the country and they pointed to a path.

"It leads to the huts of some Turkomans."

They followed the path and found the huts, which seemed to be deserted. Timur took possession of one of the dwellings, when outcry rose around them. The Turkomans, it seems, were in some of the other shelters and had taken Timur's party for thieves. Placing Aljai behind them in the hut, Timur ran to the entrance with his solitary follower. Lacking arrows, they made pretense of using their bows, but the nomads ran in to attack them.

Drawing his sword and throwing down his useless bow, Timur stepped out to meet them. As he did so the leader of the Turkomans recognized him, having known him in the Green City. He called off his men and went up to embrace the young Tatar and to ask questions.

"*Yah allah!*" he cried. "This is verily the lord of Beyond the River."

The Turkomans, lank men in evil smelling sheep-skins, being rid of suspicion, clustered around to kneel and ask forgiveness. That night they killed a sheep and feasted. The young Tatars ate from the common pot, and even the children of the tribe came as near the fire as they dared to stare and listen. Timur was plagued with questions about what was happening in the rest of the world, and had no sleep until daylight. This was an unexpected source of news to the nomads, as well as honor, and they made the most of it.

The next day Timur gave the Turkoman khan valuable presents—a ruby of price, and two suits, pearl-sewn. To return the courtesy the khan presented him with three horses chosen from the tribal string and a guide for the southern road.

In twelve days they crossed the desert, seeking the great Khorassan road. The first village they reached was deserted, ruined. It was necessary to dig for water, and when they had done so, to stay in the ruins to rest the horses.

And here new disaster came upon them. They were seen by men of a neighboring clan, who rode up and carried them off to the chieftain, a certain Ali Beg. He saw a chance for profit in Timur's capture, and took all the Tatar's belongings, putting him and his wife in a cowshed full of vermin.

Timur was not inclined to submit to such quarters for Aljai, but the guards overpowered him, and there they were for sixty and two days during the end of the dry season when the heat was a torment. Afterward Timur swore that, guilty or not, he would never keep a man in prison.

Ali Beg's bargaining for his captives brought about their release in an unexpected way. The brother of Ali Beg, a Persian chieftain, heard what was passing and wrote to the tribesman sending gifts to Timur and pointing out the folly of meddling between the lord of the Green City and the Jats.

After a long delay Ali Beg obeyed his brother and released his prisoners but with an ill grace. He kept the presents, and provided Timur and Aljai with no more than a sorry looking horse and a mangy camel.

Still Aljai of the dark tresses could smile at continued misfortune. "O my Lord, *this* is not the end of the road."

CHAPTER VII

A CAMEL AND A HORSE

IT WAS THE BEGINNING of the autumn rains, and Timur's rendezvous with Hussayn was far to the south, below the Amu river. But he could not resist making a wide circle back to visit his home. Besides, he did not want to join Hussayn empty handed. Near the Amu he had picked up some fifteen followers and horses at the residence of a friendly chieftain—Aljai could now ride in a horse litter. The sickly pony and the ignoble camel were given away to beggars.

We have a glimpse here of the young Tatar's devotion to his princess. He had set out ahead of Aljai with a few men, intending to go alone on his excursion around Samarkand. But when he came to the ford of the Amu, where armed parties were passing back and forth, he ordered his men to wait, saying that the heat was too great for travel. Accordingly they halted under some poplars within sight of the road a week or so until Aljai's slower cavalcade came up.

Aljai was astonished at the sudden appearance of her champion, but Timur, cautious now that his princess was to be safeguarded, became anxious at sight of fresh dust arising along the road. He ordered horses and litter into the river, fording and swimming the swift current between the sand bars until the danger point was passed and he had put the river between Aljai and the distant riders.

When he had hidden her away in a suburb, he entered Samarkand unnoticed with his followers at the time of evening prayer. For forty-eight days he remained here under the eyes of the Jats who were still hunting him. At night he went to the *sarais* to listen to the talk of the roads; he visited the houses of his friends secretly, with an idea of heading a sudden rising in the city where it was least expected. More than once, standing in the crowds of the mosque courtyards he saw the Jat prince ride past with his officers.

He risked his life to no purpose. Nothing could be done at the moment. The Jats had the country firmly under their hand. Overbearing and exacting, the northerners were still the visible representatives of the authority of Genghis Khan. Moreover, they were victorious.

The Tatar princes around Samarkand were accustomed to follow a military leader. They were not fanatic Muhammadans, but men trained to war, and thinking of little else. To any man who could rouse them and restrain them and give them a taste of victory they would be faithful. But the Jalairs had submitted to Ilias—Hussayn was a fugitive, with a Jat prince sitting in the hall of his palace at Kabul. And they saw no hope as yet in following the youthful Timur.

They warned Timur that his presence was known to the Jats. Again the scion of the house of Barlas had to take to his horse and escape at night.

He did not go alone. A small following had collected around him—masterless men, wandering troopers, lovers of hazard and loot, wild Turkomans and adventurous Arabs. They were poor material for an army but they made splendid partisans for the road.

They laughed when Timur led them within sight of the Green City, and camped in the abandoned summer pastureland above the white dome of his palace where the Jats could be watched, riding out to look for him. They boasted of his deeds to the Barlas *bahaturs* who had wind of his presence and arrived to salute him— Elchi Bahatur, he of the broken bow, and white haired Jaku Barlas who had a raven's instinct for scenting out happenings.

And these veterans of the King Maker's camp emptied many a cup with the young outlaw. "When God's earth is so wide," they said, "why dwell within walls?"

"Words!" Timur cried. "What will your deeds be? Are you crows, to feed from the crumbs of the Jat's table, or hawks to strike down your prey?"

"*Y'allah!*" The two Barlas men made answer. "We are not crows."

When Aljai joined them they saluted the princess respectfully. Had she not taken part in the battles of her lord? When Timur broke camp late that autumn and moved south toward the mountains to meet Hussayn they went with him.

It was no road for weaklings. For five hundred miles it twisted among the ranges that were the very bulwark of the sky—down through modern Afghanistan, vaguely mapped and only partially explored to-day. It followed a river gorge upward until the river became a bed of ice, and they had to force a path through knee deep snow.

The road led them under the glaciers of the Father of Mountains, still rising to wind swept plateaus where they pitched their round cloth tents under echoing cliffs. By day they moved in the glare of snow fields in the higher altitudes, except where the wind had cleared the pebble-strewn bed of the valley before them.

The horses wore felt blankets and the riders were wrapped in wolfskins and sables. When they came to timber they cut enough fuel to load on sledges and carry with them. At times they passed below the watch towers of a tribal citadel, where unseen sentinels wailed at them and dogs barked a thousand feet overhead.

More than once they were attacked by Afghans who did not know the men they had to deal with. Timur and his men emerged the richer by these raids. They crossed the twelve thousand foot pass between the snow summits of the Hindu Koh, and slid and clambered down the precipice path that brought them to the valley of Kabul.

This meant no respite for them, because they had to circle the city. After buying fresh horses and sheep in the villages they took the Kandahar trail which was easier going, being nearly free from snow. They reached the lower valleys of the south, and found Amir Hussayn waiting for them at the rendezvous with an army that was twin to Timur's but more numerous.

During the end of the winter they rested, and were heartened by an ambassador who came with gifts from the ruler of the nearby ranges.

There had been, it seemed, a rebellion among his people of Sijistan, and he had lost most of his hill forts. He promised reward to Timur and Hussayn if they would join him in ousting the rebels. The allies accepted the overture—Hussayn with the idea of making himself master of this southern province, Timur eager to be in the saddle again.

When the roads were passable they joined the lord of Sijistan and marched off to fight his battles—being for the moment no more than soldiers of fortune. This was the sort of thing Timur relished. They captured most of the belligerent strongholds, surprising some, storming the others on ladders.

Hussayn, however, caused trouble by pillaging the villages and then putting his own men in as garrisons. Timur was indifferent, but the Sijistanis were not pleased and the remaining rebels profited from the strained relations, sending a message to their ruler. "We bear thee no ill-will; bethink thee, if the Tatars are allowed to take our places, they will keep the whole country for themselves."

The master of Sijistan marched off at night without word to the adventurers, and joined forces with the former rebels. It was a typical about-face of the mountain clans, always suspicious, and uncertain of strangers. They attacked Timur who beat them off and charged into their array.

In this conflict, with no more than twelve warriors around him at the time, he was a target for the arrows of the Sijistanis. One shaft splintered the bones of his hand, another struck him in the foot. He paid no heed to the wounds, beyond breaking the arrows and pulling them out, but afterward they proved serious and he was forced to keep to his tent.

The Sijistanis had been defeated, and the allies gained new property and followers from the victory. Hussayn set out to the north with the bulk of the new army, leaving Timur to rest in the hills and recover from his injury.

Here he was joined by Aljai, and for a brief space the dark haired princess had the Tatar lord to herself in the camp where no one could summon him to war. Their pavilions stood among vineyards where the air was always cool, and the horses tasted of paradise in the lush grass. At night under the full moon of the month of Shawwal they lay on carpets looking down into the shadows of the lowlands. For this moon Aljai could watch Timur sitting with his boy child, the World Gripper.

And she counted the days, when Timur limped restlessly around the camp, trying his injured foot. It pained him a good deal, though he stood straight as before. And when—too soon for Aljai's love—Timur called for his armor and his saddle horse, she brought out his sword and girdled it over his loins, her dark eyes impassive with the grief that a young wife must not show before her lord.

"May God shield thee, O my husband."

whom and on his posterity be the peace). Respect
the learned *sayyids*, ask blessing of the dervishes. Be
strengthened by the four pillars of the law, prayer,
fasting, pilgrimage and alms."

Taragai left his son to his own devices, but the men
of the monastery had taken notice of the boy, and a
gray-haired *sayyid* who found Tamerlane sitting in a
corner of the hall reading a chapter of the Koran asked
his name.

"Timur [2] am I," the boy responded, rising.

The descendant of the prophet looked at the chapter
and reflected. "Support the faith of Islam, and thou
wilt be protected."

Timur considered the promise earnestly, and for a
while gave up playing polo and chess, his favorite
diversion. When he encountered a dervish squatting
in the shade by the road, he dismounted and begged a
blessing. He could not read very easily, so he confined
himself, apparently, to that one chapter until he knew
it well.

In these days when he was about seventeen he liked
to go to the mosque courtyards where sat the *imams*,
the leaders of Islam. He took his place behind the
listeners, where the slippers were discarded, and it is
related that a certain Zain ad-Din saw him there and
called the boy to him, giving Timur his own cap and
shawl girdle and a ring set with a cornelian. Zain
ad-Din was a keen mind and worldly wise, a true
leader. And Timur remembered his intent eyes and
grave voice, and perhaps also the gift.

The only leader of the Barlas clan was Hadji Barlas,

---

[2] Tamerlane is the European rendering of *Timur-i-lang*—Timur the
Limper. Timur means Iron, and this alone was his name until his foot
was injured by an arrow and he was not able to walk without limping.
The historians of Asia speak of him as Amir Timur Gurigan—Lord Timur,
the Splendid—and only as Timur-i-lang in the way of vituperation.

CHAPTER VIII

AT THE STONE BRIDGE

THERE WAS NEED OF TIMUR in the north. Hussayn, overconfident, had engaged the nearest host of the Jats and had been trounced, his men scattered. This was against Timur's advice, and the Tatar was angered. It meant that he must turn aside to the mountain clans to rally Hussayn's followers and gain new men. And his hand was not yet healed, so that he could not manage the reins and his weapons at the same time.

In a grim mood he rode with his small band, killing game for food. He was camped near the upper Amu, waiting for Hussayn, when he was discovered. The chronicle gives us a clear picture of this incident.

Timur's tents were at the edge of a stream, under the bank of a ridge. After several days of waiting, his impatience would not let him sleep. The night was clear, the moon bright, and he paced along the stream —his new habit of forcing himself to walk upon the foot that never would be quite healed. He could not grow accustomed to this wound.

When he returned to the hill the moon was dim, and the eastern sky streaked with yellow light. Timur knelt to make the dawn prayer, and when he rose he saw armed men riding past on the other side of the ridge, an arrow's flight away. They were coming from the direction of Balkh, now a Jat stronghold, and Timur went down at once to his tents, rousing his men and calling for his horse.

Alone he rode out to challenge the strangers. When

they saw him they halted and for a moment stared at him in the dim light.

"Whence come ye?" he called to them. "And whither go ye?"

"We are the servants of Lord Timur," some one answered, "and have come out in search of him. We cannot find him, although we heard he left Kumrud and came to this valley."

Timur did not know the voice, nor could he distinguish anything of the warriors. "I also am one of the amir's servants," he responded. "If it is your wish, I will lead you to him."

A rider detached himself from the column and galloped up to where its leaders waited, listening. "We have found a guide," Timur heard him say, "who will take us to the amir."

He rode forward then, slowly, until he could make out the faces of the officers. They were three chieftains of the Barlas clan and they had with them three troops of horsemen. They called to the strange guide to come nearer, but when they recognized Timur they alighted from their horses, bent their knees and kissed his stirrup.

Timur also dismounted and could not restrain himself from making gifts to them at once—his helmet to one, his girdle to another, and his coat to a third. They sat down together and game was brought in and a feast prepared on the spot. They shared the salt and Timur soon had proof of their loyalty. He sent a scout from their ranks over the river to discover what the Jats were doing. The warrior tried to swim the Amu; his horse went down and was drowned, but he himself reached a sand bar and gained the far bank. He returned with word that a Jat army some twenty thousand strong was on the road from the Green City and was laying waste the country.

The man himself had passed near his home, but had not stopped, although it lay in the path of the foragers.

"Nay," he said, "when my Lord has no home, how should I go to mine?"

The news put Timur into a fever of impatience. Up to their old tricks the Jats were pillaging, now that a force was in the field against them; he knew that the clans across the river would resent this instantly and would side with him. Meanwhile his strength was less than a quarter of the Jat general's—Bikijuk's. The old Mongol was a master at this kind of warfare, and he moved his forces on the north bank to cover all the fords.

To attempt to force a crossing in the face of such strength was a task beyond even Timur's desperation. But he did get across.

For a month he led Bikijuk upstream, until the Amu narrowed and became shallow. Here at a stone bridge he halted. The Jats, having all the advantage, were not disposed to push over the bridge, and Timur went into camp ostentatiously. That night he told off five hundred men and placed them under the orders of Mouava, an officer who could be depended upon, and Amir Musa, the ablest of Hussayn's lieutenants.

He left the five hundred to hold the camp and the bridge, himself riding off with the bulk of his forces. Close to the Jat camp he crossed the river, going on without stopping into the hills beyond that formed a rude half-circle facing the stream.

Promptly the next day the Jat scouts found his tracks, and it was clear to Bikijuk that a strong division had crossed. Apparently the numbers in Timur's old camp were still undiminished. If Bikijuk attacked the bridge, Mouava and Amir Musa were to resist and hold on, while Timur charged the rear of the Mongols.

But sagacious Bikijuk scented danger and remained quiet during the day. That night Timur scattered his men through the hills with orders to light any number of fires on three sides of the hostile camp.

Sight of these fires was too much for the cautious northerners and they left their position hurriedly before dawn, Timur collecting his men and charging into their line of march. The Jats broke and fled, Timur pursuing relentlessly.

Amir Hussayn, who had taken no part in the battle of the river, now rejoined Timur with a strong following, more than ready to offer advice.

"It is a bad plan," he said, "to pursue defeated troops."

"They are not yet defeated," Timur replied, and kept on. He greeted the clans who came out from hiding, the warriors circling their horses in joy, the women waving their loose sleeves. He slept little, because it was his task to appoint new leaders of his yet-to-be-formed army, he must conciliate old feuds, apportion the spoil gleaned from the Jats, pay compensation to the families of the slain and an allowance to the wounded. All the while he was in the saddle directing the movements of his cavalry columns northward, hastening to any point of resistance.

With such a scorching at their heels the Jat armies evacuated the country between the Amu and the Syr. Prince Ilias, assembling his divisions in the northern plain, was approached by two riders from his home-land beyond the mountains. They dismounted, and saluted him as Khan, saying that his father Tugluk had left the land of the living and had gone beyond, into the spirit world of the sky. Then they took the reins of his horse and led him back to his tent.

Perforce Ilias Khan rode off to Almalyk, his city on the road to Cathay. Bikijuk and two other Mongol generals had been taken captive by Timur in a personal encounter—a swift flurry of weapons and hard lashed ponies—and the new lord of Beyond the River was tremendously content. He ordered a feast for the veteran officers in his tent—praised them for their fidelity to the salt of the Khan, and asked curiously what they wished him to do with them.

"It is for thee to decide," they answered him calmly. "If we are put to death, many will seek revenge; if we are permitted to live, many will befriend thee. It is all one to us—when we girded our loins and put on our armor we looked for death to come."

Amir Hussayn cautioned Timur that it would be a mistake to spare a captured enemy, but it pleased the young victor, having taken the Mongols with his own hand and feasted them, to give them horses and set them free.

Meanwhile he had retaken his Green City by a trick he had learned from the desert men. Coming within sight of the walls, he had scattered his men over the countryside, ordering them to ride in all directions. Some, becoming enthusiastic, had cut branches from the poplar groves, and a prodigious dust arose. The Jat garrison, beholding all the indications of scouts and foragers in advance of a strong column, retreated at once, and the Green City was spared a siege.

One of Timur's chroniclers pauses to remark that "The Lord Timur, always fortunate in war, in this year defeated an army by fire and captured a city by dust."

Success, as always with the restless Tatars, became

more trying than adversity. Hussayn, resentful of Timur's impetuosity, exacted money and privileges by way of compensation, and Timur, moody, led the prince of Kabul to a shrine and made him swear to remain faithful to his comradeship. This Hussayn did, but he resented being asked to give the oath. Both were over-weary, and oppressed by their responsibilities and the quarreling of their followers.

The chronicle adds that "To their camp came the illustrious princess Aljai, who nursed the sick lords."

CHAPTER IX

THE BATTLE OF THE RAIN

THAT ILIAS KHAN SHOULD COME back was inevitable, and Timur went forward to meet him halfway—on the plain north of the Syr where the Mongols liked to graze and refit their horses before launching down into the Tatar countries. Ilias Khan came with all the strength of the north, a disciplined and veteran array, mounted on the best horses of Asia, well officered, well armed—their horned standards shining above the close packed squadrons of leather clad horsemen.

They were less numerous than the Tatars, but Timur knew their worth and kept in touch with them by his scouts until Amir Hussayn arrived on the scene with his mountain clans.

For once all the power of the Tatars was united in the field—the Barlas clan and the desert riders, the Jalair chieftains, the troops of the great house of Selduz, Hussayn's warriors with the Ghur clans and Afghan volunteers who had scented the war from afar. The helmeted men and the *bahaturs* had rallied to the standards.

Nearly all were mounted—only the servants and some regiments of spearmen and the herders guarded the camp behind trenches. And they were not the irregular light cavalry that modern imagination associates with Asia.

They wore armor, the fine steel mesh of Persian make, pointed helmets with steel drop and coif to fasten under the nose or chin to protect the throat. Double mail or plates covered their shoulders. Some of the horses had leather or mail body curtains and light steel headpieces.

Besides the universal bow or bows, strengthened with horn or spliced with steel, they carried scimitars, long tulwars or the straight two-edged Persian blades. Their spears were sometimes the light ten-foot lance with a small tip, sometimes the shorter and heavier weapon with an iron knob on the butt, intended for smashing through armor. Most of the riders carried iron maces.

Their unit was the squadron, the *hazara* and the regiment, commanded by *ming-bashis*, colonels. The amirs were scattered throughout the array, and upon them rested the burden of leadership in the actual fighting. About Timur and Hussayn were grouped the amirs of their personal following, the *tavachis*, or courier officers—*aides-de-camp*.

Timur had divided his host into right wing, center and left wing, and each in turn was drawn up in two bodies, the main body and reserve. The right wing, that he had made the stronger purposely—was under Hussayn's command. The point of greatest danger, the weaker left wing Timur took himself. With him he had the Barlas lords, Amir Jaku and his fellows.

Timur was hopeful, exultant in this decisive test of strength. The Tatars, beholding their own numbers, and the dignity of their array became filled with confidence. And then it rained. A true spring storm of the high steppes, lashing the ground and the men with torrents and waging a battle of its own in the sky with thunder chasing lightning. The ground, soft in the beginning, became a morass of mud; the horses, chilled and weakened, splashed around in mud up to their bellies. The river added to the inundation by flooding the gullies and lowlands. The men went about in soggy garments, protecting their weapons as best they could.

The chronicler explains sadly that this rain was a trick of the Jat Mongols, whose magicians produced it with the Yeddah stone.[1] And he adds that the Jats, forewarned as to what was coming, had prepared themselves with heavy felt shelters and felt blankets for the horses, and that they dug canals to drain their position. Which is his way of saying that the invaders came through the deluge of several days in much better condition than Timur's men. At all events, they mounted fresh ponies and moved toward the Tatar camp.

Timur advanced to meet them, and after the usual skirmishing of individual swordsmen, the advanced regiments of his left flank charged the right wing of the enemy. At once the Tatars were broken and driven back. The Jats came in a mass at their heels, and Timur's reserve cavalry wavered.

Faced by swift disaster, Timur ordered his drums to sound an advance and plunged forward with his Barlas men. Upon the sea of mud, the disordered regiments lost all cohesion and separated into yelling groups, maddened by uncertainty.

Bows were useless in that wet—horses slid on their rumps and the channels of yellow water became red with blood. Steel was the only weapon that served, and the clanging of blades, the screaming of horses, the shouting of the warriors, and the war cry of the Tatars —"*Dar u gar!*" made a bedlam of the plain.

Timur headed in toward the standard of the Jat wing commander, and got close enough to strike at the Mongol general with his ax. The blow was parried by his foeman's shield, and the Mongol rose in his stirrups to

[1] It was an old tradition that the Mongols were apt at magic. The chronicler proves the case to his own satisfaction, by explaining that the next day when one of the magicians was killed, the rain ceased.

cut at Timur with his sword, when Jaku, who had kept behind his lord, thrust the officer through with his spear. The standard came down.

Again Timur sent word to sound his saddle drums and cymbals, and the Mongols—always disheartened by the loss of a standard—began to retreat. On that plain no orderly retreat was possible, and the northern riders broke, drawing clear after a time on their fresher horses.

Riding to a hill, Timur tried to see what was happening elsewhere. Amir Hussayn had fared badly and had been driven far back, only the stubborn resistance of his reserve holding the Mongols in check. The centers of both armies had merged into this phase of the conflict.

Timur signaled his men to reform, but this was slow work. Too impatient to delay, he took what squadrons were intact near him and charged into the right of the Mongols who were engaging Hussayn. He had advanced so far that he was able to strike them almost from the rear. At this unexpected onset they drew off. Meanwhile Ilias Khan cautiously held back his reserve and seemed disposed to retire altogether.

It was a glorious opportunity and Timur sent his own courier to Hussayn to urge him to reform his divisions without delay and advance.

"Am I a coward," Hussayn cried, "that he summons me before my men?" He struck Timur's messenger in the face and returned no answer.

Time was passing and Timur mastered his anger and sent two officers who were relatives of the amir to Hussayn, to explain that Ilias was on the point of giving way and that they must advance at once.

"Have I fled?" Hussayn swore at them. "Why

then does he press me to go forward? Give me time to assemble my men."

"*Khoudsarma*," the messengers replied, "O my Lord, Timur is now engaged with the enemy's reserve. Look!"

Either Hussayn's jealousy was aroused, or it was impossible for him to get forward. Eventually Timur had to draw back, before darkness set in. He camped in the field, and, overcome by moodiness, would neither go to see Hussayn nor listen to the amir's messengers. He determined then that he would never go into battle again with Hussayn as joint commander.

The next day brought more rain, but Timur still embittered went forward and engaged Ilias, alone. He was beset by separate divisions of Mongols, and forced to retreat. The ride back through the storm over the marshes and flooded inlets covered with the masses of the dead was rendered dismal by memory of his losses. Chilled, shaken by bitterness he rode in silence, his Barlas men following him at a distance. He had been soundly defeated and he never forgave Hussayn for his failure to support him.

Hussayn sent officers to him with various plans for retiring into India but Timur in his present mood would have none of that. "Let your road be to India or the seven hells," he said. "What is it to me?"

He retired on Samarkand and saw that the city was provisioned for a siege, then went on to his own valley to recruit a fresh army while the Jats were occupied with Samarkand.

And he found Aljai dead of a sudden sickness, buried in her white shroud in a garden of his house.

CHAPTER X

THE TWO AMIRS

THE PASSING OF PRINCESS ALJAI removed the tie
that had held Timur and Hussayn together for
the last five years. Hussayn had treated his sister spite-
fully on more than one occasion, and Timur remembered it. He always brooded over personal grievances,
and now he mourned his wife. Taking his son Jahangir he moved south with the men of his clan, over the
river again, near to the spot where he had rested that
last summer with Aljai.

"To God we belong," the pious Zain ad-Din wrote
to him, "and to God we must return. To each of us
there is a place and an hour appointed for death."

But Timur was not a fatalist. The zeal of the mullahs and the imams roused no answering fire in him.
Outwardly, his calm seemed to be the peace of the
true believer, who admits that a man's destiny unrolls
before him and that salvation lies in the Law pro-
pounded by Muhammad; inwardly, Timur was tormented by questions he could not answer, and by the
savage desires that were his heritage from his ancestors.

He prayed at the appointed hours, and he took his
place in the ranks at the mosque readings, gravely at-
tentive. For hours during the nights he sat at the chess
board, moving the miniature horsemen and ivory castles and elephants over the squares—as often as not
without a companion. When he played with an op-
ponent he almost always won, and this was not policy
on the part of his officers. Timur was a master player.

To satisfy his study of the game he had a new board made with double the number of squares and pieces. On this he worked out new combinations, while the five year old World Gripper sat by him on the carpet, watching with dark eyes the maneuvers of the strange and glittering toys that engrossed his father's attention.

And to Timur thus occupied came in haste mullahs —the eyes and the secretaries of Islam—from Samarkand with a message.

"God hath lifted the collar of oppression from the neck of the believer," they said. "Reverend and courageous expounders of the Law came from Bokhara to Samarkand and roused the people of the city to bear arms against the oppressors of the faithful—until our Lords the princes should gain sufficient strength to resist them. Although the accursed enemy entered into the suburbs, the inhabitants of Samarkand, even without their two princes, defended the wall and the streets, so that the accursed enemy was driven out.

"Then by the will of God a plague spread among the horses of the Jats. Three-fourths of the horses died, so that they lacked even mounts for the couriers. They retired from the country, most of them with their quivers and packs on their backs and their swords on their shoulders. Surely never before in this world was an army of Jats seen walking afoot."

After the mullahs came officers of Timur who had been watching events, and they confirmed the fact that the townspeople of Samarkand had kept the city until the Jats withdrew, adding that the disease among the horses was so bad that Tatar cavalry following them up had avoided the infected districts.

This sudden stroke of fortune brought Hussayn back into the country. He made a triumphal entry into Samarkand, the people—full of their own success in beating off so formidable an enemy—exulting in the occasion. Carpets were hung from windows and roof parapets, the mosques were crowded and music greeted the amir in every garden.

Hussayn and Timur were now the virtual rulers from India to the Sea of Aral. Timur had, morally, an equal claim with Hussayn. He had been the real leader of the army, and his following was as great. But Hussayn was the grandson of the King Maker and son of a reigning prince. He chose the puppet Khan, the figurehead whose one virtue was that he was a *tura*, a descendant of Genghis Khan. With all the proper ceremonies the Khan was seated in his palace, and Hussayn undertook to rule as his grandfather had done.

Timur, by force of circumstances, was now inferior to Hussayn, who collected the taxes, gave judgments and apportioned out land. One thing Timur insisted upon—he must have his valley, and the district from the Green City to his river.

"As far as the river is mine," he said decisively.

He bore himself with dignity, and his generosity would endure no quarreling over exactions. When Hussayn imposed a heavy head tax upon the Barlas men, Timur protested that they had lost most of their property at the last battle, but he himself paid Hussayn the full amount, including by need or by moodiness even the jewels of Aljai—the earrings and the pearl necklaces she had worn on her bridal night. Hussayn recognized the jewels but accepted them without comment.

The final quarrel between the leaders was brought about by the turbulent amirs, their vassals. Hussayn, in setting up his puppet khan, had given the Jats new cause for invasion and in trying to reduce the amirs he made new enemies. When his companionship with Timur ceased—by whose immediate fault, no one knows—the result was civil war, and intrigue, castigated by periodic incursions of the Jats. For six years the lands of the Tatars were an armed camp.

Through the dark days of struggle, Timur moved like a disembodied spirit of war. His cold recklessness, his utter disregard for his own safety and his open handed generosity are unmistakable. Around the fires at night the caravan people told tales of Lord Timur. "Verily," said they, "he is well named, for there is iron in him—yea, unbending iron."

Perhaps the favorite story in bazaar and camp was of the taking of Karshi.

This was the city of the Veiled Prophet—now long in his grave—of Khorassan. A certain man of religion who had aroused the wonder and fanaticism of a multitude by showing them nightly at the bottom of his well the rising moon—when there was no moon in the sky. So they named him the Moon Maker, whom history knows as a trouble maker.

In Karshi Timur had built a stone fortress, and had taken some pride in it. At this particular time Hussayn's forces were in possession of Karshi, citadel and all. And Timur's men knew well the strength of the place. Amir Musa commanded the three or four thousand men holding Karshi, and they knew Musa too. He had held the stone bridge against Bikijuk. He was an experienced soldier, too fond of wine and the good things of the table, often careless but always to be relied upon in a crisis.

Timur had with him at the time about two hundred and forty men, and his officers, Amir Jaku, and Mouava —who had fought beside Musa at the bridge—and

Amir Daoud, a lover of hazard. But when he explained to them that he meant to take and hold Karshi they were incredulous. They said it was too hot a season to think of such action, and they had their families to safeguard.

"O ye men of small wit," Timur railed at them, "have I not sworn that your families shall be protected?"

"Nay, that is true," responded one of the amirs, "but they are not behind walls."

"There are walls around Karshi," Timur laughed. "Think ye—if we be masters of Karshi!"

They did think, but the prospect rendered even Daoud silent, and Jaku shook his head. "Let us first gather more strength, O my Lord. There is a time for rashness and a time for caution and thought. Musa hath followed the standards too long to be taken like a woman on a camel."

"Then go thou to the women and ask to be taught!" Timur said in his deep voice. "And I will keep with me those who held the bridge against the Horde. Thou, Mouava, and thou, Elchi! Are there others?"

Many voices proclaimed that they also had crossed the river with Timur, and had made the Jats flee without their saddles.

"Then go ye to where your families wait. Nay, go to the markets and boast thus of what is past. I will draw my reins to Karshi with others."

They knew that he would, indeed, do this if they hung back and they went off to discuss it together. Once he had decided to do something, Timur was not to be dissuaded. When he gave an order he never changed it. This singleness of purpose caused loss of life and misfortune at times that might well have been avoided; but it gave to Timur's decisions something of the immutability of fate.

When his nobles came back to join him, Jaku held in one hand a Koran, in the other a sword. "We have sworn to follow thee, O my Lord, and here is the Koran upon which we took oath. Here is a sword, and if we obey thee not, strike life from us."

So they sat down again with zeal, to discuss ways of drawing out Musa.

"O ye of little wit," Timur laughed, after he had listened a while. "If ye induce the Amir to come out with his three thousand, and ye but a hundred and another hundred and forty what will be the gain?"

"It would be better," spoke up Daoud, seeing his companions silent, "to go secretly at night, and enter Karshi and surprise Musa in his bed. Thus we could take him."

"Yea, indeed it would be better," assented Timur grimly. "And after that, will you go also to the beds of his three thousand?"

"All things are in the hands of God," Daoud defended himself. "Musa knows well that we are here, and he will not be drawn out while we are here. His Lord ordered him to maintain Karshi and Musa will do nothing otherwise."

"If I," Timur mused aloud, "should send a summons to Musa to go down to the meadows by the river and satisfy his thirst with wine, and his discomfort with coolness, would he do so?"

Daoud smiled, because it was the middle of the dry season, and they—free to choose the open camping places of the plain—were sitting coatless and damp with sweat, while Karshi must have been intolerable behind the walls. The citadel was a winter, not a summer resort, and Musa's fondness for the jug and feasting was well known. "God forbid," he said. "He would like to go, but he would not."

"Then I will not invite him," Timur made response.

And he said nothing more to his companions. In fact he seemed to change his mind about making an attempt at Karshi, because he sent couriers with greeting and gifts to the Malik of Herat in the south. He moved with his men down to the Khorassan road leading to Herat. There on the plain of ridged yellow clay along the edge of the sand dunes, he pitched his tents in spite of the heat, by the Well of Isaac.

For a month, until his galloper came back, he halted at the well all north-bound caravans. His messenger as he had expected brought back return gifts and a letter of salutation from the Malik, bidding Timur visit him. There was by that time quite a concourse about the well, and the news proclaimed by the messenger became common property.

The next day, Timur released the caravans and made evident preparations himself for departure. The merchants begged him for an escort to protect them from other bodies of his men, and he explained that he had no followers on the road to Karshi. Then he rode off swiftly to the south with his two hundred and forty— the caravans going on to the north, to cross the Amu and arrive at Karshi.

There Musa questioned them and learned that Timur had undoubtedly gone on toward Herat, evidently planning to take refuge with the Malik. Immediately Musa moved out to a pleasanter site, in the meadows Timur had mentioned, where, according to the chronicle, he "unrolled the carpet of feasting and unsealed the wine jar of intoxication." But he left his son with several hundred men to hold the fortress of Karshi.

Timur waited at his next camp a week or so, to give the caravans time to reach Karshi, then he returned to the Amu by a single forced march. He did not stop at the river, but urged his horse at once into the current and swam across, forty of his riders daring to follow him.

Then boats were sent back for the others, the forty jeering at them when they came up. They spent that night out of sight of the road—a score of men being sent at dawn to hold up all travelers on the way to Karshi. After the next sunset they mounted again and rode through the night across the open plain to a well near the outskirts of Karshi. Here they halted as long as daylight lasted, hidden in the wormwood and tamarisk growth. All of Musa's people who happened to visit the well were kept there as prisoners, and Timur set his own men and the captives to work making ladders of sorts and ropes. When darkness set in, they mounted, taking the ladders but leaving the prisoners under guard.

"We have come very fast," Jaku said, "and not all our people are up with us. This venture is important, and so it would be well to move forward slowly and take no risks."

"Do thou bring the men on slowly," Timur assented, "and I will ride ahead to look at the wall and select a place for the ladders."

Accompanied by only two men he galloped on, until they saw the loom of the towers through the trees, and dismounted. One of the warriors remained with the horses, but Timur's servant Abdullah would not leave him. The two walked forward until they saw the water of the moat gleaming before their feet. For a while they listened, hearing nothing from within the place.

Following the edge of the moat they came to the
spot where the open aqueduct of the fort crossed it—a
stone trough, knee deep in water. Into this Timur
climbed, Abdullah following. From the aqueduct he
dropped to the edge of earth that projected under the
wall on the castle side.

Along this he felt his way until he reached the
wooden framework of a gate. After listening for some
time, he knocked on the gate. What deviltry inspired
him to do so is not apparent. At all events he found
the gate to be walled up within and no one answered
his knock.

Resuming his prowl he searched until he made certain of a place where the wall had breached at the top,
an easy point of access. He then showed it to Abdullah, and assured himself that his servant would find it
again. Not until then did he return to his horse, and
ride back to his men who were waiting beyond the
walls. Forty-three of them were told off to guard the
horses—leaving about a hundred for the storming
party.

Timur again left them, to seek his breach, while Abdullah ushered up separate groups to the aqueduct and
guided them across. They found Timur sitting on the
wall, and he gave them orders what to do next.

Some were sent to round up whatever sentries might
be inside the wall. They found all Musa's watchers
asleep, at that hour near dawn. There was some fighting at the citadel itself, but Timur assembled all his
men there and—it being now sunrise—sounded his
horns from the tower.

All the inhabitants of Karshi rolled out of their quilts
to hurry to the flat housetops and learn the meaning
of this strange reveille. Not knowing what Timur's
strength might be, and utterly taken by surprise, most

of Musa's officers came in to the citadel to offer submission, and when Timur had talked with them, they
agreed to join him. Only Musa's son resisted, defending his house. But when fire was thrown in through
the embrasures he came out with his sword around his
neck and yielded himself.

Timur praised his bravery, but kept him in Karshi—
sending out the rest of Musa's family to the amir down
in the meadows.

"Our Lord's good fortune gave us the city," Jaku
said afterward. "And we who follow him have increased our glory."

It seemed to them little less than miraculous that
Timur was able, thereafter, to hold the fortress of
Karshi against Hussayn's thousands. Victory, in their
minds, was the gift of God, and defeat not otherwise.
The venerable Zain ad-Din and his mullahs warned
them of this, ceaselessly.

But these lords of Tatary were incorrigibly wayward; for hours they would sit entranced in front of
a dirty dervish who, intoxicated with fervor, screamed
at them of sanctity and the wonders of Muhammad's
paradise; at other moments they spat and gibed at all
mullahs: "It takes two preachers to make a man; one
makes only a woman."

They were troubled by visions. They would take to
horse and flee from the portent of an evil dream, or an
omen. And yet, faced by inevitable death during battle, they would cast off their helmets and shout aloud,
that others might envy them their moment of glory.
They were jealous of their personal honor, and shame,
to their spirits, was more trying than suffering. "What
is profit without honor?" they echoed the saying of the
Arabs.

CHAPTER XI

ON THE ROOF OF THE WORLD

IN THESE UNCERTAIN YEARS OF STRIFE they turned their eyes more and more to Timur. His personal daring stirred their admiration; his escapades and triumphs became their gossip. Even they who were in the field against him liked to listen to the tales of Lord Timur. His courage was the one solid thing in their restless fancies.

Several of them grew tired of Hussayn and came over to his standard. Mangali Boga, one of the older nomad chieftains of Mongol stock, rode up without so much as announcing himself and sat down among Timur's lords. Mangali had been one of his most impetuous opponents—had offered once to bring Timur in a captive, if six thousand men were given him.

"Now that I have eaten Lord Timur's salt," he said, "I will not turn my face to any other man."

Upon no greater thing than Timur's reckless leadership and the loyalty of these men was founded the dominion that history knows as Tamerlane's empire.

It was Mangali who won a battle for Timur in later years by his quick wit. The Tatars, an isolated division of them, were engaged with Kara Yussuf, chieftain of the Black Sheep Turkomans. Timur's men were hard pressed on all sides and felt the issue going against them, when Mangali withdrew from his officers and searched the ground until he found what he wanted, a Turkoman's severed head with its long beard and shaven pate.

84

This head Mangali thrust upon his lance tip and spurred into the leading Tatar ranks, shouting that Kara Yussuf was slain. The Tatars were encouraged and all the foemen within hearing correspondingly depressed. Before long the Turkomans gave way, carrying back with them in their flight the very much alive and angry Kara Yussuf.

More than once these sagacious and headstrong Tatar lords saved their master at the edge of the grave. A story is told of Elchi Bahatur, the Valiant Envoy. Like Prince Murat of Napoleon's suite, he was fond of plumed head-gear and gilded boots. Perhaps on account of the magnificence of his appearance, perhaps because of his bravado he was often chosen to go to other courts as ambassador. But he appears regularly throughout the fighting—plumes, boots and all.

On this particular occasion Timur had returned from beating off a raid of the Jats, and was searching for the hostile forces of the kings of Badakshan, in the higher ranges where the Amur takes its rise.

The mountain kings drew back steadily, up into the treeless solitude where the snow lay deep, and the projecting rocks were worn by ages of storms. Here in the gorges glaciers crawled like inanimate snakes, and the schist of the gorge walls gleaming red and purple. And here the two small armies played at hide-and-seek around the peaks, sliding down thousand foot slopes, and sitting out snow flurries huddled together like sheep.

A courier reached Timur with word that his advance guard had been cut off and captured by the Badakshanis who were retiring with their prisoners by still another ravine.

It was part of the rigid code of the Tatars that no leader should abandon his men while it was humanly possible to reach them. But the warriors with Timur could see no chance of aiding their comrades. Timur was stirred into a passion by their weariness and lack of hope. He summoned them to mount and set out with the courier for a guide, to seek for a way along the heights that would bring him out in the ravine the Badakshanis were moving down.

His men lagged along the ice-coated paths, where every now and then a horse and rider would slip and slide head over tail into eternity. Timur pressed ahead so rapidly that only thirteen were with him when he came out in the gorge and hastened to seize the summit of a pass before the Badakshan forces could reach it. With his thirteen, among them Elchi Bahatur,—he took up his position in the rocks along the ridge and engaged the advance of the mountaineers with bows.

Only fifty warriors were in the first party of the enemy, but two hundred more appeared down the ravine. Elchi Bahatur at this point executed a flank movement of his own, riding alone down the side of the ravine, and loping toward the oncoming two hundred. Sight of him in his sable cloak, bound with a flaming girdle, and his bearskin head-gear made them pause. He came, apparently, from nowhere and he was undoubtedly riding a blood stallion. His bow was in its case, his sword in its sheath of ivory inlaid with gold.

"*Hai*, ye sons of many fathers," Elchi hailed them. "Draw rein and look. That man up there is Lord Timur."

Riding in among them, as if a battle were the least thing in his mind, the Tatar pointed out to them carefully the figure of Timur in the familiar crested helmet, among the flying arrows.

"Think," Elchi advised them gravely, "if ye are

slain, even your families will call you fools. What good to be slain here—now—when Lord Timur is between you and safety? It would be better to make a truce. Much better to gather together the captives and thus gain his good-will by sending them to him."

So Elchi blandished them. And they, all uncertain, dismounted to bow before him—convinced that the Tatars were in strength, if a lord like this came among them unescorted. Elchi dismounted also, and stroked —so the chronicle has it—the backs of their necks. Soon the arrows ceased, and the captives were brought forward to Elchi who eyed them critically.

"Will ye send his own men to Lord Timur like cattle, without their swords?" he reproved the Badakshanis. "They had swords when ye took them."

The mountaineers were sadly bewildered. They could see the dreaded Timur over there on the ridge, apparently awaiting them. Their road to safety was blocked. In the end they did all that Elchi had advised—the plundered weapons were restored—and Elchi led his six hundred rescued Tatars over the ridge, and announced to Timur that the Badakshanis were waiting to kiss his stirrup.

At once Timur went down, and the men of Badakshan who had been more frightened than hostile in the beginning, swore a peace on their bow-cases. Timur and Elchi kept them occupied in talk until the lagging contingents of Tatars came up.

"This is not a fit place for sitting down," the fastidious ambassador then said. "Here there is nothing to eat or sleep in but the snow."

The Badakshani chieftains suggested that they all go to the villages, and so they trooped down from the roof of the world to feast.

This affair of Elchi the Valiant is pure gasconade.

One is reminded of Marshal Murat waving his handkerchief at the Austrians upon the bridge of Vienna, and coming over to sit on the Austrian cannon while his Frenchmen removed the mines that had been placed under the bridge.

A year or so later Elchi Bahatur died attempting to swim his horse across a river.

They knew, these lords of Tatary, that their lives would not long endure under Timur's leadership. But he shared their risks and his body bore as many wounds as theirs. Days passed with him were filled with exulting, and his nobles went singing into conflict, as the Viking berserks had done before them.

"It is a time," he said to them once, "of dancing for warriors. The dancing ground is the field of battle, the music is the battle shout and the whining of steel, and the wine poured out is the blood of your enemies."

At the end of the six years the majority of the Tatar lords had sworn allegiance to Timur. In the beginning he had been called a *kazak*, a wandering fighter who did not stay more than twenty-four hours in one spot—a word that survives to-day in the Cossacks of these same steppes. Now he was warlord, leader of a host. When Musa's people, the Jalairs, joined his standard the end was in sight. The Jalairs were half Mongol, and they could gather together an army as numerous and formidable as the army of England that had won the battles of Crécy and Poitiers less than a generation before. And Timur's eldest son had been born of a Jalair mother.

In the face of such a host led by such a warrior as Timur, the power of Hussayn melted away as snow melts before the spring rains. He was driven south of the Amu, hunted through the hills, cornered in Balkh.

The city fell almost at once, and Hussayn, hidden in the ruins, sent a last overture to Timur—a pledge that he would abandon his country and go off to Mecca, a pilgrim.

Accounts vary as to what followed. Some say that Timur promised Hussayn his life if he would come in and give himself up; but Hussayn, changing his mind at the last moment, disguised himself and hid anew in the minaret balcony of a mosque—where he was found either by the caller-to-prayer who ascended the tower the next dawn, or by a soldier who had lost his horse and had gone to the tower to look for it.

How Hussayn met his death is equally uncertain. It seems that the Tatar leaders gathered in council to discuss his fate and that Timur left the council, saying, "Amir Hussayn and I vowed friendship, and he is safe from harm at my hand." A second version is that Mouava and another officer slipped away from the gathering without letting Timur know their purpose and slew Hussayn after pretending to let him escape.

The truth of the matter is that Timur allowed his rival to be put to death. The chronicle says, "It was the hour and the place appointed for Hussayn and no man may escape his fate."

CHAPTER XII

ZAIN AD-DIN SPEAKS

TIMUR LINGERED AT BALKH with a purpose. In
this heat-ridden valley where sugar-cane grew by
the dry beds of streams, caravans plodded past India-
bound from the Land of the Sun, and the mountain
kings came down from their trails. It was a place of
memories and the dust of centuries hung in the air.

Somewhere under the clay and rubble of soft stone
lay the remnants of a temple built by fire worshipers in
the beginning of time. Strewn around underfoot were
the particles of a figure of Buddha that had stood once
in a court filled with a concourse of yellow-robed pilgrims. Men called this place the Mother of Cities—
Alexander had known it as Bactria—and now it was
spoken of as Kubat al Islam, the Metropolis of Islam.
The horde of Genghis Khan had left it a vast and uninhabited ruin, around which new shrines and mosques
had grown up—a place of graves. Subsequently Timur
rebuilt it.

Now he waited near where Hussayn lay in his
shroud, his sightless eyes turned toward Mecca. With
Hussayn dead, the Tatar chieftains must choose a new
prince. Such was the law laid down by Genghis Khan.
The law also said that the prince must be a descendant
of the Mongol Kha Khan—a *tura* of the blood of Genghis Khan.

To this *kurultai*, this council of the heads of clans,
hastened all the petty rulers from the passes of India
to the steppes of the northern hordes. And down to

the council marched imposingly the turbaned folk, the Iranian princes, the *ulama* or learned council of Bokhara—heads of academies, servants of the Church and masters of disputing. With them appeared the imams, the leaders of the faithful, among these Zain ad-Din in his white robes and voluminous turban, his shrewd eyes a little dimmed by age. Also his companion, the venerable monk Khoja Beha ad-Din, who was revered as a saint in the lands of Beyond the River. While the army and the church gathered to discuss him, Timur remained apart with his son Jahangir.

Some princes dared oppose Timur's election. "Let us now divide the lands in a brotherly manner," said the spokesman of the Badakshan clans, "each ruling his own province and uniting together to resist invasion."

Timur's veteran amirs pointed out the folly of that. "An *elder brother* is needed," they said. "If you divide, and form separate kingdoms the Jats will come and overwhelm you."

The strongest chieftains desired to return to the old order of things. "It is contrary to our code of law that any of us should be ruler; we should choose some one of the posterity of Genghis Khan to be our head, and Timur to be his deputy."

Whereupon a monk whose name was The Father of Blessings arose and made clear the choice of the church.

"It is contrary to the law of Muhammad," he began, "that *his* followers should be servants of you who are infidels.[1] As to Genghis Khan, he was a dweller in the desert who by violence and his sword conquered the Muhammadans. Now, at this moment, the sword of Timur is not less than Genghis Khan's."

[1] They were Jalair and Selduz chieftains, Tatars of the old strain. To such men the code of Genghis Khan was still the law. At this council of Balkh for the first time in the hundred and forty years since the death of Genghis Khan, the Tatar princes voluntarily departed from the old custom.

And he harangued the warriors, until out of their silent meditation grew enthusiasm.

"You all fled from Hussayn, concealing yourselves in the desert. Not until Timur advanced against him did you quit your hiding corners. He did not ask for your help to subdue his enemy, nor does he now ask it. I have spoken to you hitherto as Tatars, but I know you are also Muhammadans. And I, who am descendant of the grandson of Muhammad, in consultation with the other descendants and the leaders of the faith, look upon Timur as Lord of Beyond the River—yea and all the plains of Turan."

So spoke the church, not because Timur was a devout follower of Muhammad but because he alone seemed able to restore order out of chaos, and to resist the northern hordes who were the old enemies of Islam. What made Timur's election inevitable was the desire of the warriors—the men of the ranks—who insisted upon no other ruler.

The next day all the princes and the elders of the tribes waited upon Timur at his pavilion and bent the knee to him, taking him by the arms and leading him to the white felt upon which he was to sit as their lord and master. This was the old ritual of the Mongol clans. Thus the helmeted men gave their allegiance.

But the church had its hand in what we may call the coronation. Zain ad-Din carried from one amir to another a copy of the Koran and asked them to swear to obey no man except Timur. We moderns would call this a gesture, of submission, of acknowledgment —since Timur was already virtually their leader. But such a gesture, to these men, meant much.

From now on Timur the warrior would be Timur the Amir, and they would eat of his salt. Fidelity to him would be their honor, and treachery would bring

THE ASSAULT OF A CITY GATE. THE TATARS
HAVE BUILT AN INCLINE AGAINST THE
WALL AND ARE ADVANCING UNDER COVER
OF MAKESHIFT WOODEN SHIELDS, PRO-
TECTED BY ARROW FIRE. (*Schulz*)

TIMUR CROSSING THE AMU. THE WARRIORS
ARE LEAVING THE BARGES TO MOUNT
THEIR HORSES. CRESSETS HAVE BEEN
LIGHTED IN THE CAMP AND THE GREAT
SIGNAL-HORNS ARE IN EVIDENCE. CONTEM-
PORANEOUS. (*Schulz*)

shame upon their names and the spirits of their sons. Timur would be arbiter of their quarrels, guardian of their property. If he failed them, they were privileged to hold another council, and choose another Amir.

Standing on the carpet before the new Amir, Zain-ad-Din lifted his voice: "It is the will of God that thou shouldst conquer; thou wilt grow in power, and Islam through thee."

But the man who sat upright in the low ebony throne on the white felt, smiled at the noisy disputation of the monks from Bokhara and the assemblage of the *sayyids,* as to which should have the position nearest his right hand. There was no mark of Islam upon him; his head was not shaved, and he wore armor—linked bands of polished steel and spreading shoulder pieces and a black helmet that came down over his ears and neck, inlaid with gold.

To his new vassals he made gifts of all he had, blooded horses, robes, weapons and rich saddles. To their pavilions that night he sent trays of food and fruit. And the *sayyids* who had thronged into his tent to make manifest their affection for him, protested at his lavishness in giving.

"If I am indeed the King," he answered them, "all wealth is mine. And if I am not the King, what will it avail me to keep what I already have?"

The following day he appointed his new ministers and officers and the members of his council. Among the men chosen appear familiar names. Amir Daoud received the government of Samarkand and became leader of the *divan* or council. Amir Jaku of the Barlas clan, now gray with age, was honored with a standard and the right of beating drums before him, and was appointed one of the *tavachis,* or aides-de-camp.

In the list of regimental commanders the names of two strangers are mentioned, one of Mongol, the other of Arab descent—Khitai Bahatur, and Shaikh Ali Bahatur.

One thing was apparent from the beginning. Amir Timur would have no favorites. Many like Zain ad-Din had the right of entrance to his quarters at all times, but they influenced him no more than others. He kept all the reins of his government in his own hands, and he allowed himself to be advised but never overruled. This singleness of purpose was unusual in an Asiatic monarch, and unexpected in Timur, who had been careless of his private affairs until now.

And he was swift to strike at any opposition. Adherents of Hussayn were attacked before the court left Balkh, and the captives were chained or beheaded, their buildings burned or pulled down until nothing remained of their strongholds. He had been keeping a wary eye on the Jat Mongols, and now yearly expeditions were launched into the northern mountains, with orders to use steel and fire unsparingly. Timur was evidently convinced that the best defense of his border was an attack. And he found that a Jat Mongol on the defensive was not as formidable as one attacking.

Given a taste of their own medicine, the Jat clans abandoned the frontier valleys and moved north over the passes toward their citadel, Almalyk. Thither Timur did not follow them for the present. A new order of things was taking shape under his hand between the river Syr and India, and his wayward Tatars were given an altogether novel idea of discipline. Two of his amirs had been sent north to punish certain Jat clans; finding the pasture lands of these tribes abandoned, the amirs naturally turned back to the court, believing their mission at an end.

While they were fording the Syr, cheerful in anticipation of rest and feasting after their fruitless jaunt, they encountered a cavalry division very much like their own moving north. They asked whither it was bound.

"Verily," they were told, "to find the Jat hordes you did not find."

At first the amirs were angry, then they became thoughtful. Instead of going on to Timur they turned about and accompanied the second division. It was a year later that the united force appeared at Samarkand after staying out the winter in the higher ranges. But they brought back with them the cattle of the Jats and a tally of heads and devastated villages. Timur praised them all and rewarded them all alike, saying nothing about the failure of the first attempt of the two amirs. If he had done so they would have considered themselves dishonored, and would have withdrawn with their men from his following to start a blood feud.

Other chieftains, being aggrieved or feeling independent, did go off to their strongholds, only to find within a month or so regiments of Timur's riders quartered about their walls. They were herded out of their retirement and brought to the carpet of the Amir—and given presents. An officer who fled from a battle was sought out and deprived of his weapons—bound upon the pack saddle of an ass, face to tail. For days he was paraded in this manner through the streets of Samarkand, listening to laughter and jeers.

Prince Kaikosru of Katlan, a Persian of a distinguished family, abandoned Timur before the enemy in the desert of Khiva. The hard fighting Tatars went on into battle—it was here that Elchi Bahatur died, swimming his horse across the river at the heels of Shaikh Ali Bahatur and Khitai Bahatur—and were victorious. But Kaikosru was hunted down, seized and brought to trial by the amirs and judges, and without delay he was put to death.

"It is good to obey our Lord," the Tatars who had served Timur before now assured the new vassals. "They lie, who say otherwise."

Among the newcomers were sons of the Jat Mongols who had found resistance useless—Bayan, son of Bikijuk, who remembered that his father's life had been spared by the man who was now Amir, and Khitai Bahatur, the Valiant Cathayan, a morose and quick tempered chieftain who wore a leather tunic with a horse's mane falling from its shoulders. In a curious way he struck up an enduring comradeship with the equally hot tempered Shaikh Ali.

The two of them were in command of an advance division searching for the Jats, who were at last discovered encamped in force across a small river. The *bahaturs* halted on the near bank, and after some days sat down together to discuss what was to be done. Khitai believed in caution, and explained various maneuvers that would bring them across the stream without coming into conflict with the Jat horsemen.

Shaikh Ali listened in silence, evidently having no plan of his own. But Khitai took his silence for disapproval and perhaps for suspicion—Khitai being of Mongol descent.

"What is in thy mind?" he asked bluntly.

"By Allah," the shaikh responded idly, "I think that is how a Mongol fights."

Blood darkened the face of the warrior from the steppes, and he rose from his place. "Look," he said grimly, "and thou wilt see how a Mongol bears himself."

While Shaikh Ali raised himself to an elbow to watch, Khitai called for his horse, and without saddling it, started across the river. He rode in among the surprised Jats, and cut down the two first men he met. Then he was attacked and hemmed in by a number of riders.

Shaikh Ali's curiosity changed to astonishment. He sprang up, shouting to his servants to bring his horse. Swinging himself into the saddle he plunged through the stream. Scimitar in hand he flung himself among the circling horsemen until he was at Khitai's side.

"Thou art mad," he shouted at the Cathayan, "to draw thy rein hither. Go back!"

"Nay—go thou back."

With a muttered "God forbid," Shaikh Ali took his stand beside Khitai, and the Jats closed in around the two of them, until their followers who had scrambled after them could cut them free and lead them back. Then they sat down together again, their spirits calmed by action, and resumed the discussion in perfect accord.

CHAPTER XIII

THE AFFAIR OF THE SUFIS

To curb such men and lead them, was Timur's task. It needed wisdom and an unbending will. They said of him approvingly, "He judges rightly, and he rewards greatly." And they waited expectantly to see how he would receive the envoys sent to greet him—and to spy upon him—by his neighbors across the desert.

These neighbors were powerful and had long profited by raiding the Tatars during the years of anarchy. One, the Sufi of Kharesm, lord of Khiva and Urganj and the Sea of Aral, owed allegiance after a fashion to the Jat Khans, and he was a Jalair by birth. But he remembered Timur only as a wanderer who had struggled for life with the Turkoman tribesmen in the red sands. The city of Urganj at the mouth of the Amu was a flourishing center of trade, its walls were high and the Sufi did not lack pride.

He sent costly gifts, and Timur gave to his envoy still richer presents, requesting that Khan Zadé, the daughter of the Sufi who was noted for beauty, should be given as a wife to his son Jahangir. Friendly as this suggestion seemed, it meant that Timur chose to look upon the Sufi as his vassal—that Timur intended to claim the privileges of the Jat Khan, and the old boundaries of the Khanship.

"I have conquered Kharesm with the sword," the Sufi sent response, "and only with the sword can it be won from me."

Timur would have marched at once into the desert, but a certain devout Muhammadan persuaded the lord of Samarkand to wait until he could go and urge the Sufi to come to agreement with the Tatars. The emissary of the church was imprisoned by the Sufi, and Timur was no longer to be restrained.

He summoned his amirs to the standard, retraced the course of his former wandering—was deserted by Kaikosru of Katlan and stormed the city of Khiva without engines of any kind. His men filled the dry ditch with brush and mounted on ladders.

Shaikh Ali, the chronicle says, was the first to put his hand over the rampart, when the officer behind him, jealous of his achievement, seized him by the ankle and pulled him down into the ditch—going himself to the summit of the wall and holding off the Khivans until his companions had a footing beside him. By this mad onrush Khiva fell to Timur, and he moved against Urganj where the Sufi had taken refuge. Here siege engines were needed, stone casters and mangonels, and while they were building, a message came to his camp from the Sufi.

"Why destroy so many of our followers? Let thou and I decide our quarrel with no man's hand between us. Let him be victor upon whose hand blood runs from the sword channels."

The Sufi's envoy named an hour for the duel, and a place—the level ground outside one of the main gates of the city.

All of Timur's amirs within hearing protested instantly. Bayan, the son of Bikijuk cried out: "Prince, it is now our task to fight; your place is the throne and the canopy of command, and it is not fitting you should leave it."

All of them begged for permission to take his place

in this contest, but Timur pointed out that the prince of Kharesm had challenged him, not an officer. To the envoy he announced that he would be before the gate, alone.

Under the troubled eyes of his amirs when the appointed time came, Timur put on light link mail—his swordbearer thrust the shield high on his left arm, and girdled the scimitar above his hips. Timur placed the familiar black and gold helmet on his head and shoulders and limped out to his horse, supremely happy.

He was riding off when the aged Saif ad-Din ran out from among the officers and caught his rein, falling on his knees and crying that Timur should not go out to fight like a common man. The Amir made no response. Drawing his sword he struck at his too-zealous servant with the flat of the blade. Saif ad-Din released the rein and fell back to avoid the blow.

Alone Timur trotted out of his camp, through the line of the siege engines, already thronged with silent watchers, across the intervening plain to the closed gate of Urganj.

"Say to thy lord, Yussuf Sufi," he called to the Khivans who crowded the gate towers, "that the Amir awaits him."

It was a mad kind of daring, obstinate and admirable. Timur, the Amir, was still the lover of combat—too reckless to think of issues greater than his own mood. Sitting so in the saddle of his bay charger, Brown Lad, under a hundred bows, waiting impatiently for his enemy to appear, we see the true Timur, at once the greatness and the failing of him.

Yussuf Sufi never came forth. Timur called out at length, "He who breaks his word shall lose his life."

Then, he wheeled his horse and paced back to his

own lines. He must have been chagrined and far from content, but at his coming his amirs and lords of the regiments streamed out to meet him, and from the thousands who had watched him swelled a roaring greeting. Kettledrums thundered through the clashing of cymbals and the deep clamor of the long battle trumpets, until horses neighed and reared and cattle bellowed. There was no mistaking the feeling of his men.

Timur's angry words proved prophetic, because Yussuf Sufi fell sick presently and at his death the city was given up. It was agreed that the girl Khan Zadé should be sent to the conquerors as Jahangir's bride, and Kharesm with the great city of Urganj was made into a province to be administered by Timur's eldest son. In this way the dominion once ruled by the King Maker was extended west and north. And the western Jalairs were united to their cousins of Beyond the River.

So it was with a larger army that Timur advanced before long to pay his respects to his neighbor in the south, across the river. At least fifty thousand men trotted through the echoing defile that was called the Iron Gate, their baggage carts rumbling after them between the sheer walls of red sandstone.

The affair had begun with the usual punctilious diplomacy. The Malik of Herat was a youth named Ghiath ad-Din, the son of that Malik who had taken refuge with the King Maker aforetime. In due course Timur invited Ghiath ad-Din to attend one of his yearly councils, and this invitation meant that the Amir was ready to receive the Malik as a vassal.

Whereupon the lord of Herat expressed his pleasure at such a request and said that he would gladly go to

Samarkand if the venerable Saif ad-Din were sent to
escort him. So Timur dispatched the eldest of his
amirs to Herat. But Saif ad-Din returned alone to
say that the Malik had only made pretense of getting
presents together, and had really no intention of coming. Instead he was building a new wall around Herat.

Timur then sent an ambassador who was detained
by the prudent Ghiath ad-Din. The Tatar standards
were lifted, and the host of the helmeted men moved
south, building a bridge of boats over the Amu, highly
elated at making war outside their own provinces.
They grazed their horses in the spring meadows,
climbed over the mountain passes, and turned aside
to sit down before Fushanj—the stronghold of Herat
where Ghiath ad-Din had placed a garrison. Timur
was in no mood to delay, and a direct assault began
at once—the water ditch covered over with planks, and
ladders placed under a barrage of missiles.

To encourage his men Timur went among them
without his armor and was wounded twice with arrows.
At the heads of the storming parties Shaikh Ali, and
Mubarak—the officer who had pulled him down at
Urganj—and the son of Elchi were at their old ri-
valry. Under the steady din of the drums, the Tatars
swarmed at the walls, until some of their number,
prowling about the ditch, discovered or broke into an
aqueduct and waded into the city sword in hand.
Others surged through the opening and cleared a sec-
tion of the wall. Fushanj was a scene of headlong
pillage, the garrison cut down, the inhabitants flying.

Its fate brought gloom to Herat, and when Timur's
host met and drove back the sallies of the Malik's men,
Ghiath ad-Din the unfortunate began to bargain for
peace. He was received with honor, sent to Samarkand—his new wall razed, and his city ransomed.

The gates of Herat were carried off to the Green City, with the treasure of the Maliks—silver money, uncut precious stones, brocades and the gold thrones of the dynasty.

The taking of Herat added a great city to Timur's growing dominion, a true metropolis, nine thousand paces in circuit, housing a quarter million souls. The tally of the conquerors showed that there were in the city several hundred colleges, and three thousand bath houses, and nearly ten thousand shops. (At this time London and Paris had certainly no more than sixty thousand inhabitants each, and while there were schools in Paris, history has no record of hot baths.) But the Tatars were most astonished by the mills that were turned by wind instead of water.

The chronicle says that after this victory Timur's dominion became so secure that luxury was its only enemy. These wars in miniature, the driving away of the Jats, the overthrow of Yussuf Sufi and Ghiath ad-Din, were domestic affairs wherein gallantry and tactics played their parts and strategy not at all. They demonstrated merely that Timur had become an exceptional leader, and that he had been prompt to make himself master of the nearby powers that might have threatened him—for in the beginning he was less strong than the Malik of Herat. If he had fled years ago from Hussayn to the protection of the Malik, instead of turning back to Karshi—

But in Timur there had arisen a leader who had the instinct of a conqueror, and who was now in the fullness of his strength. He was thirty-four when he sat upon the white felt at Balkh, in the year 1369. And beyond his borders, in all the quarters of the four winds, warfare smoldered. Upon the track of the Black Plague that swept from Asia into Europe earlier in the century, unrest stirred, and dynasties fell. The trade caravans turned aside into new channels. Men sought the armed camps, and horsemen appeared in deserted fields, and flame moved through the darkness.

Into this vaster battleground it was inevitable that Timur should go.

Part Two

CHAPTER XIV

SAMARKAND

I T WAS NOW EXPEDIENT that Timur should go to Samarkand. The Green City had been the fairest spot in Beyond the River, but Timur was now Amir of a wide dominion, and Samarkand facing the gates of the north was now the central point of his lands—which stretched, more or less, five hundred miles in every direction.

Before moving his court, the Amir adorned his native city. Over the grave of his father he built a small tomb with a gilt dome; he tore down the old clay palace where Aljai's beauty had made the hours resplendent. Upon the site he constructed a greater edifice with courtyards and a lofty entrance arch. It was made of white brick and the Tatars called it Ak Sarai the White Palace. Hither came the Amir to pass his winters when he was not out in the world with his army. He was always glad to see the sun-filled meadows of his own valley, and the snow peak that was the Majesty of Solomon gleaming through the mists.

Tradition drew him to Samarkand and its half-ruined palaces, rather than to Bokhara, then a smaller place, with its academies and libraries. In Samarkand in other years Alexander reveled and slew Clytus. Here Genghis Khan had quartered his horde a hundred and fifty years ago.

"It is," said Ibn Batuta, who had traveled over more

of the world than Marco Polo, "one of the greatest, the fairest and the most magnificent of cities. It stands on the bank of a river called the Potters' River, covered with water-mills and canals that water the gardens. At this river the people gather after the late afternoon prayer, to amuse themselves and walk about. Here there are balconies and sitting places, and stalls where fruit is sold. Here are also large palaces and monuments that bear witness to the high spirit of the inhabitants. The greater part are ruined and a portion of the city is also devastated—it has no wall or gates, and there are no gardens outside the city itself."

So Timur found Samarkand, among its orchards and mulberry groves. Warmed by the sheer sunlight of the mountains, refreshed by the bracing northern air, its people lived pleasantly. Because the tawny soil yielded four crops a year, and clear water flowed in the canals—and through the great aqueduct on the embankment and from leaden pipes into every house—they had no great need to labor. They listened to the clicking of their looms that wove the red cloth desired in Europe—*kirimzi*, or cramoisy, that gave both color and name to our crimson—and the dripping of their water clocks. They made the finest paper in the world, and the trade of the ends of the world passed through their gates. It was equally good to listen to the astrologer who set up shop under an arch, or to sit and watch the dancing of a trained goat. As for the ruins, they were ruins. "What God has done," said the people of Samarkand, "is well done."

They thronged to greet Timur out of policy, and called him Lion and Conqueror and Lord of Good Fortune. His splendor widened their eyes, but they were connoisseurs in matters of apparel and they remembered that ten years ago he had passed among them like a shadow out of nowhere. Also that they—aided it is true by an epidemic—had driven off the Border Mongols. They rejoiced, the silk-robed nobles, and the saddlers and porcelain makers and horse merchants and slave traders, when Timur freed them from taxation. But he requisitioned them for labor as well.

Under his eye the breached wall was repaired, and wide avenues built from the city gates to the central market—thoroughfares paved with stone flagging. At his impatient command the hill to the south was cleared of its rambling dwellings and the foundations of a citadel laid.

Where his army camped in the suburbs from the city to the river, roads were built and gardens walled off, and cement tanks sunk into the ground. Stone—gray granite—was dragged down on ox sleds from the distant blue mountains, and craftsmen thronged into Samarkand escorted by Tatar cavalry from Urganj or Herat. Ambassadors moved sedately into the avenues between the lines of poplars, and the hostelries of the city were filled.

Even the color of the city changed, because blue was the favorite color of the Tatars—being the hue of the limitless sky and the deepest water and the highest mountain ranges. Timur had seen the glazed blue tiles of Herat, and instead of the dull clay brick, his new buildings gleamed forth in façades of turquoise threaded through with gold and white lettering.

So the city was spoken of as the Gok-kand, the Blue City.

And the men of Samarkand reflected that the Lord Timur was not as other lords. "Under the hand of Iron (Timur)" became a proverb. They drew aside now when he rode down the avenues on his charger, the long-limbed, golden-hued pacer Brown Lad, with

his lords of divisions and masters of wisdom at his
heels, crimson and silver flashing through the dust.
Seldom did they dare go before him for judgment
when he emerged from the inner door of a mosque
and stood in the shade of the arched entrance while
long-robed mullahs praised him and beggars appealed
shrilly to the Provider. For the tall Amir was patient
only with those who served him in war, and if two
citizens accused each other before him, his judgment
would be swift and the head of one might be slashed
off by a swordsman of the guard.

Long did the men of Samarkand remember the coming of Khan Zadé, the King's Daughter, from Urganj
on the Aral sea. That day the highway from the west
was covered with carpets, and the soil of Timur's camp
with brocades.

Khan Zadé came, veiled, in the litter of a white
camel, surrounded by swordsmen, followed by horses
and camels bearing her gifts. To meet her rode the
tavachis and amirs, under wind whipped standards and
billowing canopies.

That sunset when the dry wind swayed the pavilions,
yellow lanterns lighted the acacia trees in flower, and
the smoke of sandal and ambergris curled around the
mighty poles of the tents. Timur walked among the
feasters, his slaves scattered gold and pearls on the
turbaned heads of the guests.

"It was all surprising," cries the chronicler, "and
there was no place for melancholy, anywhere. The
ceiling of the great pavilion was made like the blue
sky in which shone stars of precious stones. The chamber of the bride was divided off by a curtain of gold
brocade, and it is true that the princess' bed was beautiful as that of Kaydesa, the queen of the Amazons."

The presents that the princess Khan Zadé brought

to her husband Jahangir were displayed, and Timur filled the chambers of another pavilion with gifts on behalf of his son—girdles of gold, money, uncut rubies, musk, amber, silver brocades and satins, and worked gold and silks of Cathay, robes, and the finest horses and women slaves. The chronicler pauses to mention these admiringly and to add that every day of the festival one of these chambers was emptied.

Did Timur, watching his son and the dark haired princess of Kharesm, remember that other night when Aljai had come to him in the war camp, and the kettledrums had roared? Aljai had smiled when he walked alone with her in the desert—"Surely our fate cannot be worse than this, that we should have to walk!"

Khan Zadé's fate was otherwise. The first wife of Jahangir, eldest son of a conqueror, master of a court of his own, proud of her beauty, she dared rouse Timur's anger.

"O my Lord," she said, "a conqueror is he who pardons equally kings and beggars, and if they have been guilty forgives them—because when an enemy asks forgiveness he should no longer be looked upon as an enemy. A conqueror when he gives, does not seek for any return; he does not lean upon the friendship of any one man, or cast the weight of his anger upon any one enemy, for all are beneath him and he alone has power."

"Nay," Timur responded, "for I, who am served by chieftains, am troubled by the words of a hermit."

He liked Khan Zadé's wit, though he knew she was pleading for his favor on behalf of her own kinsmen. It pleased him that Jahangir's first child by her should be a son.

He himself had taken to wife Sarai Khanum, whose husband had been Amir Hussayn. This was the custom of the older Mongols—that the women of the royal family should be taken into the household of the new ruler when their husbands were slain. And Sarai Khanum had in her veins the blood of Genghis Khan.

She was his consort, the great princess, mistress of the household "behind the tent walls." When Timur was in the field the court paid honor to her dignity. She was virile as all the Tatar noblewomen of that day, and often she rode to the hunts; about her silent fidelity to the Amir centered the loyalty of the infant grandchildren.

The men of Samarkand saw little of Timur. But tidings of him came in daily by courier or a camel rider of the frontier patrol, or with the wagon train that brought the tribute of a city that had opened its gates to him. Quiet had settled upon Beyond the River. He marched yearly to the west, along the great Khorassan road, past Nisapur and the domes of Meshed, to that other sea, the Caspian. Samarkand heard that he had put an end to the strange monks, the Sebsevars—Heads-to-the-Gibbet—who had played the part of brigands, too long.

Less was known of his march to the north. But this time he penetrated to the city of the Jat Mongols and beyond, and tales were told in the caravan *sarais* of Samarkand about the plains of the moving sands—the Gobi. Kamar ad-Din, the last Mongol who dared face him in battle, had been overthrown, even his horse captured, and had fled alone.

"Before, we stamped out the sparks of a conflagration," Timur sent word to his son Jahangir who had not gone to the north, "now we have put out the fire."

Upon the day of his return, down the thousand miles of the north road to Cathay, the men of Samarkand went beyond the outer gardens to greet him. They waited silently, clad in dark garments.

Saif ad-Din, oldest of the amirs, led a party of officers toward Timur. Upon their black cloaks they had scattered dust. Timur reined in at sight of them, and Saif ad-Din dismounted, going on foot to his stirrup and clasping it without looking up.

"Dost thou fear?" said Timur. "Then speak!"

"There is no fear in my heart," responded Saif ad-Din. "In his youth, before his strength was full, thy son is gone. Like a blown rose at the wind's touch, he is gone from thee."

Jahangir's illness had not been reported to the Amir his father, and he had died a few days before Timur's return. Saif ad-Din, the prince's preceptor, had ventured to tell Timur of his loss.

"Mount, and take the place that is thine," Timur said presently. When the old amir had done so, the signal was given to go forward, and at a foot pace—for the news spread at once through the ranks—the army entered Samarkand.

That night Jahangir's *nakaras,* the kettledrums that had announced his coming since he had held rank, were brought before Timur and broken, so that they could not be sounded again by other hands. For an instant pain tightened the wide lips of the Tatar. More than anything else that belonged to him, he had loved Jahangir.

CHAPTER XV

To UNDERSTAND WHAT HAPPENED now it is necessary to turn back nearly a hundred years and look
at Kubilai Khan. Or rather at the Mongol empires
of the day of Kubilai Khan.

The conquests of Genghis Khan had been too sudden
and too huge for any single man to dominate for long.
Although his grandson Kubilai was still the Kha Khan,
still the great Khan, overlord of his brethren, he was
actually master of no more than Cathay. From his
city of Kambalu he ruled the Gobi desert, China proper
and Korea. Elsewhere the other grandsons were at
war.

It was domestic war, savage and ceaseless and usually
without result. The various appanages of the Mongols remained intact, envoys came and went between
them, and trade flowed steadily along the caravan
routes. The long north road from Rome to Moscow,
over the steppes to Almalyk and across the desert to
Kambalu, was still open. So was the highway from
Bagdad to Kambalu. A generation after the death
of Kubilai a venturesome Arab marabout Ibn Batuta
outwandered Marco Polo. In 1340 nuncios of the
Pope Benoit XII traveled to the court of the great
Khan in Cathay. At Almalyk, the reigning city of the
Jat Khans, there was an almost forgotten but flourishing Christian mission.

But already one link of the Mongol chain of empire
had snapped. Down in the southwest the Il-Khans

had ruled from Jerusalem to India. To these Il-Khans as late as 1305 we find ambassadors journeying from Edward I of England and James II of Aragon, and the Greek Emperor of Constantinople and the King of the Armenians—to retain the good-will of the "very great and illustrious Mongol Lord."

At this time, softened by luxury and attacked by the Iranian princes—Arab and Mamluk and Persian—the Il-Khans fell. Anarchy succeeded. Meanwhile the great Khan in Cathay had been cast out by the Chinese, and his Mongols driven back slowly into their native steppes, the Gobi. Their strength sapped by Chinese civilization, they had lost the secret of victory; surprised and obstinate, they were penned beyond the great wall again, to rebel at times but never to march as conquerors upon the highways.

The smallest of the Mongol appanages had been that of the Jats—as the descendants of Chagatai, son of Genghis Khan, came to be called. The King Maker had lopped off the southern half of their lands around Samarkand. And now, in 1375, Timur the Amir had ousted them from their mountains around Almalyk.

Timur in his advance north had not only crossed the mountain barriers, he had put himself astride the great highways of Asia. Without knowing about it, or probably caring in the least, he had marked the end of the barbarian inroads from north Asia. Scythians, Alans and Huns—Turks and Mongols, they had all come out of the limbo of the steppes. They had been his ancestors, and he had prevailed over his foster brothers. The gentleman was driving the barbarian into the desert.

In this decade, 1370-1380, three quarters of the old Mongol dominion vanished from the map, and the highways were closed. But the most formidable quarter remained intact. This was to the north and east of Timur and it was called the Golden Horde.

It had grown up around Juchi, the eldest son of Genghis Khan. It had been dubbed the Golden Horde because Batu the Splendid, the son of Juchi, had covered his great domed tent with cloth-of-gold. It had fared well indeed because the steppes of mid-Asia and Russia were perfectly suited to the needs of these nomads; it had increased and its cattle had multiplied and it had worried Europe exceedingly for a hundred and fifty years.

At Timur's birth the Golden Horde was at the height of its power. Life in the open plains, seasoned by constant raiding, had kept these nomad clans fit and more than aggressive.

They wandered over the snow countries, whipped by the winds from the northern tundras—the women and children keeping to the covered carts that were towed by oxen, the warriors riding beside them. Whole cities moved in this fashion, smoking kitchens on wagons, domed mosques of gray felt adorned with banners. Sometimes they retired to a many-towered fortress of pine logs, up north where the blue timber marks the limit of the grasslands.

They were half pagan. Long-haired shamans, girdled with strings of iron images, squatted beside mullahs, and the tame bears of conjurers slept under the mosque wagons. Uncounted horse herds filled their changing pastures, and the sheep were numbered by the dogs that drove them.

Only the ruling families were Mongols. The rest were the offspring of all the north that our ancestors called the Land of Darkness. Their names sound like the roll call of the Hyperboreans—Kipchaks (Desert

Men), Kankalis (High Carts), and Kazak Kirghiz, Mordvas, Bulgars, Alans. Among them were gypsies and Genoese—merchant traders—wanderers out of Europe, a few Armenians, and plenty of Russians. They were largely Turks and Tatars, but it is simplest to call them men of the Golden Horde.

They were cousins of Timur's Tatars—slant-eyed and thin-bearded, nervous and acquisitive. They dressed in sables and padded silks and had excellent armor. And they were less barbaric than the Russians of their day—they minted coins for the Russians to pay back to them as tribute, and supplied the counting machines to calculate what was due them, and the paper on which they made out the charters of the Russian grand princes.

Russia was ruled by them from a distance—from their city of Sarai on the Volga, and Astrakhan. To them went the Russian princes with gifts and tribute, and as a rule they only entered Russia when the tribute failed, to burn and slay and fill their saddle bags with what they fancied.

The political balance of eastern Europe was in their hands, and not long since they had raided suddenly into the heart of Poland, under a Khan who had married the daughter of a Greek Emperor. To their court at Sarai went the agents of the industrious Venetians and Genoese who had established trading posts throughout their territory.

The only check to their power was given by Dmitri, the great prince of Moscow who had recruited a host of 150,000 Russians, boyards and swordsmen. At the river Don he arrayed his standards against Mamai of the Golden Horde and defeated him. A glorious day for the Russians, but a day soon ended. And they had cause to say "We who have taken up the sword have suffered more than our fathers who bent the neck of submission."

It happened at this time that one Toktamish, a prince of the Crimea, fled from his kinsmen of the Golden Horde. For refuge he went to Timur. And at his heels came a chieftain on a white horse, the ambassador of the Golden Horde.

"O Tamerlane," [1] cried the herald, "thus says Urus Khan, lord of the east and west, lord of Sarai and Astrakhan, master of the Blue Horde and the White Horde, and the Khans of Sibir—thus says he: 'Toktamish has killed my son and sought refuge with you. Surrender him to me, or I will make war upon you, and a battlefield will be chosen.'"

Nothing could have suited Timur better. Already his conquests overlapped those of the Hordes, and a struggle for mastery was inevitable. To have a prince of the royal house of Genghis Khan on his side was a stroke of sheer good fortune, and in any case Timur would never have given up a man who had sought sanctuary with him.

"Toktamish," he replied, "has put himself under my protection. I will defend him against you. Go back to Urus Khan and tell him that I have heard his words and I am ready."

He feasted Toktamish, and called him his son—gave him two fortresses on the northern frontier, and officers and men to aid him. The two cities, it happened, Timur had taken from the Hordes. To all this he added an imperial outfit—weapons, gold, furniture and arms, camels, tents, drums and banners.

[1] Outside his own borders Timur was spoken of as Timur-i-lang, Timur the Limper. Only two rulers presumed to address him so to his face, and one of them was Urus Khan. At this time Urus was Khan of the White Horde, lying east of the Golden, where Mamai still ruled, but the two peoples were presently united under Toktamish.

Thus equipped Toktamish sallied forth, and was soundly whipped by the Hordes. Again Timur out-fitted him, and again he was trounced, swimming back alone across the Syr on Timur's charger, Brown Lad, hiding wounded in the brushwood until an officer of the Barlas clan on scout duty found him and assisted him to the court. Then the wheel of fortune turned.

Urus Khan died, and Toktamish became the chief claimant of the throne of the Golden Horde. Sup-ported now by half the northern clans, strengthened by part of Timur's host, he began to taste victory. Headlong, cruel and untroubled by scruples, he passed across the steppes like a black wind storm. He drove out Mamai and took up his quarters at the reigning city, Sarai on the Volga.

He demanded tribute from the Russian princes, who were too mindful of their victory of two years ago at the Don to play the part of submission again. By fire and blood Toktamish sealed his mastery over them, marching through the smoke of burning villages toward Moscow, which he besieged, tricked and sacked, leaving the Grand Prince grieving. To Toktamish at Sarai then came the sons of the Russian princes as hostages, and the Genoese and Venetian nobles to sue for trade privileges.

Again the wheel revolved. Toktamish, master of the Golden Horde, was not Toktamish the fugitive. He had seen the majesty of Samarkand and the pavil-ions of the Tatars. He turned upon Timur without warning and without concerning himself about such an abstract thing as gratitude.

Some of his nobles, it seemed, advised against this. "Timur's friendship hath aided thee. Only God knows if thy fortune may not change again, and thou wilt not have need of his friendship."

But Toktamish felt assured of the result—moreover Timur had taken Urganj that had belonged in times past to the Golden Horde. Toktamish moved to war with all the caution and the careful preparation that had been taught by the tradition of his race. Some detached forces of the Golden Horde appeared near the Caspian sea where Timur was then engaged. But presently into Timur's camp galloped a courier weary and swaying in the saddle. He had come nine hundred miles, from Samarkand, in seven days. And he reported that Toktamish with the main body of the Horde had crossed the Syr and was invading Timur's home-land, a few marches from Samarkand.

So swiftly did Timur return along the great Khorassan highway, leaving foundered horses in his wake, that he appeared upon the scene before Toktamish could reach Samarkand.

Several of the frontier fortresses had held out against the invaders from the north. Omar Shaikh, the eldest of Timur's sons, had encountered them in battle and had shown rare bravery, although he was defeated, his men scattered into the hills. Tidings of Timur's approach found Toktamish's divisions separated, their work half done. They burned a palace in the suburbs of Bokhara, and withdrew beyond the Syr.

But Timur's home-land had been invaded and partially laid waste—crops trampled, horses and captives carried off. And when the horned standards of the Horde appeared, other standards were raised in revolt. On Timur's left, the Sufis of Urganj—Khan Zadé's relatives—took the field. On his right in the high valleys of the ranges the Jat clans mounted their horses and rode down to pillage.

The real struggle for mastery was at hand. Toktamish, born of the seed of Genghis Khan, upholder of
the Yassa, champion of the nomads, arrayed at his
side the Mongol powers. Timur, son of the chieftain
of a small clan, had at his back no more than his own
following of clans bound by loyalty to him.

Meanwhile Toktamish had vanished into his steppes
as swiftly as a fox slips into a covert. Where he would
strike again, there was no telling.

Timur called before him all those who had held
command and had been defeated by the Horde. He
rewarded the leaders who had shown daring, and one
who had fled from the battle he ordered punished in
his own way—trimming the offender's hair like a
woman's, painting his face red and white and sending
him barefoot and in woman's garments to walk the
streets of Samarkand.

Then, in the worst of a bitter winter, Toktamish
came down with a formidable host toward the river
Syr. A European monarch in Timur's situation would
have withdrawn into Samarkand and left the outlying
districts to take care of themselves. But Timur had
never once allowed himself—not even when defending
Karshi—to be penned behind walls.

He had only a portion of the army with him—the
rest were off clearing the eastern passes of Jats. To
retire on Samarkand and leave the Golden Horde to
face the rigors of the winter in the open seemed obviously the safest course. But to give a leader like
Toktamish the run of the country would have meant
disaster; the northerners were quite at home in winter
marching, and the Sufis and the Jat Khans would have
joined them. Timur's amirs advised retiring to the
south and waiting until he could gather together the
scattered divisions.

"Wait!" cried their Amir. "Wait—for what? Is this a time to wait for the morrow?"

Himself at their head, he divided his forces, and ordered them up to the Syr. They rode through rain and snow, the horses up to their bellies in the drifts. They attacked the outposts of the Horde, filtered through the divisions of Toktamish, and drove in his foragers. Under Timur's maneuvering they appeared to be the advance of a yet greater host.

When Toktamish found them circling to his rear, he was certain that stronger bodies must be supporting them. Unwilling to risk being cut off from the northern road in such a season, he withdrew swiftly, and Timur ordered detachments to follow and keep in touch with him.

When the roads had dried out in the spring Timur moved out himself, but to the west. He struck into the country of the Sufis and laid siege to Urganj. Regardless of slaughter, the great city was carried, and given to the sword. No dueling upon this occasion! The walls were mined and torn down, the palaces and hospitals burned, and the site left in smoking ruins filled with charred bodies. The surviving inhabitants were taken to Samarkand.

With them he turned back, and passed into the east, harrying the Jat clans before him to Almalyk, driving them so far that for years they would not cause trouble on his borders.

Not until this was done, his flanks cleared, did he devote himself to the struggle with Toktamish. And instead of awaiting the Golden Horde in his own country, he mustered his regiments and reviewed them on the great plain by Samarkand. There he explained to them his purpose. He meant to ride north into the lands of the Golden Horde, and there meet Toktamish.

CHAPTER XVI

THE WAY OVER THE STEPPES

THIS DECISION invited certain disaster. Napoleon
doing likewise more than four hundred years
later left the *grande armée* of France dead in the snows
of Russia and Poland, although he took Moscow.

Timur had not yet encountered the Golden Horde
in the field. Toktamish's host was more numerous
than his own, and slightly more mobile—since it would
have an immense stock of fresh horses to draw upon.
Timur's men were capable of living off the country—
given some water and any kind of grazing. But the
Golden Horde had lived off that country for generations.

To enter it Timur would have to feel his way
through sand deserts and clay steppes and sterile hills;
over such terrain it would not be possible to transport
provisions to serve for more than two or three months.
And if then he met Toktamish he would be obliged
to give battle with the barren lands at his back. A
defeat would mean the inevitable loss of the greater
part of his host, and in all probability his own death.

Peter the Great sent a Russian army in 1716 south
over this country against Khiva and the Turkomans,
and the Russian general Prince Bekovitch Cherkassi
(the Circassian) died in the desert with most of his
men, the rest being made slaves. A century later
another army under Count Perovski tried it in winter
when an ample water supply was assured—and the
survivors came back the year after, leaving ten thou-

sand camels and as many carts and a large part of its men in the icy plains behind it.

These wastes of Asia are still forbidden ground to expeditionary forces of any size. And Timur could not go around. By marching due west, around the Caspian, he could strike the cities of the Golden Horde. But nothing was more certain than that Toktamish would be master of Samarkand before Timur had penetrated the Caucasus valleys. And Timur could have no idea where Toktamish might choose to meet him—at the edge of the border deserts, or fifteen hundred miles away at the Black sea, or up near the Baltic, or even under the rising sun where the Gobi lies. As a matter of fact Toktamish chose to do something quite different and equally unexpected. And Timur's service of information had failed, his provisions given out and he and his army had entirely lost their way before he saw the horned standards of the Golden Horde.

By all the canons of military strategy Timur invited failure. But he was right. He acted upon his knowledge of human nature, and not by bravado. A moment's reflection will recall that Toktamish had lived at his court for some years, and had twice fled from a pitched battle. Timur understood thoroughly the strength and weakness of the Mongol temperament, and plan of action.

He must have known that in the end he could never win a defensive war against a cavalry leader like the Khan; that as long as Toktamish held power in the north, Samarkand would be menaced. Timur simply chose to risk everything to bring the struggle to a final issue in the country of the Golden Horde where Toktamish least expected him.

Nothing is more clear than that throughout his

career the Amir of Tatary followed three fixed rules: never to involve his own country in the maneuvering of any campaign; never to allow himself to be put upon the defensive; always to attack as swiftly as hard driven horses can travel.

"It is better," he said once, "to be at the right place with ten men than absent with ten thousand." And again, "It is good to go swiftly and break an enemy's power, before he has mustered his full strength. No greater army should be taken than can be maintained on the way."

In the beginning, until they left the muddy Syr behind them they were on familiar ground. They passed from one frontier fortress to another and moved slowly through the barrier range, the Kara tagh. Here—it was the end of February—deluges of snow and rain held them up in camp, and hither came envoys from Toktamish to present Timur with nine splendid horses and a falcon with a jeweled gorget.

Timur took the falcon on his wrist and listened in silence to the tale of the ambassadors. Toktamish, it seemed, admitted his obligation to the Amir of Samarkand, and his error in making war, and wished to enter into a peaceable alliance with Timur. This was no more than a feint at diplomacy, to be treated as such.

"When your master," Timur replied to the ambassadors, "was wounded and oppressed by his enemies it is well known that I aided him and called him my son. I took his part against Urus Khan, and many of my horsemen died. All this he forgot when he saw himself powerful. When I was in Persia he betrayed me, and destroyed my towns. Since then he sent another great army into our country. And now, when we march against him, he would save himself from punishment. Too often has he broken his oaths. If now he sincerely desires peace, he must send Aly Bey to negotiate with my amirs."

Aly Bey, the chief minister of the Golden Horde, was not forthcoming, and the march northward was not delayed. The women of the royal court were sent home with the officers who were to defend Samarkand, and Timur's host moved out from the shelter of the hills into the White Sands.

For three weeks it marched over the wind-billowed dunes, still bleak with the passing of winter. In the cold before dawn the *kourroun*, the seven-foot trumpets, sounded their summons and the divisions saddled up and mounted. Tents were stowed in the heavy carts that had wheels higher than a man's head. Beside the carts moved the strings of baggage camels, grunting and snarling under their loads. In the carts also were the equipments of the squads—ten men were in a tent —two spades, a saw and pickax, sickle and ax, a coil of heavy cord, a cooking pan and an oxhide. Provisions were of the lightest—flour, barley, dried fruit and the like. On entering the White Sands, each man was limited to some sixteen pounds of flour a month.

Every soldier had been furnished an extra horse. All were mounted and armed with cuirass of link mail, helmet, shield and two bows—one for long distance, one for rapid shooting. Each man had thirty arrows, scimitar or two-edged sword and whatever smaller side-arms suited his fancy. Most of the regiments carried long lances slung at their shoulders; some had the heavier javelin, or thrusting spear.

The divisions moved in a set formation—it would have been suicidal to divide, and they camped in the same order. Every officer could be found in a certain position and a certain distance from the amir's standard. So there was little confusion even in the dark-

ness. Although they rode at ease, the amirs of *tumans*
—lords of divisions—kept their regiments in approxi-
mate battle position. This wide-flung array allowed
the horses to take advantage of what little grazing was
to be had, where a green scum was appearing in the
sand.

An hour or so before noon the *kourroun* sounded
again and they halted to rest the horses. Already the
weaker beasts were dying off from lack of water.

Late in the afternoon they made camp in a region
picked out by the scouts in advance. Timur's horsetail standard surmounted by the gold half-moon was
set up in front of his pavilion poles, and his curtained
tent palaces rose around it.

Then followed a rather stirring thing, the Tatar retreat. As each lord of division brought up his regiments and encamped, his kettledrums rolled. Mounting again and assembling his divisional officers, he rode
to the central standard, his drummers going before him
with the band—flutes, pipes and horns.

At the piercing note of the pipes, shrill and so swift
that the ear could hardly follow it, the horses pranced
and were reined in cruelly. Cymbals clashed, and a
band of chosen singers, heads thrown back and eyes
shut, wailed a chant of daring and delight of war.

In the red glow of sunset, trotting over the dark
sands, their wild, fur-tipped heads tossing above the
manes of the horses the amirs sought the standard.
Steel gleaming under crimson and sable cloaks, shrill
song echoing the thudding hoofs, they passed before
Timur. With a jangling of silver-weighted reins and
a single deep throated cry they greeted him:

"Hour-ra!"

When the last division commander had come and
trotted by, his thin dark face alight with pride in his

own splendor and the magnificence of his lord, Timur dismounted and went to dine with his entourage. Even in the desert he was dressed in the richest embroidered silks and the finest of brocades.

After dark to his quarters came the supervisors of the march lighted by lanterns with reports from the scouts who had been miles out on the wings and in advance. Timur was told the condition of the horses, and the number of sick.

He pushed over the sands rapidly, and tolerated neither delay nor straggling. A man who fell behind had his shoes filled with sand and hung about his neck, and was obliged to walk afoot the next march. If he lagged again, he died.

At the end of three weeks they entered rolling grassland, where mists filled the gullies. Here, upon the bank of a river in flood they camped to rest the horses, and they swam the river by divisions. They called it the Sari Su, which means the Yellow Water.[1]

They were amazed at the extent of the prairies, which seemed to them like the sea itself in its rolling monotony. When they neared two mountains that they christened the Big and Little, they halted while Timur climbed the larger elevation and stared with his officers at the vista of the green steppes stretching to the skyline beyond the purple shadow of the mountain. It was then early in April, the grass tinged with the blue of cornflowers. Partridges ran through the wild wheat, eagles circled overhead. Through the veils of mist shone the gold of distant freshet lakes. And in all this time, the chronicle says, they had not seen a man or any cultivated land.

[1] There were no maps, of course, and these steppes are only vaguely landmarked to-day. Timur's actual course is a matter of conjecture after he crossed the Sari Su. Apparently he turned a little west at this point, toward the Urals.

Some traces were visible—camel tracks in the damp earth, charred remains of a fire, or the dung of a horse herd. Here and there they rode over human bones, washed out of a shallow grave by the winter storms.

Daily now the Tatars hunted in advance of the army. They brought in wild boars, wolves and a few antelope. Meat was very scarce—a sheep sold for a hundred *dinars kopeghi*, dog dollars. Timur ordered that no meat should be baked, or bread. The common fare was a kind of stew of meat and flour. This in turn yielded to a thick soup seasoned with herbs.

To hearten the men, who were beginning to suffer, the amirs ate with them out of the common pot. The gleanings of the hunters, an occasional trove of birds' eggs, and an increasing amount of herbs went into the soup, which was soon limited to one dish a day. The army marched with an eye to the earth for roots and quail. The ration of flour was almost exhausted.

The horses, thanks to the excellent grazing, were in tolerably good condition, but they could not be sacrificed for the pot. A man dismounted was a man out of action in this country, and to lose any large number of horses meant disaster. As the situation grew worse the officers began to ponder what lay ahead of them. To turn back now would be hazardous, because it meant recrossing the deserts with weakened men, and the near certainty that the Golden Horde would appear out of its limbo of invisibility and make of the retreat a nightmare. In this crisis Timur gave orders to his *tavachis* to permit the commanders of the wings to throw out the great hunting circle.

Hitherto scattered riders had brought in what game could be shot ahead of the divisions. Now a hundred thousand men spread themselves in a thirty-mile line.

While the center remained stationary, the distant ends of the line galloped in a half-circle, driving all four-footed beasts inward. Other regiments moved around the wings, to close the narrowing gap in the north.

Once the circle was closed, it moved inward upon itself. Not even a hare could slip past the half-starved Tatars, and as the beasts felt themselves driven there began a mad tumult of racing deer, charging boars—gray wolves slipping through the brush, bears lumbering away from the riders, stags racing with antelope.

Some of the things that turned up within the closing net surprised the Tatars. The chronicle mentions a kind of stag larger than a buffalo that they had never seen before—almost certainly elk. Timur entered the circle first, as the rule of the hunt ordained, and shot with his arrows some antelope, and deer. His mastery of the bow always roused his followers to admiration. Most of them could only draw the long bow to their chests, but Timur's great strength of arm and shoulder could draw the feathered end of an arrow to his ear.

For once meat was plentiful. The Tatars slew only the fatter beasts, and feasted memorably.

Timur gave them no time to taste idleness. The next day the *tavachis* rode out with orders to assemble the divisions for review. And an hour later Timur appeared, garbed for ceremony, his white ermine head-gear gleaming with rubies, the ivory baton tipped with a gold ox skull in his hand, and his staff at his heels.

At his coming the lords of divisions dismounted and bowed to his stirrup, following him on foot down the length of their commands, beseeching him to notice the stature and strength of their men, and the good condition of the weapons. He looked into dark faces familiar to him—the bronzed Barlas men, the lean Selduz Turks, the soldierly Jalair clansmen, and the wild hillmen of Badakshan with whom he had fought on the Roof of the World.

He was not content with this. Later in the day the great kettledrum by the standard sounded its thunder, bred of a six-foot brass basin and taut bull's-hide. The drums of the encampment answered, and at once the mounted division separated into regiments that moved into battle formation. Probably never before or since did these steppes of Siberia witness a review of such a host. The officers galloped to their new posts and from one wing to the other, miles distant, arose the shout that heralds a charge.

"*Hour-ra!*"

The army was fit and in excellent spirit, and the next day it took up the march again.

CHAPTER XVII

THE LAND OF SHADOWS

Fog rolling away before them, green-gray wisps of alders hemming in the streams, yielding moss and treacherous swamps underfoot, red creepers twining over gray rocks. It was a place of silence. Hawks winged over the tree-growth, but no songbirds greeted the sun. The sky was no longer the royal blue of Samarkand. Sometimes shallow mounds loomed in the mist—graves or barrows of some voiceless and vanished men.

"It is called the Land of Shadows," Ibn Batuta said of this place, "and the merchants that venture hither leave their goods and go away, returning to find furs and leather in place of what they left. No one sees the people who live in this place. Here the days are long in summer and the nights are long in winter."

It was the abode of the Cimmerians, the country of the Hyperboreans, the dwellers of the north. And the wandering tribes, supposing that they existed at all, must have fled from the approach of Timur's host. In the south Toktamish had taken pains to clear men and cattle from his path, but here the army was entering a region seemingly uninhabited.[1]

All the scouts, the chronicle says, sent out for information wandered like vagabonds in this great desert. It was not, of course, a desert; but to the Tatars accus-

[1] They were approaching the fifty-fifth degree of latitude, which lies on this continent north of Lake Winnipeg. Apparently they crossed the Tobol north of its springs. It is conjectured that the next river was the Ural. At the Ural they turned due west, crossing what is now the boundary of Europe.

tomed to the burning light of the clay barrens with their familiar wells and river cities, this gray and wet expanse without human life appeared more formidable. Especially were the mullahs upset, who found it impossible to follow the daily routine of prayer.

The early dawns—no sun being visible for hours— brought them out with the cry to prayer before the hours of the night were done; between the twilight and the sleep prayer hours passed, and the short darkness gave the men little rest.

Whereupon the imams held a solemn council at which it was decided that the routine of the prayers could be changed. Meanwhile Timur had detached a division twenty thousand strong to look for the Golden Horde. Nearly every officer of the host volunteered to go with this advance, but Timur gave the command to that youthful warrior Omar Shaikh, his son. The twenty thousand disappeared over the plains, and after a few days a courier rode back with word that they had come upon a large river, and another following at his heels reported the discovery of five or six fires not yet quite extinguished.

This was the first tangible clew to the enemy, and Timur acted upon it instantly. He summoned experienced scouts, sent them at a gallop after his son, to comb the prairies—himself riding after them with a small escort. The river proved to be the Tobol, that flows into the Arctic, and the fires were upon the far bank, to the west. Timur swam the river, joined his advance and took command.

The scouts came in with tidings that some seventy fires had been lighted nearby within the last day or so, and horses had passed over the ground. Timur then called upon Shaikh David, a Turkoman with a name for raiding and unexpected deeds, to search the country to the west. The Shaikh departed at a gallop and after two days and nights found what he sought, a group of thatched huts. He rode around the place and lay hidden for a night, being rewarded at daybreak by seeing a horseman ride out toward him.

He overpowered the man, bound him and drove him back to the advance division which had drawn closer. But the captive knew nothing of Toktamish—had only seen ten riders in armor camped in the brush near his dwelling.

Sixty Tatars were detached with spare horses to round up the ten riders. At last Timur had information to act upon. The prisoners told him that the Golden Horde was camped a week's ride to the west.

Timur's long march to the north would puzzle a modern strategist, but this was warfare without rules and without palliation. To display weakness or to leave himself open to a surprise attack by the Horde would have been fatal. He knew that unseen eyes had watched his advance, and that the Khan was well informed of his movements. Time meant everything to Timur, who must force the Horde to battle, or bring his own army into cultivated land before the end of the summer; delay was Toktamish's finest weapon and he made full use of it.

By his rapid movement to the far north Timur disconcerted the Horde which was forced to move opposite him and keep between him and its home-land, while the tribes were assembling from the far western steppes, from the Volga and the Black sea. With his full strength Toktamish would have double the number in Timur's host.

Then began the wary maneuvering of armies bred in the steppes. Caution was all-important in the face of

an enemy who could cover a hundred miles in a day—
who would remain invisible until he had chosen the
moment to attack.

Timur's actions show that he realized the hazard he
faced, his men suffering from privation. For six days
he moved west by forced marches, and reached the
bank of the Ural river. From his prisoners he learned
that there were three fords within a short distance, but
after looking at one he gave command to swim the
river elsewhere, at the point where the army had halted
—going over himself with the advance and penetrating
at once into the scattered woods.

Here they took more prisoners who said that they
had been sent to join Toktamish at the river but had
not found him. Two days were needed to bring the
Tatar host across. When his men were all over, Timur
investigated, and found that a multitude had encamped
at each of the three fords. Toktamish had lain there
in ambush, hidden in the fringe of beech and alders,
and had retreated when Timur crossed elsewhere.

But the Horde was never more dangerous than when
it seemed to be retreating.

Timur ordered his men to remain within their regimental lines, to light no fires at night. As soon as
darkness set in cavalry detachments were sent out to
circle the camp. For days they pushed westward
through the shallow valleys of the Urals, forcing their
way through marshes. Out in the open again they
made forced marches, until the day when all the bands
broke into frenzied tumult and the warriors rode forward singing.

The scouts had come up with the rearguard of Toktamish. But not with Toktamish himself. The master
of the Golden Horde had the fresher horses and the
better stock of provisions, and a last trick in his quiver.

While his rearguard skirmished daily with Timur's scouts, the Golden Horde turned north again. It could not shake off the Tatars now but it could keep ahead of them, clearing the country of game as it rode farther beyond civilization, deeper into the land of shadows. The tree-growth through which the armies passed was no longer beech and oak, but birch and dark evergreens. And the forests began to yield to the damp tundras.

Timur's men were gnawed by hunger and depressed by the slaying of three chieftains and many men who had been cut off by the riders of the Horde. They knew the issue now was one of extermination, either way. But they had everlasting faith in Timur.

Then rain came, and snow—although it was the middle of June. For six days the hosts were held in their tents. Timur was first afield. Omar Shaikh's twenty thousand riding ahead and sweeping away the outposts of the Horde, he made a forced march and at the end of the seventh day saw for the first time the horned standards, the massed herds, the domed tents and the throngs of his enemy. His divisions being already in battle formation, it was only necessary to give one order. And the order he gave was to dismount, set up the tents and cook all remaining food for a hearty meal.

His march of eighteen weeks and nearly eighteen hundred miles was ended. Half a mile distant the Horde massed for battle, its wagons moving to the rear. Neither army could disengage now—one of two swordsmen who had crossed blades could not turn and run. Toktamish's men were amazed when the Tatars went into camp as indifferently as if they had all the northern tundras to themselves; but Timur was resting his horses and strengthening his men.

His outposts were vigilant enough, and he allowed no lights to show after darkness set in; but he held no

last hour council. The lords of his personal following
slept on the carpets around him, the couriers stood by
their horses with the entrance guard. Timur sat by an
oil lamp in his armor, dozing at times, passing the hours
with his miniature warriors of the chessboard.

All arrangements had been made—the army was
drawn up in seven divisions, as it had been so often on
the march. The left wing had its advance and main
bodies, likewise the center; behind the center Timur
held aloof with the regiments of his guards and picked
veterans. The worst of the army held the center, but
on the right wing, under nominal command of Timur's
young son Miran Shah, were the distinguished amirs,
leaders of the heavy cavalry. Here too were the berserks, the fellowship of the death-seekers, Shaikh Ali
Bahatur and the rest of the *tulu bahatur*, the "madly
valiant."

And here, upon Timur's strong right flank, he had
directed the first attack to be made at dawn. Gray-
haired Saif ad-Din led five thousand riders forward
in a headlong charge, to the cry of *"Dar u gar!"*—
"Hold and slay!"

Toktamish's line extended in a half-circle, its wings
overlapping the Tatar flanks. And the extreme left
of the Horde swung in and drove at Saif ad-Din.
Even the seven-foot horns and the great kettledrum of
Timur's headquarters could not penetrate through the
tumult to those two-mile-distant flanks. The battle, except where Timur could appear in person was in the
hands of the amirs, the lords of divisions.

Another corps charged in to support Saif ad-Din, and
the whole right flank moved forward at a gallop behind
flights of arrows.[2] The Horde gave way before the

[2] Timur had formed his veteran Tatar cavalry on the right wing as
usual. It had its own advance and reserves, and the ablest generals were
always to be found in its leading lines. It maneuvered by divisions, and

impact of the heavy cavalry. Timur ordered his center forward to support Miran Shah.

What happened at the center is uncertain. Over the whole plain masses of horsemen were locked, swirling and meeting with a rending impact of steel and smitten flesh, under the deadly flashing of arrows. Wounded men clung grimly to the saddle; the dying still wielded their weapons. No mercy was looked for—men struggled until the blood drained out of them and their bodies were tossed at last from the saddle, to be trampled into the soft earth.

On the left the Tatars, outnumbered, drew back under successive charges; the Selduz clan was scattered and broken; Omar Shaikh still defended his standard. To this point rushed the headlong Toktamish, penetrating to the rear of the Tatar center.

Timur, who had followed up the advance of his center, saw the horned standards between him and the battle on the left.

He turned back with his reserve and smashed into Toktamish's flank. Under this sudden impact, beholding the horsetail standard approaching him over the gleaming helmets of Timur's guards, Toktamish felt that the end was at hand. With the nobles who were near him, he turned and forced his way out of the struggle, racing to the west without thought of the

as a rule it broke the opposing left wing completely. The Tatar conqueror was apt to hold his left wing refused, until the right had completed its advance. He himself commanded strong reserves in the rear of the center.

With his reserves he could either follow up the charge of the right wing, or move to the support of the weaker left. He seldom was in motion at all until near the end of a battle. His center was apt to be entrenched, and Timur used it mainly to go forward after the smashing impact of his splendid cavalry.

He liked nothing better than a ranged battle on an open plain, and he was capable of swinging the whole front, on the pivot of his reserves, to advance obliquely after the right wing, the left *following* the center. The formation of his main army was a permanent one, and every division knew its position and duties.

thousands of his men still on the field. He was racing with the shadow of death.

And at his going, the great horned standard of the Horde fell.

CHAPTER XVIII

MOSCOW

THE TATARS MARCHED AT LEISURE. They had captured Toktamish's camp and no longer lacked for horses or provisions. Seven regiments out of ten had been told off to pursue the fugitives—for the other nobles of the Golden Horde had fled with their men when the standard went down. The remnants of the Horde were harried east to the marshes of the Volga, where multitudes perished under the Tatar swords. The chronicle says that a hundred thousand died in the battle and the flight; however this may be, the slaughter was great.

Again the hunting line was thrown out, but this time to comb the country on either side the Volga for loot. Down to the warmer south the Tatars moved, gathering up the herds of oxen, sheep and camels, swelling the masses of their horses. They took the ripe wheat from the fields, and examined every wooden village for beautiful girls and young boys. Swinging around through Russia they found wealth that surprised them—bars of gold and silver, white ermine skins and black sables—more than enough to last each soldier and his children for their lives.

Every man had by now a mule load of woven cloth, and silver fox and vair skins, and a string of unshod colts. In fact, every man had more than he could manage, and had to abandon a good deal. The various commands united again in the lower steppes, and Timur gave permission for a week's festival.

The place delighted them—the high grass through which the warm wind rustled, the whisper of the great river. The mist was a thing of the past, and under a brilliant moon every blade of grass stood out distinct, and the clouds that passed over the sea of grass cast shadows.

The monotone of night insects, the gentle flight of stray birds, the warm fragrance of the earth made a luxury of idleness, and Timur did not gainsay them. He sat with his amirs in the pavilion that he had taken from Toktamish, silk hung, its poles plated with gold. Rose water was sprinkled upon the silk underfoot, and meat was served to the warriors by the captives.

They called in the minstrels with lutes and two-stringed guitars, and they made a song of their deeds— "Tidings of the Conquest of the Desert" they called it. But when the food was taken away and the wine cups were brought out, the music changed. It softened, sank to the low strumming of the *balalaika* and the wailing of the flute.

Wine was carried in then to the victors in golden bowls, honey mead, date wine and spirits. And the bowls were brought by the hands of captive women, hundreds chosen for their bright faces and fine figures. As was customary, their garments had been taken from them, their dark hair loosened upon their shoulders. And they were made to sing the love songs of their people before the Tatar lords took them off and violated them.

When the days of festival were ended at the Volga, Timur left the army to follow him under command of Saif ad-Din, and returned to Samarkand by forced marches. And the city, that had had no news of him for eight months, thronged out to greet him exultantly.

The menace of invasion had passed, and from this year men spoke of Samarkand as The Protected.

Timur had left Toktamish to his own devices and the vast northern portion of the empire of the Golden Horde to the mercy of Providence. He had, it is true, chosen a Mongol officer for Khan of the subjected regions. But this was no more than a gesture of authority. And the consequence was that Toktamish returned.

We find him three years later harrying Timur's frontier which was now north of the Caspian. To him Timur wrote in exasperation:

"What devil is in thee, that thou canst not keep within thy border? Hast thou forgotten the last war? Thou knowest the tale of my victories, and that peace and war are alike to me. Thou hast made proof alike of my friendship and my enmity. Choose, and send to me word of thy choice."

Again the dour Toktamish tried the issue of battle, and never was Timur so near defeat. We have a glimpse of him cut off with a few men, his sword broken, so hard pressed that his men dismounted and formed a ring about him, until a Tatar named Nur ad-Din brought up three of the enemies' carts and formed of them a sort of barrier that Timur defended until aid could reach him. His son Miran Shah and the great amir Saif ad-Din were both wounded in this battle.

But it was the end of the Golden Horde. Toktamish fled to the northern forests; his clans scattered—moved out bodily, some to the Crimea, some to Adrianople, and even into Hungary. Many joined Timur.

Ghastly was the fate of mighty Sarai on the Volga. This time Timur did not spare the cities. He retraced his steps, drove the inhabitants of Sarai out to perish in the mid-winter cold and made a flaming torch of the wooden buildings. He stormed Astrakhan at the Volga's mouth—defended, tradition says, by a massive wall of ice blocks upon which the inhabitants cast water until the whole froze together. Reminding the garrison that they were to die in revenge for the burning of the Bokhara palace, he put them all to the sword, and thrust the governor under the ice of the river.

Moscow had reason to be afraid when Timur's standards moved along the Don. The Russian grand prince and the army took the field with little hope. And sleighs sped to Vishaigorod, to fetch the ancient image of the Virgin. In procession, the image was drawn back to Moscow between lines of kneeling people who cried out as it passed.

"Mother of God, save Russia."

And to this the Russians attribute their deliverance. For Timur turned back at the Don.[1] No one knows just why. Moscow's gain was the loss of the European settlements on the sea of Azov. The soldiery of the Venetians, Genoese, Catalans and Basques fell under the Tatar sword, and in their slave ports and trading posts crowed the red cock—fire.

Under a gray sky and a winter sun, Timur marched over the ruins of the Mongol empire. It was the twilight of the Golden Horde that the seed of Juchi had

[1] It must be remembered that Toktamish's army had gutted Moscow seven years ago, and that Timur had in turn despoiled the Golden Horde of its possessions. Moscow, with its fifty thousand-odd inhabitants was no more than a roadside town, to his mind. The majority of histories persist in saying that he sacked Moscow, but the Russian annals are clear on this point.

What did happen, however, four years later, was that Witold, Duke of Lithuania, led a kind of mad crusade against the Tatars remaining in southern Russia, and two khans of Timur's court terribly defeated the host of Lithuanians, Poles, Galicians and the Grand Master of the Teutonic Knights. (Further details of this little-mentioned battle are given in the notes.)

It was Timur's sword that made it possible for the Russians to cast off the Mongol yoke.

ruled—the passing of the law of Genghis Khan. Except in the Gobi desert and the northern tundras the Mongol Khans were no longer masters.

Leaving the far north for the last time it pleased Timur to complete the march around the Caspian, to open a way through the barrier of the Caucasus.

With new additions to his host—the Kipchak, desert men, and the Karluk, the dwellers in the snows—he moved down upon the gorges and forested walls that had proved an invulnerable bulwark to other armies. It was necessary to cut a road as he went, and storm the rock nests of the warlike Georgians, who disputed his path with their usual courage.

It took all of one summer to do this, for Timur had called upon his men to accomplish what seemed beyond human skill. The forest at one place—great firs towering above the lesser growth and the trunks of fallen giants, amid a lacework of creepers and ferns— was so dense that the wind did not penetrate it, and except for spots of sunlight the murk of twilight hid the ground. Here a way had to be cut through the heavy timber.

Nearby, a mountain clan had withdrawn to a place that looked impregnable. It was a height, with cliffs on every side and the summit so high that the Tatars became dizzy looking up at it, and no man could shoot an arrow to it. Timur refused to pass it by—to leave one stronghold intact upon his new road.

He called on his Badakshan men to examine it for a possible approach. They were bred to the mountains, and had hunted horned sheep over such cliffs. From crevice to ridge they went and returned to Timur to report failure. Still the Amir would not go on. He studied the place from another height, and ordered ladders to be built and roped together.

The ladders were raised against the three-hundred-foot cliff by ropes led from the taller trees. The tops of the ladders reached a ledge part way up, and from this ledge the Tatars raised the ladders again to another foothold. They helped each other by ropes—those who were not knocked off by the stones cast down by the defenders.

Some of them climbed to a pinnacle from which they could reach the cliff summit with their arrows, and when others gained a footing on the height the Georgians surrendered.

In this way the army penetrated to the long valleys that led down to the sea. Before them lay Al Burz, the barrier range of northern Persia, with fortresses as strong as those of Georgia. One by one Timur summoned them to submit, sparing the people who did so.

Two of his sieges here are memorable in tradition —Kalat and Takrit. The first was a mountain table-land, having springs of good water on the summit and grazing ground for herds. It sprang out of a nest of gorges that made impossible the encampment of an army beneath it. The gorges proved impassable and the cliffs impregnable and the summit beyond reach. Here in later years Nadir Shah stored his treasures.

Assault failing, Timur posted detachments of his men in all the gorges and went on. Eventually an epidemic drove down the defenders, and the place was taken, and its gates and paths restored for future use.

The other citadel, Takrit, was built on solid rock facing the river Tigris. It belonged to an independent clan that raided the highways with impunity. Takrit had never been taken by assault.

When Timur approached, the chieftains of the castle decided that they would not yield the place to him. All avenues up the rock were stoned in and cemented.

At once the Tatar drums rolled for the attack. The outworks below the ridge were carried quickly enough, and the defenders withdrew into the castle. Timur's engineers then set to work to build stone casters. Long timbers were bolted in place, and the machines set up. It was found that these mangonels could send their rock projectiles over the wall, and one by one the roofs of the buildings were broken down.

But this kind of a barrage did not bother the defenders very much. At that height the stones could do no damage to the massive wall itself. On the third night the regiment of a certain Sayyid Khoja ascended the tower of an outer bastion and took it, but did not gain a footing near the wall.

Under cover of temporary roofing that was raised higher on posts, the Tatar engineers and miners went to work, erecting a scaffolding until they could stand directly under the foundation of the wall along the face of the rock.

Different sectors were told off to the separate divisions of Tatars, and seventy-two thousand men began to labor at the rock with steel bars and sledges. They excavated by relays, keeping at the task day and night. One division tunneled about twenty feet into the rock, shoring up the top as it advanced.

The besieged were alarmed by the mining, and sent out gifts to the Amir of the Tatars. But Timur said that the chieftain, one Hassan of Takrit, must come forth and give himself up. This Hassan did not see fit to do.

So the great kettledrum sounded the assault, the props under one portion of the wall were soaked in oil and buttressed with piles of brush and set on fire. The heavy timbers burned through and that sector of the wall collapsed, bringing down with it many of the defenders. The Tatars charged up the mass of rubble, but encountered desperate resistance. Timur ordered the timbers to be burned under two other sections, and black smoke welled up around the doomed citadel.

When the new breaches were opened, the heavily armored regiments carried the attack through them, and the men of Takrit fled to the height behind the half-ruined castle. Hither they were pursued, Hassan bound hand and foot and lugged down. The civilians were separated from the soldiers and spared, but the warriors of Takrit were divided among the Tatars and put to death.

Their heads were cut from the bodies, and of the heads two pyramidal towers were built, cemented with clay from the river. Upon the foundation stones of the towers this legend appeared. *Behold the fate of lawless men and evil doers*—although truth might have written, *Behold the fate of those who opposed Timur's will*. The breached wall was left standing, and men journeyed hither by day to gaze upon the handiwork of the Tatar, and the testimony to his power. But not by night, for it was said that spirit fires appeared upon the summits of the skull towers, and only the wild boars rooting through the brush visited the site of Takrit after darkness.

In seventeen days Takrit the impregnable had fallen to Timur.

He was master of the north, of the Aral and Caspian seas, of the mountain region of Persia and the Caucasus. For twenty-two hundred miles the great Khorassan road ran through his lands. Fourteen cities, from Nisapur to Almalyk paid him tribute.

But this had taken its toll of life. The council of the amirs had thinned; the fellowship of the *bahaturs* had grown less. Khitai Bahatur had fallen in the snows of the Syr—Shaikh Ali Bahatur, who had flung his helmet at the Golden Horde, had been stabbed by a Turkoman spy. And Omar Shaikh, Timur's second son, had been struck down by an arrow in the Caucasus. Death, that seemed miraculously to spare the conqueror, had taken another child from his side.

This time Timur showed no emotion when he was told of the fate of Omar Shaikh.

"God gave, and God has taken away," he said, and issued orders to return to Samarkand.

On the way he stopped at the great Ak Sarai, the white palace now finished in all its detail, in the meadow near the Green City. Here for some time he rested quietly and would have nothing of the court.

He went over to inspect the tomb he had built for Jahangir, his first-born, and ordered that it should be enlarged for the body of Omar Shaikh. In the last years Timur had grown more silent, more inclined to brood over his chessboard, and he spent less time than ever in Samarkand. He said nothing to any one of his plans, but after the death of Omar Shaikh, he started on the first of his far-flung invasions.

CHAPTER XIX

THE CUP COMPANIONS

UNTIL NOW the Tatar conqueror had not looked to the south. With India, beyond the Hindu Koh, he had little concern except in the way of trade. And the chain of salt deserts separated him from the land of Iran.

And Iran was a seat of grandeur, mostly in ruins. Witty and wine-loving princes sat upon the marble throne-stones of the dead who had been giants of Islam —jackals in the lair of lions.

Naked pilgrims, drying themselves in the sun— dervishes whirling to the patter of drums, but mindful of coins cast into their bowls—lords of men riding on mules under slave-borne canopies. Too often the silk prayer carpets were wine soaked, and white beards stained with hemp juice.

It was a brittle land, dust plagued, a land of sheer beauty when the full moon rose over its walled gardens, and an abomination when the fever wind blew in from the desert floor, rattling through the shade trees. Within it stood the mass of pillars that had been Persepolis, and the yellow marble floors where the girl slaves of Semiramis had danced.

Hafiz of Shiraz said of his country that it had rare musicians, because only a rare musician could play a tune for the drunk and the sober to dance to at the same time.

Iran—the Persia of to-day—had endured wealth too long. The rich were suspicious, the poor arrogant.

147

A king blinded his sons, and smiled at his brother's death, saying that now at last they truly shared the earth—he above and his brother below it. Here, said one satirist, the fool is fortune's favorite, and the learned man is one who has not sense enough to earn his own living—a lady is one who has many lovers, and a housewife one who has few.[1]

Here wool-clad Sufis debated mysticism with the poets. And here were found the *sakis,* the cup companions.

Mummers, rhapsodists, jugglers of words and praise, beggars in silk—these were the cup companions of princes. And among them a fellowship of inspired poets. These pleasure loving Persians gave homage to the forbidden Daughter of the Grape, and they loved better to sing of chivalry than to put on armor.

> "We are no other than a moving row
> Of Magic Shadow-shapes that come and go
>   Round with the Sun-illumined Lantern held
> In midnight by the Master of the Show."

They could stone a mocker of their faith, and still dispute over the cup the futility of faith. They were the Greeks of Asia, the sybarites and, in another moment, the fanatics. The Tatars they hated, calling them heretics.

The late Shah, the patron of Hafiz, had had more than the usual fondness for the wines of Shiraz and for a life of backgammon, beauties and candles. Near the end of his days he recalled that he had sworn an alliance with Timur long since. He made solemn preparations for his own funeral—watching the making of his shroud, and the building of his coffin. And to

[1] From *Persian Literature under Tartar Dominion,* by E. G. Browne.

Timur whom he had never seen, between whiles he dictated a letter, dwelling impressively upon his coming death:

"Great men are aware that the world is the theater of inconstancy. Men of learning are never given to trifles—nor transitory pleasures and beauties—because they know the passing away of all things. . . .

"As to the treaty between us, designing never to break it, I look upon the gaining of the Imperial Friendship as a great conquest, and my chief wish—dare I say it—is to have in my hand this treaty with you at the Day of Judgment, so that you should not reproach me with breaking my word. . . .

"Now I am called before the tribunal of the Sovereign Master of the Universe, and I thank the Divine Majesty that I have done nothing wherewith my conscience can reproach me—notwithstanding the faults and sins which are inseparable from life and the depraved nature of man—and I have tasted all the pleasures I could reasonably expect during the fifty-three years I have stayed upon earth . . .

"In brief, I die as I have lived, and I have abandoned all the vanities of the world. And I pray God to give his blessing to this monarch [Timur] as wise as Solomon and as great as Alexander. Although it is not at all necessary to commend to you my loved son Zain al Abaidin—God grant him a long life under the shadow of your protection—I leave him to the care of God and your Majesty. How could I doubt that you will keep this treaty?

"I also beg of you to say the final prayer for your devoted friend, who is happy in departing out of this life in friendship with you, that through the prayers of a Prince so great and fortunate, God may be merciful to me and raise me up among the saints. This is what we pray your Majesty to carry out, as our last will, for which you will be answerable in the next world."

It seems that a similar letter was sent with similar presents to the Sultan of Bagdad. In due course of time the Shah of Persia died, and ten princes began to scramble for the pieces of the kingdom. One got Isfahan, another Fars, another Shiraz and so on. They set up shop as monarchs; some coined money but all raised taxes and fought for what they had not already claimed. These princes were of the family of Muzaffars and they gave new point to the proverb, "To hate like cousins."

Then in the year 1386, when the hazy sun of winter dimmed the glare of the desert floor, down came Timur from the north. He was accompanied by seventy veteran divisions marching at ease, and the splendor of the first city, Isfahan, widened their eyes—a place of domes and arch-shaded streets, and bazaar-crowded bridges. Ibn Batuta who passed that way before them said of the imperial city, "We journeyed among orchards and streamlets and fair villages where the road was bordered with pigeon towers. This is a very great and beautiful city, although suffering from the wars of religious sects. We found here splendid apricots, melons and quinces that the people preserve like our figs of Africa. The people of Isfahan are of fine stature; their skin is light and tinted with rouge. They are, otherwise, amiable and rival each other in the feasts they give. In truth, they invite you to share only their bread and milk, but upon their silk-covered dishes you will find the costliest sweetmeats."

Timur approached Isfahan prepared for war, but not inclined to it. He remembered the Shah's exhortation, but his only grievance was that the Muzaffars had detained his ambassador without cause. For some years he had watched their discords and had decided to come down to look for himself.

Out to greet him advanced the grandees of Isfahan, the uncle of Zain al Abaidin at their head. They were given presents and seated on the carpet of the Amir, while the fate of Isfahan was discussed.

"Thy people are granted their lives," Timur said, breaking through the fencing of courtesy, "and thy city will be spared from plundering, if a ransom is paid."

The ransom was agreed upon—the Muzaffars understanding perfectly that an army of this size would not come a thousand miles to go back empty-handed. They asked that envoys be sent in, to receive the money, and a noble from each Tatar division was told off to go to each quarter of the city. A high amir went with them, to take charge of the transaction.

The next day Timur made a formal entry, riding in state through the main avenue, and out again to his camp, leaving detachments in command of the city gates.

All went well enough until that night. Seventy thousand soldiers had marched for two months or so without anything in particular to divert them, and they looked longingly at the lights of Isfahan. Detachments that were sent in on duty, lingered in the bazaars, and many of their comrades in the camps invented cause why they should visit the city. More and more filtered in, to the wine shops.

What happened next is variously told. It seems that some of the more unruly spirits among the Persians assembled under the leadership of a blacksmith. A drum was beaten, and shouting was heard—the rallying cry of Islam.

"Ho, Muslimin!"

At this the people came out of their houses, and
mobs formed in the streets. Fighting began at once
between these throngs and the until-then-peaceable
Tatar soldiery. In some quarters of the city Timur's
commissioners were protected by the more responsible
spirits, in others they were put to the sword.

Having started blood flowing, the mob went on to
greater things. It cleared the streets and fell upon the
guards at the gates, who were cut to pieces, and the
portals closed.

When this was reported to Timur the next morning,
he fell into a violent rage. Apparently some three
thousand Tatars had died, among them a favorite amir,
and the son of Shaikh Ali Bahatur. He ordered an
immediate advance on the walls. The Persian grandees
in his camp tried to mediate, but went unheeded. The
mob, having played at warfare, now had to defend itself.

But the Tatars stormed the gates, and Timur ordered a massacre, bidding every man of his army bring
out the head of a Persian. The quarters of the city
that had not joined in the rioting were not molested,
and some attempt was made to safeguard the *sharifs*
and venerable men. Elsewhere the citizens were
hunted down. The slaying lasted through the day,
and the unfortunates who had hidden in the darkness
and fled from the walls were tracked through the snow
the next morning and cut down.

Many Tatars who wished to have no hand in the
massacre bought heads from the soldiers. The chronicle relates that the price paid at first was twenty dog
ducats, but that this fell to half a dinar when the quota
was reached, and then to nothing at all. The grim
trophies were at first piled on the walls, then made
into towers along the main avenues.

In this way died seventy thousand or more of the people of Isfahan. The slaughter had not been planned beforehand. Timur was forced to take vengeance for the deaths of his men; but his vengeance had been ruthless beyond all anticipation. It frightened the other Muzaffar princes into silence and surrender—except for Mansur, who rode off to the mountains.

Shiraz and the rest paid ransom quietly; Timur's name was read in the *kutbeh*, or public prayer for the king, and to each Muzaffar he gave a grant of authority, signed with the *tamgha*, or red hand print. They were now his governors, and he their liege lord. The lands of Iran were theirs indeed, but by his sufferance. He discovered that the Iranians had been taxed too heavily, and this he remedied.

And at Shiraz, tradition says, he sent for Hafiz, the illustrious poet, to come before him. The Persian man of letters appeared in plain garments as a token of poverty before the conqueror.

"Thou hast written a verse," Timur said sternly, "in this manner:

'If my mistress of Shiraz would take my heart in her hand,
I would lay before her feet Bokhara or Samarkand.' "

"O Lord of Kings," Hafiz responded, "that is my verse."

"With my sword," Timur mused, "and after years of conflict have I taken Samarkand; now I am taking from other cities great ornaments for Samarkand. How is it that thou wouldst bestow it upon a wench of Shiraz?"

The poet hesitated, then smiled. "O Lord, by reason of that same prodigality I have fallen into the sorry plight in which you see me."

The ready answer pleased Timur and he sent Hafiz richer from his presence.

More than one of the minstrels of Iran went back with him to Samarkand. But he had reason to regret the cup companions of the south. Miran Shah, his third son, had always been headstrong, given to wine and skepticism—brave enough upon occasion but savagely cruel. Only when he joined the army under Timur did he keep himself within bounds.

Years later Timur gave the government of the Caspian region to Miran Shah, only to hear when returning from a year's campaign in India that his son was nearly insane. The Tatar officers reported mad deeds in the great cities—wealth scattered from windows to the mobs, and drinking bouts held within the mosques. They explained that Miran Shah had suffered from a fall from his horse, and had said, "I am the son of the man who rules the earth. Is there no deed by which I also may be remembered?"

And he had given orders to pull down the walls of the hospitals and palaces of Tabriz and Sultaniah. The word of Timur's son was unalterable law to the Tatars and the demolition began, to be followed by wilder whims. At his command the body of a celebrated Persian philosopher was dug up and reinterred in the Jews' cemetery. Miran Shah's mind was unsettled by the fire of wine and the poison of drugs.

"Nay," said the officers, "he is afflicted of Allah— did he not strike his head upon the earth when he fell from the saddle?"

When they had left, a woman came to Timur's gate. She was veiled and clad in dark garments and without attendants. But one whispered word opened the doors to her, and bent the heads of the guard and sent the chamberlain of the palace in haste to Timur.

"The King's Daughter waits to greet thee," they said, "alone."

It was Khan Zadé who appeared in this manner to Timur—she who had been the bride of his first-born, Jahangir. She had hastened to his quarters, waiting impatiently until the officers had been dismissed. And the black robes of fresh mourning showed to advantage the fair face when she drew aside her veil and threw herself down at his feet.

"O Amir of amirs," she cried, "I have come in from the city of thy son, thy son Miran Shah."

Boldly she spoke to the conqueror, she who had used her wit to safeguard her kinsmen who had been scattered by the Tatar storm long since. In her voice echoed the triumph that she dared not put in words. With her attendants and personal court she had taken up her quarters in a city under the protection of Miran Shah. She had remonstrated with Timur's son when his mad humor became destructive. In spite of the resistance of her men, he had taken her into his house. He had fed his mad hunger upon her beauty. And then had taunted her with wantonness.

"Lord Timur," she cried, "of thee I seek protection and the justice of a king."

Khan Zadé's husband was no longer living—he whom Timur had loved and had looked upon as his successor. By the code of the Tatars, the throne should now revert to Miran Shah, the eldest living son. Since the days of the desert khans it had been ordained that the first four sons born to a ruler should be his heirs. Jahangir and Omar Shaikh were in their graves, and there remained Miran Shah and the youngest, Shah Rukh, son of the empress Sarai Khanum, the Princess of the Palace. But Shah Rukh was little older than Khan Zadé's children—born of Jahangir. And he was unlike his brothers, a gentle boy who loved his books better than the conflict of authority.

The succession lay between Miran Shah and Khan Zadé's sons. Timur had entrusted to the elder prince a wide government—and Miran Shah made havoc with debauchery. Perhaps Khan Zadé had planned beforehand the fruits of her visit to Miran Shah—perhaps her beauty had been the flame that caused the conflagration.

Years later there centered about the youthful Khalil a struggle that not even Khan Zadé could have foreseen.

For the present, her courage was admirable. She had appealed to Cæsar, against his own son. Fearless, she stood before Timur. And he did not delay judgment. To Khan Zadé he gave what she had lost in property—and new retainers to serve her, and he paid her the honor due to the wife of Jahangir. Although he had just come in from a hard journey, he ordered his officers to prepare at once to ride to Sultaniah.

There, after he had investigated the havoc wrought by Miran Shah he condemned his son to death. The high amirs intervened—even they who had suffered at the hand of the wayward prince. Miran Shah was brought before his father, a rope around his neck.

And Timur consented to let him live; but all authority was taken from him. Broken in spirit, a shadow without power, he was compelled to remain in this province where others now ruled.

Soon afterward the good knight Ruy de Gonzales Clavijo, journeying from the court of Castile to Samarkand, passed through Sultaniah and what he heard there he has related simply in this fashion:

"*When Miran Shah did these things, he had a woman with him named Gansada. She left him in dis-*

guise and traveled day and night until she came to Lord Timur, whom she informed of what his son had done; for which he deprived his son of the government. This Gansada remained with Timur and he treated her honorably, not allowing her to return; but Miran Shah had by her a son, named Khalil Sultan."

Upon the companions of Miran Shah the wrath of the conqueror fell without restraint. Rhapsodists, jesters—distinguished poets as well—the cup companions were hailed to the execution platform. And there the jester turned to his more notable fellows, by the steps that led to the swordsman's block. Even at this moment he must have his quip.

"You had precedence in the company of the Prince—go before me also here."

CHAPTER XX

DOMINION

IN THE YEAR 1388, at the age of fifty-three years, Timur was undisputed master of that breeding ground of revolt, Central Asia and Iran. He was emperor in everything but in name. His only title was Amir Timur Gurigan—Lord Timur, the Splendid. His nominal sovereign was still the Khan, the *tura*, of the blood of Genghis Khan.

This puppet khan had nothing whatever to do. He commanded, it seems, a division of the army, and a palace had been fitted up for him at Samarkand. No doubt he appeared at certain ceremonies—the sacrifice of a white horse when an alliance was to be made binding, or the yearly review of the army when two hundred thousand men rode past the horsetail standards. But his name appears only rarely in the annals, and his prestige dimmed steadily before the brilliance of the lame conqueror. He lived happily enough with his fleshpots, enjoying the martial pageantry in which his own part diminished with each year.

Nor had Timur's growing empire a name. He was still addressed as the Amir of *Ma-vara'n-nahr*—Lord of Beyond the River, although his name was read in the public prayers throughout his still-to-be-christened dominion.

His mastery was due to a simple thing. The men of Central Asia had been ruled by the chieftains of the tribes. If they did not like their own "white beard" they migrated to another's domain, and placed their lives between the hands of the new lord. Dissatisfied, they might select one of their own fellowship as leader —themselves partakers of his salt. Then they would fight furiously in defense of their new choice.

Proud of their own name, and clan—intensely jealous of their personal liberty and whatever privileges custom accorded them—they were yet at home with despotism and intolerant of anything else. Children of nomads, worshipers of kings, they could recite—the worst looters of the lot, squatting like vultures by the hill trails—the glories of Solomon, and the deeds of Alexander whom they called *Duhl-carnin*, "Of the Two Worlds," and tales of Mahmoud, he of the golden throne. They traced their pedigrees with satisfaction back to Noah, and claimed descent from the patriarchs.

They knew every tomb and its history, along the great pilgrim roads, and the Old Testament they knew also. Their ability to quote matched their range of vituperation, which was not surprising since it included pedigrees that dated to the Flood. For written law they cared not a jot, but they would shed blood for intangible tradition. At usury they mocked, and an oppressive tax collector would die with a knife in his back.

They had fought Timur until even they had seen the uselessness of it, and then they had come in to share his salt. To govern them a hand of iron was needed.

Never before had they been united. Mahmoud held many of them together around his standard; Genghis Khan rode through them and gathered them together, until, at his death, they divided again under new chieftains.

In only one thing were they united now—in willingness to obey Timur. To bring them together was like leashing wolves. No code of laws would serve the jade hunters of Kashgar, the predatory hillmen of the Hindu Koh, the warlike remnants of the Jat and Golden Hordes, the Iranian knighthood of the Land of the Sun, and the chivalrous Arabs.

To hold them in check Timur became himself the law. All commands came from him direct to his new peoples. All who dared had access to him; he would allow no favorites to govern for him. When a kingdom was conquered, or when it submitted of its own accord, it was given to one of his sons or a high amir of the army as an appanage—a feudal grant.

It became a province of the new empire, governed by a *daroga* or administrator who was responsible to Timur. A magistrate as well as the *daroga* was appointed. The warriors who joined the army went of their own consent, but laborers and artisans were impressed at need. The former rulers or princes were taken to the court and given independent rank and duties to perform. If then they caused trouble they were put in chains or slain.

Timur's restless energy was impatient of failure. Where he passed over a ruined bridge, the governor of the district was ordered to repair it. Old caravan *sarais* were put in order, and new road houses built. The roads themselves were kept open in winter, and guard stations erected at intervals along them. The officers of the road guards were responsible for the post horses, and for the safety of caravans journeying along their stretch of the highway. These caravans had to pay a sum in silver for the protection given them. The Spanish envoy Clavijo has left a description of the great Khorassan road.

"They [the travelers] slept in large buildings erected by the roadside, where no people live. Water was brought to these buildings from a great distance by pipes underground.

"The road was very level, and there was not a single stone to be found on it. When they arrived at a stopping place they were given plenty of meat and fresh horses. The lord [1] had horses waiting at the end of each day's journey, at some places one hundred, and at others two hundred; and thus the posts were arranged as far as Samarkand.

"Those whom the lord sent in any direction, or who were sent to him, went on these horses as fast as they could, day and night. He also had horses in deserts, and he caused great houses to be built in uninhabited places, where horses and provisions were supplied by the nearest villages. Men appointed to take care of these horses were called *Anchos*.

"When ambassadors arrive, these men take their horses, remove the saddles and place them on fresh horses, and one or two of these *Anchos* go with them to take care of the horses. At the next post they return.

"If a horse becomes tired on the road, and they meet another at any place belonging to any other man, they take it in exchange for the tired horse. The custom is that even merchants, lords or ambassadors must give up their mounts for the service of any one who is going to the great lord, and if a man refuses, it costs him his head, for such are the commands of Lord Timur.

"They even take horses from the troops, or from the son or the wife of the great lord himself.

"Not only was the road thus supplied with post horses, but there were messengers on all the roads so that news could come from every province in a few days. The lord is better pleased with him who travels a day and a night for fifty leagues and kills two horses

[1] Timur.

than with one who does the distance in three days. The great lord, considering that the leagues were very long in his empire of Samarkand, divided each league into two, and placed small pillars on the roads to mark each league; ordering all his Zagatais to ride twelve or at least ten of these leagues, in each day's journey.[2] Each of these leagues was equal to two leagues of Castile.

"In truth it would scarcely be believed unless it were seen, the distances which these fellows travel, day and night; they sometimes go over fifteen and twenty leagues in a day and night. When their horses are knocked up they kill and sell them; we found many dead horses on the road which had been killed by hard riding."

Clavijo adds that at some of the post stations they saw fountains which were packed with ice in the hot season, with brass jugs placed in readiness for any one to drink from.

Up and down the post roads couriers carried messages to Timur—reports from the camel corps on the frontier, dispatches from generals beyond the border, tidings from the *darogas* of the cities. Throughout every province, and in the caravan cities outside the empire, secret service men wrote periodic reports to the Amir, giving him the gist of what was happening— what caravans were on the roads and what actions had taken place. What his officers did was related truthfully—any one who falsified such a chronicle was killed out of hand.

---

[2] Fifty to seventy-two miles. Clavijo's Zagatais are the Chagatais or Jats of the annals. This account of the post roads is quoted, slightly condensed, from *Narrative of the Embassy of Ruy de Gonzales Clavijo to the Court of Timur at Samarkand, A. D. 1402-1403.* A publication of the Hakluyt Society. This account is apparently the source of the strange statement to be found in some general histories, that Timur ordered every noble in his empire to ride sixty miles every day.

Timur's service of information was complete, and probably swifter than anything of the kind until the days of railroads.

He dealt with the question of land and property as decisively. His soldiers received their pay from the army treasurers, and were not allowed to levy tribute on the inhabitants. No soldier could enter a civilian's house without cause.

Waste land, and real property left without heirs, belonged to the throne. A farmer or man of means who undertook to irrigate and cultivate waste land—to build dwellings or bridges—was entitled to possess the land without taxation the first year. The second year he might pay what he thought just; the third year he was assessed.

Taxes were collected after the crops were taken in. The usual rate was one third of all produce, or its value in silver. It was higher upon irrigated land, and lower upon crops that depended upon rain. Farmers also paid for the use of the large reservoirs.

Merchants coming into the empire with goods paid duty as well as the road tax, and this became quite a source of income because at that time the caravans from the far east bound for Europe avoided Egypt, where the Mamluks were bitterly hostile to the Christians and all pertaining to them.

Trade was carried westward over the great north road through the Gobi, past Almalyk, to Samarkand, and thence through Sultaniah and Tabriz to the Black sea and Constantinople. This was the great Khorassan road. It branched also more to the north, to Urganj or across the Caspian to the Genoese posts along the Russian frontier. A third route ran south through Persia to the ports near India.

There was little commerce by sea. At times the Arabs navigated around India to the Golden Chersonese and Cathay, and Chinese vessels frequently hugged the coast as far as Bengal. But these were intermittent ventures of ship owners and wealthy travelers. On the other hand river traffic was heavy—down the Amu to Urganj, down the Indus throughout the length of India to the sea, and also upon the Tigris and Euphrates.

By now Timur had opened two gateways into India —from Kabul through the Khyber pass, and from Kandahar into the barren gorges that led to the Indus. In a single campaign he had subdued the king of Sijistan, whom he had once served as gentleman-adventurer and in whose service he had been lamed for life.

In another campaign he had crossed the desert country from Shiraz to the ports on the Persian gulf. From these ports ships went up to Bagdad and down to the mouth of the Indus.

To the west, he had stormed the citadel of the Black Sheep Turkomans, and the marble city of Mosul. So he held the strongholds of the upper Tigris, fifteen hundred miles from Samarkand. Here he could consolidate into his empire the great *entrepôt* of trade, Tabriz. This was a metropolis of more than a million souls, where the north-and-south trade crossed the Khorassan route. And from Tabriz alone he gained revenues that were larger than the yearly revenues of the king of France.[3]

Apparently in such a city the inhabitants paid no head tax, but the city council gave a yearly sum to

[3] All available evidence indicates that Tabriz was the largest city in the world, outside China, at that time. Samarkand, Damascus and Bagdad were smaller, although their public buildings were more notable. But these surpassed Rome or Venice in size and splendor at the end of the fourteenth century.

Timur's *daroga*. It was tribute, but so long as it was paid the city was not molested.

To the merchants of the caravans Timur's government was a boon, because they could travel through his lands, under effective guard, for five months and pay only one customs tax.

To the small landholder and peasant, his coming was a benefit to the extent that it brought freedom from oppression at the hands of the nobles. Timur was clear enough on this point. A ruined man was of no use to anybody; a devastated kingdom was no gain to his treasury. By the treasury the army was strengthened. And the army was the fabric of the new empire. It took water where it wished and marched over cultivated lands—gathered in crops along its line of march when it needed grain. And the peasant suffered accordingly.

Timur was intolerant of weakness. He tried to lay the swarm of beggars that infested every city by forbidding them to beg and granting them doles of bread and meat. They took the doles as largesse and went out to the streets again with their whining cry—*"Ya huk! Ya hak! Allah u kerim!"* and their bowls into which the devout tossed bits of food at cooking time. Dervish and mountebank, blind man, leper and rogue, they still begged. For this was the unalterable custom of Islam, and Timur's soldiers slew them in vain.

With thieves he was more successful. Every magistrate in the towns and every captain of the road guards he made responsible for theft within their district. Any article stolen they had to replace themselves.

But Timur's code of law amounted to no more than his own will. Outside his own country his regulations were still new, and not established as yet. Here and there revolt simmered, and he was constantly on the march to quiet unrest. Under his dynamic energy the army grew into a disciplined machine, accustomed to victory and guided by veteran commanders.

This was his pride and by it he had now determined to conquer all of Asia.

CHAPTER XXI

IN THE SADDLE

IN THESE YEARS the lame conqueror tasted to the full the truth of the proverb, *"He who sets his foot in the stirrup must mount to the saddle."*

Seldom now could he be found at Samarkand, or hunting in the hills. The first empress, Sarai Khanum, moved in dignity, black slaves bearing her train, and her maidens supporting the jeweled feathers of her head-dress on either side. Under her feet new court-yards came into being, blue-tiled, immense. And Timur, who had planned them with Persian architects, would appear for no more than a few days, to stir his builders into a fever of activity, to receive the ambassadors from China and India and Bagdad, to listen to the salutation of his grandsons, to feast hugely and be off again.

When he was on the road, he made use of two sets of pavilions, sleeping in the first curtained palace, while the second was carried on by pack animals, to be set up at the next stage. So he would always find the imperial quarters erected, the carpets spread, the barrier curtains up on the bamboo posts, the silk ropes taut and the wide fly hoisted into place against the heat of the sun. About his quarters would be the tents of the *kulchis*, the twelve thousand warriors of the guard.

The officers of the guard were chosen from the *bahaturs*, the mighty men of prowess. They were spared no ordeal, and never went without an inspiring reward.

"The soldier of long years," Timur once said,

"should not lack either rank or payment. For these men, who give up permanent happiness for perishable honor, are worthy of reward." He was insistent upon that. As he had once written down the names of the thousand who followed him, he now caused to be recorded the personnel of his divisions, and even their sons. Any action of distinction was placed upon the service record by the secretaries.

The man of the ranks was promoted to be a leader of ten for personal bravery; the leader of a squad became captain of a company. And certain insignia were awarded—a girdle, or an embroidered coat with a collar. Sometimes a horse and sword. To the regimental commanders a standard and drum were given, and to the high amirs, or marshals, a divisional standard and a lion standard, and drum. Such amirs were entitled to take with them a hundred horses.

When they gained a victory these amirs were accorded more material reward—the feudal grant of a city with its revenues, or in some cases a province. Promotion was by merit only, although the high amirs seem to have been men of royal blood. Old Jaku Barlas was one of the few to survive and be retired in splendor—the rank of Lord of Amirs and the government of Balkh being his perquisites.

Timur disliked the man who made excuses for failure, or who hung back in a crisis, or made certain of a way of retreat before going forward. And he was impatient of stupidity, saying more than once, "A wise enemy is less harmful than a foolish friend."

A certain chronicler called the Arab has drawn a clear picture of him, at this time.

"This conqueror was tall. He had a massive head, a high forehead. He was as remarkable for his physical strength as for his courage. And by nature he had been well endowed. His skin was white, and his complexion vivid. He had stalwart limbs, the shoulders large, the fingers powerful. His beard was long, his hand dry. He limped with the right leg, and he had a deep voice.

"In middle age his spirit was as firm and his body as vigorous, and his soul as daring as in the past—like enduring rock. He disliked lying and jesting. But he looked for truth even when it was disagreeable to himself. He was not depressed by misfortune, and prosperity did not stir in him any exultation.

"He carried for device upon his seal two Persian words, *Rasti Rousti,* that is—Strength is in right. He was very taciturn in conversation, and never spoke of slaughter, of pillage or the violation of women's sanctuaries. He loved brave soldiers."

Timur's hair turned white at an early age. Others speak of his skin as dark, but to an Arab it would have appeared light. It is interesting that this description is given by Ibn Arabshah who had been carried off as a captive by Timur and who hated him.

Few names upon the rolls of Timur's host were honored as unexpectedly as that of a certain Tatar berserk, Ak Boga—the White Paladin. He was, it seems, a warrior remarkable for stature and strength, who carried an iron shield, and a heavy five-foot bow. A leader of ten, but master of only one horse—notable for his ability to drink down a ram's horn full of mare's milk mixed with spirits.

It is said of him that in the second Persian campaign Ak Boga without any companions had quartered himself upon a roadside village—more exactly, in the tav-

ern. Being in enemy country his horse was kept saddled at the door. To him thus ensconced at table with
loosened girdle, came one of the headmen in haste
saying that forty or fifty Persian riders were dismounting near the village tank.

"Well," responded Ak Boga, "go and gather your
fighting men and then we will attack them."

The headman protested that the horsemen were too
numerous, and that Ak Boga himself would better think
of flight. But the Tatar paladin had not thought of
this at all.

"If we do not attack them," he pointed out, "how
can we seize their horses and their saddles? By Allah,
you have no wit. These Iranis are jackals; they will
run at sight of a wolf like me. I have seen them run.
Go, and bring your men to this place."

While he finished his potations the villagers talked
it over. They were afraid of the horsemen, but they
were in awe of the armored giant. In the end a score
of them came to the tavern on their ponies, and Ak
Boga adjusted his girdle, put on his helmet, tied the
leather flaps under his beard and thrust his shield on
his arm. "When I give the war shout," he explained
to his new recruits, "ride in like devils—don't stop to
pick dust out of your eyes."

With the villagers following him he rode down the
street to the mosque and the roadside tank. At sight
of the Persians watering their horses he began to ply
his whip and roared out his battle cry.

"Hour-ra!"

But the prospect of facing bare weapons was too
much for the villagers, and they turned and raced back
the way they had come. The berserk, now thoroughly
roused, was in no mood to turn back. He carried out
his charge alone.

Either the Persian detachment thought that he was the advance point of a strong body of Tatars, or they were thrown into panic by the sudden shout. They mounted in haste and fled the other way. Ak Boga galloped after them, lashing his horse. The riders scattered and drew away, being better horsed—so the story runs—and although Ak Boga shouted to them to pull up and fight, he had to turn back in the end, victorious but empty-handed.

"The Iranis are jackals," he told the villagers, "but you are hares."

In this campaign Timur was marching rapidly south into Persia. The Muzaffar princes, left as governors of the different cities, had plunged into civil war again. Out of the confusion Shah Mansur emerged master of Isfahan and Shiraz. He was the one who had not come in to submit to Timur, and now he had made himself overlord of his cousins—had taken captive and blinded with a heated iron the luckless prince Zain al Abaidin.

On his way to quench the fire of revolt, Timur had stopped to exterminate a nest of the curious assassins [1] of the mountain country, who gained their courage from hashish, and whose daggers were feared by the rulers of near-Asia. With him he had no more than three divisions, one commanded by Shah Rukh, the others by his eldest grandsons, born of Khan Zadé.

At his coming Shah Mansur threw half of his men under one of his lieutenants into the White Castle, the sanctuary of Iran that had proved impregnable since the day of the mythical Rustam. Here also the blind Zain al Abaidin was confined, and hither Timur directed his march.

[1] The Ismaelites, as the followers of this sect were called, had troubled the crusaders from Europe, who coined the word assassin—*hashishin*—to describe them. Marco Polo, journeying past their strongholds, spoke of their leader as the Old Man of the Mountain—Shaikh al Jabal. At this time Timur was also engaged in subduing the Arab and Kurdish clans.

The White Castle was actually the summit of a mountain and the chronicle describes it clearly:

"The Persians put their trust in this place because it was the top of a rock mountain and it was reached by only one narrow road. This mountain summit was a beautiful smooth plain, a league long and as broad. Here are rivers, and fountains, fruit trees and culti-vated ground, and all kinds of beasts and birds.

"The princes had built here many pleasure houses, where they had no reason to fear fire or flood—much less mines or assaults by battering rams and engines. No king had ever undertaken to besiege it, because of its height and the impossibility of bringing up battering rams. Its hard rock could not be dug, and it seemed inaccessible and impregnable. The way which leads to the top of the mountain is so planned that in any nar-row place three men may withstand a thousand.

"Not content with its natural strength, the Persians had fortified the turnings of the road with great stones joined with mortar. As the cultivated ground could yield food enough for its inhabitants, and the cattle and fowl had enough to subsist on, they could not be starved out. Only death had power over its people."

Timur attacked the White Castle the day his forces came beneath it. His camp was pitched on the summit of an adjoining ridge, and then his Tatars rode up the slope to the place where sheer rock walls rise. They dismounted and divided, spreading like ants over the detritus, and assailing the lowest towers at the turning of the road.

From his height the Amir could look down upon the tiny helmets creeping upward where arrows glinted in the sun, and the heat rose in exhalation from the maw

ONE OF TIMUR'S PERSIAN FOLLOWERS. THE
LIGHT WEAPONS ARE IN DISTINCT CON-
TRAST TO THE HEAVIER ARMS AND LONG
BOWS OF THE TATARS. (*Schulz*)

TIMUR HOLDS COURT IN ONE OF HIS PALACE
GARDENS. PAINTED A GENERATION AFTER
HIS DEATH. HERE, AS OPPOSED TO THE
LIFE-PORTRAIT OF THE FRONTISPIECE, THE
CONQUEROR HAS BEEN PERSIANIZED, REP-
RESENTED WITH WHITE SKIN, TRIMMED
BEARD AND CROWN. (*Martin*)

of the valley. Beside him the kettledrums thundered, and from time to time there was audible the swelling shout of his men as they clung to their footholds beneath the arrows and the rocks that the defenders cast down.

At nightfall nothing had been gained. No other path up had been discovered, and the officers looked grim when they counted the bodies carried down from the ground under the towers. The Tatars spent the night in their positions or rather perches under and on the face of the cliff. And at sunrise the officers led them to the assault again, wielding pick-axes among the men, until they fell and were carried into the valley bed. Again Timur's kettledrums urged them on.

Then men who had climbed abreast one of the towers heard a stentorian shout high over their heads.

"Our Lord conquers! The dogs of Iranis are spayed!"

On the summit of the cliff two hundred feet above them and beyond arrow shot of the road stood Ak Boga. He had forced his way up a crevice at a place that had gone unheeded by Persians and Tatars alike because it looked unclimbable. But Ak Boga, his shield and his bow slung on his back, had climbed it and was announcing the fact to all who could hear.

Propping his shield against the rocks in front of him, he made such good use of his bow that he held off the Persians who happened to be near. At sight of him thus situated, Shah Rukh who had joined the men on the road, ordered an immediate attack on the towers, to hold their defenders in place, while the Tatars nearest the cleft scrambled up to support Ak Boga.

They found the summit deserted, the Persians fleeing and Ak Boga trundling in pursuit, sword in hand. When they appeared on the skyline, Shah Rukh's standards were lifted under the towers and the drums in the valley roared that the end was in sight.

The Persians left the towers to go up to the height, but they were taken in the rear by Timur's men who had climbed the cliff and they were picked up and thrown, man after man, from the summit. Shah Mansur's officer followed them, and lay, a lifeless bundle of garments on the rocks below. The White Castle had fallen.

When the fighting had ceased Ak Boga was searched for, found, and brought to Timur. He was given silver money, rolls of brocade and silk, tents and fair women slaves and any number of horses, mules and camels so that he departed from the presence of his lord in a daze, shaking his head when he looked at what followed him. When he was stopped and praised by others he said:

"God be my witness, yesterday I had no more than one horse and how can all this be mine now?"

He was promoted to the command of the rearguard of Muhammad Sultan's division, and he rode in magnificence for the rest of his life; and from that day he would never turn his back upon the place where Timur was. Whenever he made ready to sleep, he was careful to place his feet toward the pavilion of the Amir, and he requested that when he died his body should be laid with its feet toward the abiding place of his lord.

When Timur took up the pursuit of the Muzaffars it was reported to him that Shah Mansur had fled. After detaching the right and left divisions, his two grandsons, Muhammad Sultan and Pir Muhammad, commanding, he hastened toward Shiraz with the main body, thirty thousand strong. Shah Rukh who always attended him was with his staff as usual. They were astonished to come upon three or four thousand Persians drawn up in the gardens outside a village. These cavalry regiments were armored, the men wearing breastplates of leather lined with iron, the horses barded with quilted silk.

What had happened was that Shah Mansur, fleeing toward Shiraz with this mounted force, had stopped at the village and asked what the people of Shiraz were saying of him.

"By Allah," he was told, "they are saying that *some* who carried big shields and heavy quivers have fled like goats before wolves, leaving their families to the foe."

Enraged by the taunt, Mansur had wheeled his horse and led his men back along the road. In desperation he now hurled his cavalry against Timur. Some of his regiments fell away in disorder, but two thousand broke through the Tatar array and gained heights in the rear. Not content with this, he charged back at Timur's standard.

The Amir had drawn a little apart with some of his staff to watch this unexpected onset, and Mansur turned toward him. At once the Tatar officers around Timur were locked in hand-to-hand fighting with the Persian horsemen.

Timur stretched back his hand for his lance that was always carried behind him; but the lance bearer had been beset and had gone off, taking the weapon with him. Before he could draw his sword, Mansur rode against him.

Twice the Persian prince slashed with his sword at the Tatar conqueror. Timur bent his head, and the sword's edge glanced off the steel helmet, sliding harmlessly down his mailed arms. Timur kept motionless in the saddle, until one of his bodyguard thrust a shield over his head, and another lashed his horse between the daring Mansur and his foe.

Mansur turned at last to escape but was hunted down by some of Shah Rukh's followers, and Shah Rukh rode back with the severed head of the prince, casting it down before Timur's horse.

It was the end of resistance in Persia, and the doom of the Muzaffars. Timur ordered that all the survivors of the family should be sought out and chained. Later they were put to death.

Only Zain al Abaidin and Chelabi—who had also been blinded by their kinsmen—were kindly treated and sent back to Samarkand where land and dwellings were allotted to them and they could enjoy peace. Out of Shiraz and Isfahan the skilled mechanics, the artists and distinguished men of letters were gathered and sent to Samarkand to Timur's growing court.

CHAPTER XXII

SULTAN AHMED OF BAGDAD

IT WAS INEVITABLE that an alliance should be formed against Timur. Too often had he come out of the east, out of his deserts, sweeping over cities like the black wind storm, and leaving them dismantled. Like the wind, his coming could never be anticipated.

Ambassadors hurried between the kings of the west. The Emperor of the Turks, off in Europe, was indifferent for the moment, but the Sultan of Egypt—master of Syria, Damascus and Jerusalem—and the Sultan of Bagdad exchanged pledges to withstand Timur. And Kara Yussuf, whose Turkomans had been harried west by Timur, was more than ready to join his standard to theirs.

Bagdad lay in the path of the Tatar's advance. The city was no longer the heart of the Muhammadan world as in the days when Haroun the Blessed drank with the Barmecides; it lay, inert and massive, on the two banks of the Tigris—still thronged with pilgrims and wealthy merchants. It was, said the son of Jubair, filled with vanished traces and the shadows of other years—like a woman whose youth is past. And, like an old woman, it looked drowsily down into the river that was the mirror of its beauty.

Its Sultan, Ahmed the Jalair, was still called Protector of the Faithful, and still the black garments of the Koreish were seen in the great mosque. But the real guardian of Bagdad was the Mamluk, Sultan of Egypt. Ahmed fed his soul with suspicion and his

177

passions by cruelty; he was afraid of the treasures that lay in his coffers, and more afraid of the slaves that guarded them. And in his fear he turned his eyes east when dust swirled over the plain, to look for the coming of Timur's Tatars.

He sent the Grand Mufti to the lame conqueror with presents such as only he could give—and he forwarded similar gifts to his ally at need, Kara Yussuf. One account has it that Timur sent back the Mufti with a courteous answer, another that he sent back the head of Shah Mansur. It might have been either way. He did not want Ahmed's gifts—he wanted the submission of Bagdad, with his own name read in the prayers and stamped upon the coins.

Meanwhile Ahmed made preparations for a service of safety. He kept in touch with his Turkoman allies and with Damascus, and he selected with care a body of men and swift horses to serve as escort for himself, his family and treasure if he had to flee. And at his frontier eighty miles away he posted watchers with carrier pigeons who were to send him word of any sign of Timur's approach.

Apparently Timur's spies brought him the tale of Ahmed's preparations. At any rate, he decided to take Bagdad. First he detached a cavalry division to stir up the Turkomans and keep them occupied. Then he moved up himself as if to join in the campaign.

Instead of doing so, he left the highway and advanced by forced marches through the hill country. At night his men lighted cressets and pushed into the defiles, Timur traveling in a litter. The bulk of his forces fell behind, and he kept with him only a picked force with a herd of remounts.

Ahmed's watchers in the hill villages saw the dust of his coming and messenger pigeons were loosed with

warning that Timur was within sight.   Entering the
village the Tatar had the people called before him and
asked if they had sent word to Bagdad.   They were
afraid to deny it, and Timur ordered them to send a
second message.

"Say that the riders you have seen were Turkomans
escaping from the Tatars."

Again pigeons were freed, and Timur rested some
hours.   Then he selected a few hundred men and the
best of the horses and rode eighty-one miles over the
plain without dismounting, into the suburbs of Bagdad.

Sultan Ahmed had started his preparations for flight
when the first message came—sending his possessions
and entourage across the river and calling his escort to
arms.   The second message did not entirely deceive
him.   He lingered in the city himself until it was certain that Timur was approaching.   Then he crossed the
Tigris and destroyed the bridge of boats.

Timur's troopers galloped to the palaces that had
once been the abiding place of the Kalifs.   They traced
the lord of Bagdad down to the river, and swam their
horses across.

Ahmed had no more than a few hours' start, and the
race to the Syrian desert began—the Tatars finding and
sending back to their lord the splendid state galley
called the Sun in which the Sultan had feasted at night
on the water.   For a day and a night and another day
the Tatars pushed their horses over the dry marshes
until they reached the reeds of the Euphrates.

Here they had to search for boats, and they rowed
across, the horses swimming beside them.   Evidently
they had gained upon the fugitives, because they found
Ahmed's personal baggage and most of his treasure
abandoned, the pack horses grazing unattended.   They
had passed all the villages and no remounts were avail-

able. The men of the ranks had fallen behind steadily, being worse mounted than the leaders, and presently the Tatars found themselves no more than forty or fifty men, nearly all amirs and regimental commanders. They had promised Timur to bring back Ahmed and they kept on, into the clay ridges of the waste land.

Meanwhile the Sultan had thrown back a detachment to guard his road, and the Tatar officers found themselves confronted by a hundred or more horsemen. With their bows they broke up a charge of the Sultan's followers, and galloped on when the Bagdadis retreated.

A second time they were attacked, and they dismounted, shooting over the backs of their horses until their adversaries scattered again. After that all traces of the fugitives were lost and the amirs, tormented by thirst, their horses done up, had to turn aside to look for water.

Ahmed reached Damascus alive, but his women and sons fell into the hands of the Tatars who brought them back to Timur. Bagdad paid a ransom, and acknowledged Timur's lordship. A governor was left there and the invaders withdrew as suddenly as they had come. Before they left, they poured all the wine of Bagdad into the river. And Timur took with him to the concourse of Samarkand all the astrologers and architects.

The Sultan, himself a man of letters, wrote a mournful couplet upon his misfortune:

> "Men say Thou wert Lame for the Fight.
> But surely I proved not lame in my flight."

The storm had passed over, leaving Sultan Ahmed nearly bare of gear and honor alike. At Cairo the lord of Egypt sheltered him, gave him new women and slaves. To Cairo came also envoys from the Tatar court.

"In the days of Genghis Khan," said the envoys, "the ancestors of our Lord fought with your ancestors. Then a peace was agreed between them. Afterward all Iran became the prey of misrule and civil war. Our Lord hath restored peace in Iran, which borders upon your dominion. So he sent ambassadors to you, that merchants may come and go and quarrels not arise. The praise to Him who is sole Lord and Master of Kings."

It pleased the monarch of Egypt to put these envoys to death. By seizing Bagdad Timur had drawn too near the powers of the west, and the forces of the Mamluks were set in motion. At this moment they gained an unexpected and a formidable ally.

A Tatar army had interfered in the affairs of Asia Minor, thus drawing upon Timur the anger of Bayazid, Sultan of the Turks. The alliance was now complete, and it seemed that Timur's westward march had ended. With the Turkomans and Syrian Arabs supporting their flanks, the Sultans felt their way eastward, meeting little opposition, as far as the Euphrates and the Caspian sea.[1]

The Mamluks of Egypt marched down the Tigris, and entered Bagdad, escorting the fugitive Ahmed. He was duly installed again in his palace, this time as governor for Egypt. When the Mamluks had withdrawn from Bagdad, and the Turks from Mosul, sat-

---

[1] This was the year when Miran Shah's drug-inspired vagaries were making chaos of the Tatar province south of the Caspian, and Timur was engaged elsewhere, first in quelling the last onset of Toktamish in the north, and then departing for the march into India. To have followed his campaigns in chronological order would have required a route book and a constantly changing map. As a consequence each phase had been dealt with separately until now.

isfied with their achievements, Ahmed was left to his own devices. He sent spies to Samarkand to gain tidings of Timur and his men returned with strange tales.

"We have seen what we have seen. The city is not as it was formerly. Now it has blue domes and marble courts where once camels were tethered. Verily we saw the lord of the Tatars, at the building of a *sarai*. He was not pleased with what the builders had done, and he gave command to tear it down. Thereafter for the space of twenty days he came each day upon his horse and watched, and—God is our witness, this thing happened as we say—in the twenty days the palace was erected to the last stone of the arch and the bricks of the dome. The arch is the height of twenty and four lance lengths, and fifty men can stand in its breadth."

"And what more?" the Sultan asked.

"He sits in talk with the imams of the Sunnites and the Alyites, saying to them—"

"What are his words to me? What doeth he?"

"By Allah and the Companions, may your highness favor us! He hath departed into Ind."

Although he knew Timur must be more than a thousand miles away, Ahmed could not feel at ease. He had not forgotten that mad flight over the barren lands with the amirs at his heels. He began to distrust his ministers and more than a few he put to death with his own hand. He moved his quarters into the almost deserted women's palace, and surrounded himself with Circassian Mamluks and negro swordsmen.

From the balconies, from behind the marble fretwork that had screened his wives, he watched the throngs that passed over the bridge of boats. Secretly he had eight horses put in a stable across the Tigris and guarded by the few followers he trusted. Then he declared that no one would be admitted into his presence. No slaves came into the chambers, and Ahmed passed his hours going from embrasure to embrasure, distrusting those who watched for him.

His fear gained such mastery over him that at last he had his meals brought to him on a single tray and left at the *sarai* door. When the chamberlain who brought them had departed, Ahmed opened the door and took in the tray.

By nights he made trial of his way to safety, going out heavily cloaked and crossing the river to where his horses waited. To him thus guarded came a folded missive written in beautiful Persian—a verse of praise from the immortal Hafiz whom he had invited long since to visit him:

"Ahmed, son of Sultan Owaiss,
  The King and son of a King!
Lover of wine-filled days,
  To thee may fortune bring
The throne of Khusru and the glory of Genghis Khan."

A year passed and Ahmed had begun to feel secure when the quiet of his solitude was broken by the roar of a great drum.

Part Three

CHAPTER XXIII

THE PROTECTED

FOR TEN YEARS no breath of war had disturbed the city of Samarkand. And in ten years, under the impetus of Timur's will, much had been done.

He had taken a Samarkand of sun-dried clay and brick and wood and made of it a Rome of Asia. He had adorned it with whatever pleased his fancy in other lands; he had peopled it anew with captives, and installed within it the scientists and philosophers of his conquests. Every victory had been commemorated by a new public building; the scholars had been provided with academies and libraries, and the artisans with guilds in the trading centers. There was even a menagerie for strange beasts and birds, and an observatory for the astronomers.

This city had been Timur's dream. He had never been too deep in a campaign to overlook any materials or works of art that might beautify it. The white marble of Tabriz, the glazed tiles of Herat, the silver filigree work of Bagdad, the clear jade of Khoten—it was all here now. No one knew what would turn up next, because no one but Timur had a hand in the planning of the new Samarkand. He loved it as an old man loves a young mistress. At this time he was off plundering India to enrich Samarkand. The results he had achieved in ten years are worth looking at.

At this particular time, a day in early spring, 1399, Timur was absent in India, and he communicated with the city by courier, by way of the Khyber pass and Kabul. Riding in from the south highway, from the Green City, the couriers had passed through a plain where the groves were filled with tents and huts. The throngs in these camps were the overflow of late arrivals, captives, hangers-on and fortune seekers drawn to the new Utopia—a bedlam of tongues, and a babel of varied prayer. Here were gathered Christians, Jews, Nestorians—Arabs, Malakites, Sunnites and Alyites. Some looked on with haggard eyes, others were intoxicated with excitement and suspense as if with wine.

Here, too, were the picket lines of the horse and camel traders, where armed guards sat in the wind-tossed chaff. On one side of the road near a well stood a small stone building without color or dome—a church of the Nestorian Christians. Beyond these cantonments of strange people began the estates of the nobles, the white of a palace wall gleaming through the light green tendrils of elms. Still a mile from the city wall, the couriers entered the suburbs where they could read the giant lettering on the blue façade of a distant academy—"God is great and there is no God but He."

The road enters two lines of sentinel poplars. But off on the left there are streams and bridges and a labyrinth of garden plots—outskirts of the palace called Heart's Delight, where the stone cutters are still at work. At one side within the sycamores and blossoming fruit trees, stands a wall five hundred paces long, which is no more than one side of a square, each side having a single ogival arched gate supported by rearing stone lions.

Within, gardeners from Persia are at work with pots and picks, while slaves clear away the débris of cement. Beyond a marble colonnade rise the walls of the central palace. It is three stories in height, and some celebrated architects competed in drawing the plans.

Skilled painters are still at work upon the entrance hall. Each artist has a segment of the wall to himself, and a bearded Chinese who scorns color draws with a hair brush beside a court painter of Shiraz who is nothing if not flamboyant. Beyond them stands a Hindu who is not much at drawing but knows how to apply gilt and silver tissue on cement. Overhead the ceiling is a mass of flowers, but the flowers are all mosaics. The walls shine brilliantly—white porcelain, newly cleaned.

On the north side of the city a garden very similar to this was completed before Timur left for India. And the chroniclers who write down the daily transactions of their master have this to say about it:

"Our Lord erected his pavilion there for one night. He built it for plays and festivals on days of rejoicing. He chose a model from the designs of the architects. Four amirs watched the building of the four pavilions in the corners. Lord Timur was so intent upon this building that he stayed a month and a half to make certain it was finished swiftly. A piece of Tabriz marble was laid in each corner of the foundations.

"The walls were painted in fresco by artists of Isfahan and Bagdad with so much care that the Chinese paintings in Timur's cabinet of curiosities are not as fine. The court was paved with marble, and the lower walls within as well as without were covered with porcelain like this. The name of it is the Garden of the North."

Within the circuit of these garden palaces lies the main city, its walls five miles in circumference. At one of the gates—the Turquoise Gate—a courier takes the right of way from a cavalcade of priests on mules. He is a horseman in armor, his pony dark with sweat, flecked with foam. The man's bloodshot eyes glare out of a mask of dust and the arm that flicks the pony's flank with the whip moves mechanically. A courier from the army in India.

Loiterers at the gate hasten after him, following the way that he opens, through the quarter of the Armenians where sallow-faced men stand in dark furs, up into the street of the saddle makers, smelling of hides and oil, as far as the palace of one of the governors where secretaries are waiting to copy out the dispatches. Lingering, the throng may hear some of the news—for rumor is never penned within walls. The dispatches, it seems, are urgent.

"A command of our Lord." But the nature of the order is not apparent. Officers of the governor ride out, and tongues wag.

Armed Tatars bar the way to the citadel hill where the imperial women have their courts. But the women have also garden courts dedicated to each of them, and in one of these to-day there is a festival.

The building is in a wilderness of rose and tulip beds, and the visitor notices that it is roofed with a Chinese pagoda-peak. One chamber opens into another through arches, as far as a room hung with rose colored silk—walls and ceiling ornamented with plates of silver gilt bearing designs in pearls. Silk tassels swaying with the wind appear like a moving curtain.

Here are divans under canopies of silk supported by spears. Rugs from Bokhara and Farghana cover the floor. In every chamber stand tabourets of gold, cast in a single piece, bearing vials of scent, set each with different stones—rubies, emeralds or turquoises. Also gold pitchers of honey mead, clear wine or spiced wine, the inside of the pitchers being a mass of pearls. One of the pitchers is flanked with six cups and through the wine in the cups gleams a ruby two fingers in width.

But the festival is in the pavilions, shaded from the sun. There sits gray-haired Mouava, and a few Tatars, and many Persians of royal blood, and visiting chieftains of the Afghans and Arabs. When they were all seated and expectant, Sarai Mulkh Khanum appears.

Before the empress advance black slaves, and beside her walk her ladies with downcast eyes. But the Princess of the Palace moves erect under the weight of her crimson head-dress that is shaped like a helmet, heavy with its precious stones and embroidery and the broad circlet of gold about her brows. The summit of this head-dress is a miniature castle from which rise white plumes. Other feathers fall about her cheeks, and between them tiny gold chains gleam.

Crimson, too, is her loose robe, trimmed with gold lace. Fifteen women bear in their hands the long train. Sarai Khanum's face is coated with white lead, and veiled after a fashion with sheer silk; her black hair is spread behind her shoulders.

When she is seated another princess appears, younger and less resolute, but composed and respectful to the elder. Her dark skin and wide eyes show that she is a Mongol—the daughter of a Mongol Khan, and Timur's last bride.

To these ladies of the palace advance cup-bearers, holding goblets on gold trays, white cloths wrapped about their hands so that they should not touch even the tray. They kneel, and when the princess has sipped from a cup they retire backward, and others come forward to serve the amirs. And these empty their goblets, turning them upside down to show that no drops remain within and that they had thus honored fittingly their hostess.

Timur's residences are elsewhere, beyond the citadel quarter. Here are the pavilions of the officers of his staff who did not go with the army to India, and his magistrates and the keepers of the treasury—a castle built apart, at the edge of a ravine. This serves also as arsenal and laboratory.

It houses collections of fine and odd weapons, and the drafting room of the engineers, with tables covered with models of catapults, mangonels and fire throwers —counterweight and torsion, both. Here are the rooms where swordsmiths weld and test new blades, and a thousand captive artificers work steadily upon helmets and body armor alone. At this time they are perfecting a light helmet with a broad nasal piece that can be pulled down to guard the face or thrust up out of the way.

Within the treasury it is not permitted to go, but not far away is the Hermitage, a kind of den and curio house of white marble near the animal park where Timur sleeps at times. In the courtyard stands a tree that flashes in the sun—its trunk gold, its branches and leaves worked out of silver. But the fruit! Hanging from the boughs are lustrous pearls and selected precious stones of every color shaped like cherries and plums. Even birds are there, of red and green enamel upon silver, their wings extended as if they were pecking at the fruit. Inside the treasury building is a miniature castle with four towers encrusted with emeralds. These are toys—things of fancy, but symbolic of the wealth that lies at hand.

The traveling mosque is gone. It was a light structure of wood, blue and crimson, a high stairway leading to it, and light let in through colored glass. It could be taken to pieces and packed in the great carts, and there it is stowed at present, being set up daily for Timur's hour of prayer alone, while he marches through India.

By now it is mid-afternoon and the markets are hot, crowded and full of noise and dust. The Tatars can buy there anything from manna to a young woman; but many of them are going past the bazaars out to the tomb of Bibi Khanum—turning aside into the alleys to avoid a train of camels just in from the Cathay trunk road, bearing loads of odorous spice in hemp bales. This spice is bound for the Hanse towns by way of Moscow, and the bales are marked with Chinese characters and Arabic lettering, as well as the stamp of the Tatar customs officers.

Like the larger palaces, the Bibi Khanum quarter is on a low hill surrounded by slender poplars. The buildings—a mosque, with its companion academy and quarters for teachers and disciples—are so large in scale that only from a distance can their proportions be realized and they are not yet completed. The mosque appears about the size of St. Peter's at Rome—without the central dome, but with flanking towers two hundred feet in height. To reach it, the visitors cross a stone-flagged plaza, and circle a marble tank. Here sit dignified figures, mullahs wearing the huge turbans that the Bokhara men affect, and philosophers who have studied natural law, and are disputing about it with the mullahs who know only what the leaves of the book unfold.

"Who taught Avicenna his skill in medicine?" asks a black-robed Arab. "Did he not observe, and make experiments?"

"And write in a book also?" adds a hook-nosed philosopher from Aleppo.

"Verily, he did," assents a third. "But he had read Aristotle's Law of Nature."

"True," put in one of the mullahs who was not too sure of his knowledge among distinguished strangers, "yet in the end, what was his conclusion?"

"By Allah," the Arab smiles, "I know not the end of his book, but he came to his own end by overmuch love of women."

"O ye of little wit!" a deep voice speaks. "What was truly his end? The great physician, dying, ordered that the Book should be read aloud, and thus he opened the way of salvation."

At this the man from Aleppo lifts his head. "Harken, ye who spoil the carpet of contemplation with the spittle of argument—I have a story to tell of our Lord Timur."

While heads turn in his direction, he explains that he was present at a discussion two years ago, when the learned men of Samarkand and the Alyites of Iran sat before Timur in his camp. "I heard our Lord ask a question—whether in that war his own men who died, or the enemy would be called martyrs? Indeed, no one dared to answer, until a kadi raised his voice and said that Muhammad—upon whom be blessing—had answered before them, saying that not they who fought in defense of their lives, or they who fought because of courage alone, or they who desired glory alone would see his face after the day of judgment. Nay, only he who fought for the words of the Book would see his face."

"And what said our Lord?" demanded a mullah.

"He asked the kadi how old he was. And the kadi said two-score years. Then our Lord said only that he himself was aged three-score and two. And he gave presents to all who had argued."

For a moment the listeners meditate upon this, fixing all the words in their minds so that they could repeat it to other audiences.

"*I* think," the Arab observes, "that thou hast seen this anecdote in Sherif ad-Din's history."

The man of Aleppo defends his own version. "What my ears heard, I have said. Sherif ad-Din took it from me."

"The flea said, 'This garment is mine!'" The Arab scoffs. "O Ahmed, were there no others at the discussion?"

"If thou doubtest the faith of our Lord Timur," Ahmed cries suddenly, "look!"

And his long-sleeved arm points overhead at the façade of the mosque of Bibi Khanum, with its turquoise tiles and gilt inlay now softened by shadow—dark against the burning blue of the sky. A massive work, clear-cut as a cliff rising from the desert floor, and marred by no clumsy buttresses.

But the Arab is not to be outdone. "By Allah, I see. It was built by one of his women."

She who built it—or for whom Timur raised it—lies in a small domed tomb in an adjacent garden. The body of Bibi Khanum is beneath a square slab of white marble there in the entrance where throngs move in and out, and the dark Tatar swordsmen stand on guard. Her name is no more than that—the Blessed Princess.

The visitors have heard that the body is the well loved Aljai Agha, brought hither from the Green City. But some say that this princess came from China [1] and

---

[1] We cannot be sure who Bibi Khanum was, so many legends have gathered about the name. Timur never married—as many histories say—a woman of the royal family of China. But he did take as wife the daughter of the Mongol Khan. But at the date of this marriage some of the Bibi

others will tell at length how thieves came one night to take precious stones from the casket and were struck by a serpent that lived in the tomb, so that guards coming to take their posts the next morning found the bodies of the thieves outstretched.

The shadows grow longer across the plaza, and the men of Samarkand make an end of discussion and the affairs of the day. Some go off to the bath houses to be stripped and soaked and scrubbed and shaved and kneaded and led into the warm room to dry by degrees while their shirts are washed, so that they may dress again in clean garments to go forth to eat—at the palace of an amir, or into the suburbs by the river. This is the rendezvous of all the Tatars who seek amusement. They follow their noses into booths where quarters of mutton are roasting, and rice and barley cakes are piled up. Then on to other stalls where sugar candy and sun-dried melons and figs may be bought for the half of a silver coin. Usually the end of the promenade is a wine shop where they may sit and watch the throngs and the endless shows of the board walk.

Along the river stand the cotton booths of the shadow plays, where puppets quarrel and strut upon a lighted sheet, and the magic lantern throws its pictures. Rope dancers pass over the heads of the watchers, and tumblers spread their carpets underfoot. Some of the Tatars prefer the groves of lilac and pomegranate trees where crimson and blue lanterns glow, and the wine pitcher circles among the feasters kneeling about a carpet. The gossip of the day is exchanged, the news debated. A musician improvises upon a guitar, and a poet, looking about him, quotes a little-known astronomer who used to sign himself the Tentmaker:

Khanum buildings had been erected. Obviously it could not be the great princess, Sarai Khanum.

"We are but chessmen laboring amain,
The great chess-player Heaven to entertain;
The while It moves us on the board of life—
Then into the box of death we go again."

CHAPTER XXIV

THE GREAT LADY AND THE LITTLE LADY

SAMARKAND was built according to Timur's fancy. Unlike other conquerors of his race, he did not copy Persian art as it existed. He looked at Persian buildings, and carried off artisans from the south, but the monuments of Samarkand were Tatar in conception, not Persian. Their ruins—and the kindred ruins of Timur's other cities—remain to-day the finest expression of Tatar art. And even the ruins have an imperishable beauty.

Grotesque at times, and often hideous in details—sometimes gleaming magnificence upon the façades, and unfinished cement and brick in the rear—they have perfect simplicity in design. Timur longed for mass. At least twice he ordered a completed work torn down and erected again on a larger scale. He delighted in color.

In him was the somber humor of the Tatar race, and the almost voiceless poetic sense of the nomad. His buildings were stark and magnificent. Timur had the desert dweller's pleasure in foliage and running water. It is noteworthy that his palaces were built for the gardens.

And Samarkand had its public square. A place for prayer and talk, a concourse for politics and news, a rendezvous for the great lords and an exchange for the merchants. It was called the *registan*—the square.

On its four sides loomed the buildings created by Timur's will, churches and academies. It covered the summit of a low rise, under the citadel height, and it was always gay with streamers and the dripping of fountains. On the day after the reception of Sarai Khanum, it was crowded at sunrise because rumor had reported the arrival of a courier the day before.

"No word is yet known," the grandees agreed, "save that the message was from our Lord. And this silence —is it not a cloak to cover calamity?"

They recalled that the high amirs had been reluctant to go to India, until roused by Timur. And that even his grandson, Muhammad Sultan, had said: "We may subdue Ind; yet Ind hath many ramparts. First, the rivers; and secondly, wilderness and forests; and thirdly, the soldiers clad in armor; and fourthly, the elephants, destroyers of men."

"Ind," said a Tatar lord who had been there, "is a land of sudden heat, not like our heat, but breeding sickness and sapping strength. There, the water is bad and the Indus speak a language that is not like ours. What if the army should linger there too long?"

In this Tatar Forum there were wise counselors and men who had governed kingdoms before Timur's coming shuttled them into other tasks.

"With the gold of Ind," they vouchsafed, "we could subdue the world."

They knew that the empire beyond the mountains was the treasure house of Asia, and that Timur meant to gather in its resources. They suspected, too, that he meant to open a road into China. Had not two other Tatar divisions been sent to explore the Gobi beyond Khoten? They had reported not long since that it was two months' march from Khoten to Kambalu. And they had investigated Kashmir, where the mountains were a barrier into China.

These counselors bethought them that only recently

Timur had taken in marriage a young daughter of the Mongol Khan. And not long ago the emperor of China had died.

"In the world," some one pointed out, "there are six rulers of such power that we do not mention them by name. So the marabout Ibn Batuta said, and he visited all in turn."

"Six?" laughed an officer. "There is one, and his name is Amir Timur."

"Nay," asserted the more experienced, "the marabout was right. He described them thus: the Takfur of Constantinople, the Sultan of Egypt, the King of Bagdad, the Lord of Tatary, the Maharaj of India, and the Fagfur of China.[1] Until now our Lord of Tatary hath overcome no more than one other of these rulers, the Sultan of Bagdad."

Moodily the Tatar officers pondered their wars of forty years—the aged Saif ad-Din and Mouava were in the *registan* that morning. In those forty years, only one of the greater princes of the world, it seemed, had fled before Timur. And now Sultan Ahmed was returned to Bagdad.

Indeed the news from the west was all bad. Revolt simmered along the Caucasus, and the Sultans had reoccupied all Mesopotamia. If by any chance Timur should be defeated in India! Timur's people were so accustomed to victory, that nothing else was looked for. Had not the army, ninety-two thousand strong, gone down the Khyber pass, and built a bridge across the Indus. Multan had fallen, and now Timur moved against the Sultan of Delhi.

[1] Takfur—emperor. Ibn Batuta's list would startle a European, but except for the fact that the Greek Emperor and the Sultan of Bagdad were exalted more by past reputation than by power, his account is accurate. Europe, divided into a dozen small kingdoms and dukedoms, had not yet begun its conquests. The last of its crusaders had withdrawn. The Asiatics believed that Constantinople was the reigning city of Europe.

The Tatars at the head of the home government mused upon the fighting ability of the elephants, that they had never seen.

That morning word spread swiftly through the *registan*. The courier's message was known. Had not the citadel guards searched all night because of it?

"The message of our Lord was a command, to put to death the courtesan Shadi Mulkh."

All Samarkand wondered who Shadi Mulkh might be, except the few who knew, among them the old general Saif ad-Din.

This eldest of the amirs had brought back with him from Persia a black-haired girl not long since. A creature with the full eyes and white skin of the harem-bred. And Khalil, the youthful son of Khan Zadé, had been intoxicated with her beauty. At his plea, Saif ad-Din had given the girl to him. So Shadi Mulkh, trained in the arts of a courtesan, had passed into the arms of Timur's youngest grandson.

Khalil, stirred by the passion that filled his life, spent his hours at the feet of his new mistress. He dreamed of a marriage in state, before the grandees and the royal princesses.

But this request Timur had refused instantly, and had ordered Shadi Mulkh to be brought before him. Frightened, the girl had fled, or Khalil had hidden her, and then the army had gone off.

Now from India the conqueror had sent command to put Shadi Mulkh to death. Khalil could not aid her, nor could she hide from the search that penetrated all of Samarkand's gardens. One sanctuary alone might save her life. And so, veiled, she hastened to the palace of the great princess Sarai Khanum, mistress of the court. There she flung herself down, catching at the feet of the elder woman, begging wildly to be saved from death. She had not the stoic courage of the Tatars.

What passed between the women we do not know. But the picture is clear—the beautiful girl, henna-stained, tears smearing the black kohl from her eyelids upon her cheeks—the impassive empress, stern in the traditions of the Tatar conquerors. Shadi Mulkh, a thing created for pleasure, maddened now by fear. And Sarai Khanum, at once the widow and wife, the mother and grandmother of reigning princes, about whom had centered the anxieties and stress of fifty years.

Shadi Mulkh at last cried out that she was with child by Khalil.

"If that is true," the great princess said, "the Lord Timur will spare thee."

And she sent Shadi Mulkh to the care of her own eunuchs, forbidding her to see Khalil until her case was brought before Timur.

A slight affair, this love of a boy for an unknown courtesan, but upon it rested the future of an empire. Between Sarai Khanum and Khan Zadé there was bitter antagonism—for Khan Zadé's influence was little less than the prestige of the elder princess. And Khan Zadé was ambitious, and much more clever than Sarai Khanum. Men called them the Great Lady and the Little Lady.

It would have been much better if the Great Lady had let Shadi Mulkh be put to death. Later, Timur confirmed her decision and the courtesan lived.

Into Samarkand rode a courier who made no secret of his message, for he reined in a rearing horse to shout at guard house and *sarai* and gate:

"Victory!　Our Lord has conquered!"

Others came with fuller stories, grim enough.　Before meeting the Sultan of Delhi the Tatars had massacred, they said, a hundred thousand captives.　They had broken the army of India in battle, and had taken Delhi.[2]　The elephants—so rumor ran—had been scattered by flame throwers.

There was festival in Samarkand, and the *registan* was crowded nightly.　Especially the Church rejoiced.　With northern India underfoot—the treasure house broken into, the Hindu rajas driven into their hills, the leaders of Islam dreamed of a new Kalifate, and a dominion that stretched from Bagdad to India.　Under Timur's protection there would be peace, and wealth, and upon such sureties the power of the imams would grow.

The next spring the army returned, by way of the Green City, and the Black Throne, where a garden of dark marble had been built upon a mountain top.

Under the Turquoise Gate of the city carpets had been spread, and crimson cloth upon the street leading to the citadel.　From roof parapets and garden walls flamed silks and embroidered cloths.　Shop fronts were decorated, and the people clad in their brightest colors.

Down the road went the resident amirs, the visiting lords and the princesses, to give welcome to their lord.　Thither rode Sarai Khanum with her court, her eyes searching the throngs of mailed riders for the face of Shah Rukh, her son.　And there too Khan Zadé waited the appearance of her two first-born, Prince Muhammad Sultan and Prince Pir Muhammad.　When the

---

2 Timur's conquest of India was no more than a short campaign.　He did not wish to besiege Delhi, so he maneuvered in the plain and entrenched himself with all the appearance of uncertainty and fear.　The Sultan of Delhi was deceived and gave battle in the open, which was just what Timur desired.　Once the Indian army was defeated he sacked Delhi at leisure and moved south on the Hindu border cities.

princes rode past the slaves tossed into the air gleaming gold dust and pearl seed, and precious stones under the hoofs of Timur's horse.

And then upon the watching multitude fell stark amazement. Their great heads nodding above the dust, their huge forms painted in many colors, appeared the leaders of the elephants—ninety-seven teams of them, laden with the treasure of their former masters.

So Timur made his eighth triumphal entry into Samarkand. Among his gleanings from India were plans of the Jumna mosque and two hundred masons to help him build one like it. The chronicle relates that the first thing he did upon dismounting was to go to the bath.

CHAPTER XXV

TIMUR'S CATHEDRAL

To COMMEMORATE THE CONQUEST OF INDIA, Timur wished to build something new and notable. Evidently he had already made up his mind what it would be, because he entered Samarkand on the twentieth of May, and on the twenty-eighth he was superintending the foundations of the great mosque that came to be called the King's Church.

It was to be of cathedral size, large enough, the chronicle says, to hold all the people of the court. There was little sleep thereafter for architects and artisans. Five hundred stone cutters were sent to the hill quarries, and stone blocks began to appear down the road, dragged on massive wheels by the newly acquired motive power, the elephant teams. The problem of applying elephant power to the building itself was laid before the engineers, and they devised hoists and pulleys to fill the need.

When the walls were up the Indian masons were set to work inside, all two hundred of them. Timur passed from war to building with perfect detachment. Having finished with India, he thought of nothing but the new cathedral. Perhaps two hundred thousand human beings had died along the route of his battles that last winter, but the memory did not trouble him. Victorious generals were appointed the duty of overseeing the erection of towers and pillars.

Within the cathedral four hundred and eighty stone pillars went up; doors of worked brass were set in place

—a marble ceiling laid, and polished. Gilt iron and silver went into the pulpit and reading desk. The decorations were inscriptions from the Koran.

In less than three months the caller-to-prayer was crying from the minarets of the new towers, and from the pulpit prayers were read in the name of the Emperor.

Timur never took to himself formally the title of Emperor. He was still Amir Timur Gurigan—Lord Timur, the Splendid. He did not claim to be a *tura*, a ruler of imperial descent. His documents began with the short phrase "Lord Timur hath given this command—" or even more briefly, "I, Timur, servant of God, say this—"

But his grandsons, all born of women of the imperial line of the Tatars, bore the titles Mirza and Sultan—Prince. To them Timur had given empires as fiefs. Muhammad Sultan was ruler of the Jat dominion, Pir Muhammad of India—Shah Rukh, his gentle son, ruled in Khorassan and was building palaces of his own in Herat. The sons of the disgraced Miran Shah had their court in the west, which was at present much the worse for disorder.

Timur had given no hint whom he would name as his successor. The aging Sarai Khanum hoped in spite of all likelihood that her son Shah Rukh would be given the imperial throne. Khan Zadé spared no intrigue or cajolement on behalf of her youngest son Khalil. But neither dared speak openly to the old conqueror. And to his grandsons he was an inflexible arbiter, a passionless judge.

Untroubled by the ambitions of the women, Timur sat in the saddle watching his elephants at work. It occurred to him that the existing bazaar was too small for the traffic of the city, and he commanded suddenly that a wide street should be opened from the *registan* to the river, and fitted up as a street of trade. This, he said, should be done in twenty days. He entrusted the task to two nobles, promising that their heads would fall if the work were not done as he ordered.

Naturally, the two overseers went to work. Along the line Timur had pointed out an army fell to wrecking houses. Protests were vain—the owners fled with their clothes and what else they could gather while their walls came down.

Workmen were drafted from outside the city—loads of lime and sand requisitioned. The débris was carted off, the ground leveled, the street laid out and flagged and drained. Laborers were divided into two shifts, one for the day, the other to carry on by torch-light. They seemed, the chronicle says, to be so many devils toiling beside flames, and the noise was unending.

The broad street was finished, the arcade built over it, the shops erected—windows pierced through the domed roof. Merchants were summoned in haste to cart in their goods. Before the limit of twenty days the new street was crowded, and Timur, riding through it, was satisfied with the work.

It had an aftermath. The ousted owners made a plea to certain judges, and one day while they were playing chess with Timur these judges ventured to suggest that since he had caused the houses to be demolished, he ought to make amends to the owners. This enraged the conqueror. "Is not the city mine?"

Fearing that they would be given to the swords of the guards, the judges made haste to assure him that the city was indeed his, and all he did was right. After a moment Timur responded:

"If it is right that the people should be paid, I will pay them as you desire."

Apparently in all this time he had given no thought to another war. In reality he had been gathering information. He had every reason to rest content with what he possessed. He had gutted India, the north was under his hand. True, the western line of the Tigris had been taken from him; but no power of the west would dare attack the heart of his dominion.

He was now sixty-four years of age. Although his body seemed as vigorous as ever, he had been struck down at times by illness; his mind was as alert as in middle age, but he was given to long silences, and his temper had hardened. He had built his cathedral, but the leaders of the Church could not influence him. All his life he had been troubled by an inward conflict. The faith of his devout father, the catechizing of his preceptor Zain ad-Din, the law of Koran—these influences were in conflict with the heritage of his nomad ancestors, the lust for battle and the reek of destruction under his hand. And now it seemed as if he reverted to the code of the nomad. "A man's path is only one." Struggle and victory and the glory of possession.

The kings of the west were the pillars of Islam—the Kalif was in Cairo, the Protector of the Faithful in Bagdad, the Sword Arm of the Faith in the person of the Emperor of the Turks. To them the Tatar was a barbarian and more than half a pagan.

To march against them would be to divide the world of Islam, and to put a million men under arms. The Church was desperately urgent for peace; it called Timur Ghazi, Victor for the Faith, and prayer for the new Emperor echoed in the cathedral.

But there was a third side to the old Tatar's somber character. He was still the Timur who had gone alone to the gate of Urganj to fight a duel. He would never remain quiet if challenged. Now chieftains under his protection had been ousted from the threshold of Asia Minor; his son's lands had been invaded, and Bagdad taken from his governor. All this was a clear challenge.[1]

In May 1399, he had entered Samarkand, and in September he set out at the head of his army. For three years Samarkand did not see him.

[1] In addition, Timur was now pondering the invasion of China. He did not feel free to move against China in the east while the alliance in the west was threatening his frontier.

We can see at this point, as clearly as if they were so many moves upon a chessboard, the plans of the old Tatar. His object was first an alliance with the Mongol khans of the Gobi, then an invasion of China. To do this he would have to leave Samarkand for years. First he removed from the board the Sultan of Delhi, its nearest possible enemy; with the spoils of India he launched into the west, and cleared his frontier there. It is clear that he did not wish a conflict with the Turks, as long as they remained in Europe. When they advanced into Asia he went to meet them. The moment the western powers were crushed he turned back to Samarkand, and organized in two months his great expedition to China.

CHAPTER XXVI

THE WAR OF THREE YEARS

THE SITUATION confronting the Tatar conqueror was peculiar. To reach his enemies it was necessary to move west more than a thousand miles. Here the frontier of the allies, as it might be called, extended along an immense half-circle from the Caucasus mountains to Bagdad.

It was like a very pliant curved bow drawn back to the limit of its arc. And the Tatar host advancing along the great Khorassan road was moving in from the feathered tip of the arrow toward the head of the arrow and the center of the bow. Timur was moving west very much as Napoleon moved east in the summer of 1813 against the half-circle of allies, before the battle of Leipzig and the disastrous although brilliant retreat to Paris that overthrew the French leader and brought to an end the First Empire.

Like Napoleon, the Tatar conqueror had the advantage of a veteran army, himself sole commander, against a divided enemy. But the country over which they maneuvered was not the same at all. Instead of the level, cultivated lands of Europe with their network of roads and open villages, Timur was faced by all western Asia with its rivers, and mountain ranges, its deserts and marshes.

He had a choice of few routes, and once started along a certain road he had to keep going. And on these main caravan roads there were fortified cities, each with its army to defend it. Also, he had to march with an eye on the calendar—to think of crops and grazing for the horses. Some countries were impassable in winter, others forbidden ground in the hot season. Napoleon himself was turned back by one of these fortified cities, Acre, and the heat of the Syrian desert.

Along the half-circle of the frontier a dozen separate armies awaited the Tatars—the warlike Georgians had emerged from their fastness in the Caucasus. Next to them, an expeditionary force of Turks occupied the headwaters of the Euphrates. Kara Yussuf was on the prowl as usual with his Turkomans—a powerful Egyptian army held Syria, and down in the south lay Bagdad. If Timur moved on Bagdad, the Turks could attack his rear from the north; if he attempted to penetrate the lands of the Turks in Asia Minor, the Egyptian army would be at his back.

So he could not at first penetrate to the strongholds of the Turks in Europe, or the reigning city of the Mamluks in Egypt. He could not force either of the two great Sultans to give battle, while they could invade Asia at any time they wished.[1]

Above all was the question of water. The army had its camel trains, and Timur had brought along the elephants. But in the main it was an army of cavalry, with an extra horse to each man. To route anywhere from fifty thousand to a quarter million horses required care and exact knowledge of the country. While he marched Timur consulted his geographers and merchants daily; ahead of the main forces moved scouts,

---

[1] The difficulty of this terrain was evidenced by the checks suffered by the Allied powers in its invasion during the great war. The Russian armies penetrated little farther than Erzerum from the north, while a British army was forced to surrender near Bagdad in the south. In Syria the British and Lawrence's Arab clans were nearly two years in capturing Damascus.

These expeditions had command of the sea behind them and were better equipped than the Turk, the solitary defender of 1915-1918. In Timur's day the Turk was comparatively more powerful and was allied to the Mamluks, Circassians, Georgians and Turkomans, all formidable fighters—not to mention the Syrian Arabs.

and ahead of them scattered observers to report the position of the enemy and the water question. Beyond
the observers, spies went over the borders.

At first Timur advanced leisurely, and in state. Sarai
Khanum and two other imperial princesses and several
grandsons were with him. The great Khorassan road
saw the splendor of the Tatar court.

Meanwhile officers were making the city of Tabriz
into a base for operations in the west and the plain of
Karabagh a remount station for the horse herds. Timur
himself indulged in letter writing. In particular he
sent missives to the Tatar Khan who was then in power
in the Russian steppes—a certain Idiku. He received
a surprisingly frank reply.

"Lord Timur," Idiku wrote, "thou hast spoken of
friendship. For twenty years I lived at thy court, and
I know thee well, and thy tricks. If we are to be
friends, it must be with the sword in hand."

Nevertheless, the Tatars of the steppes kept out of
Timur's way and remained neutral in the coming
struggle.

To Bayazid, surnamed the Thunder, Emperor of the
Turks, Timur wrote courteously, but requested that no
aid be given to Kara Yussuf and Sultan Ahmed—who
had put themselves under the protection of the Turks,
and were then in active alliance with Bayazid. With
Bayazid as yet he had no personal quarrel; he respected
the military power of the Turks, and possibly he wished
to leave well enough alone in this quarter if the Turks
would remain in Europe.

Bayazid's answer was not conciliatory. "Know, O
bloody dog named Timur," it said in effect, "that the
Turks are not accustomed to refuse shelter to friends
or to shun battle with foes, or to resort to lies and tricks
of intrigue."

This drew a retort from Timur, who alluded to the fact that the Othman Sultans were sprung from the Turkoman nomads. "I know your origin." He added that Bayazid should think carefully, before venturing against elephants that would crush him—although Turkomans were never noted for good judgment. "If you do not follow our counsels, you will repent it. Consider, therefore, and do as you see fit."

To this Bayazid returned a long summary of his own victorious career—how he was conquering Europe, the stronghold of the unbelievers, how he himself was the son of a martyr for the faith, and the true champion of Islam. "Long have we wished for war with you. Now, the praise be to God, it is at hand. If you do not come to seek us, we shall pursue you to Sultaniah. Then will we see who will be exalted by victory and who will be cast down by defeat."

Apparently the Tatar conqueror made no immediate response. Later, he wrote briefly, saying that Bayazid could avoid war if he gave up Kara Yussuf and Sultan Ahmed at once.

The Thunder answered promptly and violently—so much so that the chroniclers of the Tatar conqueror have not dared to repeat the letter as it was written. Bayazid inscribed his own name at the top in gilt illumination and wrote Timur-i-lang—Timur the Lame —beneath in small black letters. He promised among other things to violate Timur's favorite wife. A letter that goaded the old Tatar into fury.

But while this animated correspondence had been taking place, Timur had accomplished a great deal.

First sending back the imperial women with their courts out of harm's way to Sultaniah, he left the bulk of his forces to mobilize at Karabagh, and sent sep-

SCALE IN ENGLISH MILES

0   100   200   300   500   700

THE EMPIRE—The dominion of the Tartar conqueror can only be approximately indicated
from Delhi to Moscow. Much of it was merely tributary; or

arate divisions against the Georgians in the Caucasus on
his right.   Roads were cut through the wooded defiles
again, the Christian armies shattered, and the unhappy
country laid waste in a ghastly fashion with fire and
sword.   Churches were burned, and even the vineyards
torn up.   No terms were offered, or respite—as in
other years.   In the field against massed enemies, Timur
was merciless.

In such fashion the fifteenth century dawned.   With
the melting of the snows, Timur's main divisions were
on the march into Asia Minor, by way of the valley of
Erzerum.   By midsummer 1400 he had taken all the
cities as far as Sivas.

Sivas was the key of Asia Minor.   The frontier army
of the Turks retreated in haste, while the Tatars assailed its walls, mining under them and propping up
the foundations.   Then the props were burned, and
whole sections of the wall came down.   The Muhammadans of the city were spared but four thousand Ar-
menian cavalrymen who had harassed the Tatars were
buried alive in the moat.

This done Timur ordered the fortifications repaired.
He scattered contingents of Turkomans who had come
upon the scene and hastened down by forced marches,
to surprise Malayta, the gate of the south—entering
it the same day that the Turkish governor fled with his
men.

Then, instead of advancing farther into Asia Minor
he ordered his divisions to prepare to march south
against Syria.   His amirs came to him in a body, to
protest.   Only a year ago, they said, they had ended
the war in India, and since then their men had marched
two thousand miles, in two new campaigns.   The enemy
in Syria was numerous, the cities were fortified, and
their men and beasts needed rest.

"Numbers mean nothing," Timur cried. And under the lash of his will, the army moved south.

It stormed Aintab, and found the army of the Egyptian Sultan awaiting it at Aleppo. Here it moderated its advance, crawling forward each day, digging trenches and building barriers around its camps. The Mamluks and Syrians accepted this as a sign of weakness and moved out of the walls to give battle. At once the Tatars advanced from their barriers and attacked, the elephants in the center—archers and flame throwers in the elephant castles.

Before the onset the allies broke. The Tatars forced their way into Aleppo, stormed the citadel on the height —and marched on, to Damascus. It was now January 1401.

Damascus bargained for terms, hoping for time in which a second army could be got together to oppose Timur. When the Tatars moved past, they were attacked from the rear by new forces of the allies. At first there was confusion, but Timur formed his divisions, drove home his charges, and cleared the field.

Then he turned back upon Damascus, and the great city was given up to the looters. Fire broke out, and raged for days, burying in its ruins the bodies of the slain.

The survivors of the Egyptian armies fled through Palestine. By order of the Egyptian Sultan one last attempt was made to check Timur. An assassin, dosed with hashish, tried to reach the lame conqueror with his dagger. The man was seized, thrown down and cut to pieces.

During the carnival of destruction at Damascus, Timur ordered that plans be drawn of a curious dome that had caught his attention. It covered a tomb that could be seen from the plain, and it was unlike the squat pointed domes that the Tatars had known. Swelling out from the base, it tapered to a slender point. In shape it was like a pomegranate.

Apparently it differed from all other work of the architects and its stateliness pleased the Tatar conqueror.

This bulbed dome of Damascus—destroyed in the fire—became the pattern of Timur's later buildings and those of his descendants. Transported in another century to India, it forms the summit of the Taj Mahal, and the palaces of the Moghuls. In Russia it is found upon every church.

CHAPTER XXVII

BISHOP JOHN GOES TO EUROPE

A T DAMASCUS Timur once more executed an about
face. As he had refrained from venturing far into
the lands of the Turks, he now turned back from the
Syrian desert. One division was sent down the coast of
the Holy Land, to pursue the Egyptian contingents as
far as Akka—the Acre of the crusaders, and later the
stumbling block of Napoleon. Several more were ordered due east to invest Bagdad.

Timur himself returned the way he had come as far
as Aleppo. It was now March 1401. More slowly—
because there was a limit to the endurance of even
Tatars, he moved over to the Euphrates, and allowed
the divisions with him to hunt. The chronicle mentions that the meat of roe-buck gave to wine an added
flavor.

Here he established fuller communication with his
base, and received messages from the amirs in command there, also the reports from Samarkand and the
weekly news from Sivas—on which he bestowed some
thought. Sivas was the gateway of the Thunder, and
Timur had wasted no time in bringing his main strength
back within two hundred miles of it.

But from the amirs before Bagdad he had a message
that sent him to the southern road. The commander
at Bagdad, it seemed, had defended the city. Sultan
Ahmed had fled to join Bayazid, leaving orders that
if Timur appeared in person before the city, it was to

be surrendered; but unless Timur came, it was to hold
out until the Turks could advance against the Tatars.

So the conqueror went south at once, traveling by
forced marches in a litter.

His arrival before the city was announced to the Sultan's officers within.   One who knew Timur by sight
was sent out to make certain that the conqueror himself
was present at the siege.   Faraj, the Sultan's commander in Bagdad, chose to disobey his master's orders.
Possibly he was afraid to yield the city after having
closed the gates against Timur—possibly, with the summer heat making a furnace of the Tigris valley, he believed that the Tatars would have to withdraw.   But
he must have known that for forty years the Tatars
had not abandoned the siege of a fortress.

The men of Bagdad trusted that the massive stone
walls would hold out against the Tatars.

The last thing Timur wanted was to invest Bagdad.
For nearly two years his divisions had been in the field
without respite; his main strength was gathered at his
base, Tabriz, against the coming of the Turks, and
there he had planned to be at this time.   His terrific
marching had at last failed to keep up with the sun,
and he was caught on bare, heat-ridden plains, faced
by shortage of food and grazing.

But Bagdad was the key of the Tigris, a rallying
point for the armies that might come out of Egypt and
the last stronghold of his enemies in Asia.   In an hour
he changed his plans, and couriers galloped out from
his quarters with orders to Shah Rukh to move down
from the north with ten veteran divisions and the engineers and siege train.   A corps of observation was
thrown into Asia Minor to watch the Turks, and an
order sent back to Samarkand, to Prince Muhammad

to advance to the west with the army that had been left
in the reigning city.[1]

When Shah Rukh arrived, Timur ordered a formal
review of his mounted divisions before the walls of
Bagdad. With standards raised and bands playing a
hundred thousand Tatars paraded before the eyes of
the inhabitants. The spectacle had no effect and Timur
set to work savagely.

A bridge of boats was thrown across the Tigris below
the city, to enable the besiegers to move from one bank
to the other and to cut off escape by the river. The
suburbs were stormed and leveled and occupied; the
circuit of more than twelve miles was closely invested.
From distant forests large tree trunks were hauled and
of these pyramids were built on nearby elevations. On
the summits of the pyramids the siege engines were
placed so that stones could be shot down at the walls
and the city within.

Meanwhile the miners began their burrowing under
the foundations. In a few days whole sections of the
outer wall came down. But behind these breaches the
Bagdadis had erected inner walls of stone and cement,
defended by fire missiles.

Timur's generals begged him to order a general assault. The heat was becoming a nightmare. In that
lifeless air birds, the chronicle relates, fell dead out of
the sky. The soldiers laboring in the reflected glare of
the burned clay of the ground under the heated walls
were literally baked within their armor.

[1] From the autumn of 1399 to the autumn of 1401 Timur's every move
was planned against the possibility of Bayazid's approach. At this time,
while Timur was preparing to besiege Bagdad, Bayazid was actually crossing leisurely from Europe to Asia. Had the Emperor of the Turks displayed more energy, and appeared upon the scene before Bagdad fell, he
would have found Tabriz—an open metropolis—deserted by the Tatars.
The Tatar corps of observation could have reported his movements to
Timur, who would have been able to unite in a few weeks with the reinforcements from Samarkand.

The old Tatar would not consent to have the great kettledrum sound the general assault. A week passed, while the siege engines kept up their battering—the soldiers retiring to shelter between mid-morning and late afternoon.

But it was in the full glare of noon without warning of any kind that Timur struck his blow. At this hour when the defenders except for a few watchers had deserted the outer wall, picked regiments of Tatars ran out from cover with ladders. The surprise was a success. Nur ad-Din, who had saved Timur in that last struggle with Toktamish, gained the summit of the defenses and planted there his standard of horsetails with its crest—a gold half-moon.

Then the great drum roared and all divisions upon that side of the city moved forward. Nur ad-Din descended into the streets and behind him the Tatars drove a wedge of mailed warriors. By mid-afternoon, in all the torment of merciless heat, the Tatars were masters of one quarter of the city, driving the Bagdadis toward the river. The city across the river now lay open to assault, and the scenes of terror that followed may well be passed over in silence. Timur's men, maddened by suffering and their heavy losses, appear like demons exulting in slaughter.

Their chronicler says that Bagdad, called *Dar essalam*, the Abode of Peace, might better have been called in that day the palace of havoc and hell. Faraj, its commander, fleeing in a boat, was killed by arrows from the bank, and his body dragged ashore. A hundred and twenty columns were built of severed heads, and perhaps ninety thousand human beings perished.

Timur ordered the walls to be razed and all buildings burned and pulled down except mosques and the various edifices of the Church.

So passed Bagdad from the pages of history. Its ruins were occupied later, but it remained from that day a place of no importance in the affairs of the world. Letters announcing its overthrow were sent to all the cities of Timur's dominion, and to Bayazid, the Thunder.

Sultan Ahmed, its absentee master, returned after the storm passed over. Timur, hearing of this, sent down a cavalry column to try to capture the evanescent prince. The chronicle relates that Ahmed fled again in his shirt up the river, and thereafter remained safe under Bayazid's wing.

Leaving the main army with the baggage and siege train to follow at leisure, Timur hastened back to Tabriz with Shah Rukh and a few generals. Bagdad fell in June, and in July 1401 he was again at his base. His grandson Prince Muhammad reported himself as far as Nisapur on the great Khorassan road with the reinforcements from Samarkand. Shah Rukh was within reach of the base. The first campaign was over.

Timur had marched from one end of the arc of his enemies to the other. In fourteen months he had fought two major battles and any number of smaller engagements, and had taken by assault nearly a dozen fortified cities. As a feat of arms it was remarkable, and it eliminated all of Bayazid's allies before the Thunder appeared on the scene.

It was now too late in the season to move against the Turks, and the Tatars were well enough content to postpone the reckoning until the next year. In due course Prince Muhammad's drums were heard on the road leading to the great camp and Timur's veterans rode out to stare in amazement.

The divisions from Samarkand blazed under their eyes in a new magnificence. Every standard was a different color—green, red and so forth, and all the horsemen of a division had cloaks and caparisoning and even shields and bow cases of the same color. The survivors of Timur's veterans who had galloped from India to the Black sea and down to Palestine and back again were loudly scornful of the new conceit, but secretly envious.

Timur interested himself in reopening an ancient canal that the Greeks had dug from the river Araxes. He also made a study of the trade routes of Africa and Europe. And by the hand of John, bishop of Sultaniah, he sent a letter to Charles VI of France—*"Roydefransa,"* with expressions of good-will.[2]

To him came the far-wandering agents of Genoa, eager to gain the good-will of the invincible Tatar before their rivals of Venice. They brought with them a secret appeal for aid from the Christian Emperor at Constantinople who was then at the mercy of Bayazid.

[2] Nothing in Timur's two letters to the King of France justifies the often-repeated remark that he offered to share the world with Charles—except the circumstance that the good Bishop John convinced Timur that Charles was the greatest of European monarchs, as Timur was the master of Asia. Timur said that he was marching against Bayazid, who was Charles' enemy, and hoped that merchants could be exchanged between his people and the French. He added that John would speak for him in everything "except matters of religion."

CHAPTER XXVIII

THE LAST CRUSADE

To UNDERSTAND WHAT NOW HAPPENED it is necessary to look at Europe for a moment. For two generations the Greek Emperors of Constantinople—no more than the ghosts of the old Roman Emperors—had seen their power pass to the Turks who had emerged from Asia Minor, and were now overrunning the Balkans, and the shores of the Black sea.

At the field of Kossova, the new conquerors, the Othman Turks, crushed the stalwart Serbians, and thereafter penetrated into Hungary. They were dour and disciplined fighters, full of fire and doglike in their devotion to their emperors. Their cavalry, especially the *sipahis,* was more than good, but their massed infantry, formed around the *janissaries,* was superb.

They had intermarried with all the Levant, and out of their Christian slaves—Greeks and Slavs—they were forming a new race. Bayazid had the virtues and faults of his people. He was turbulent and courageous, able and cruel. Upon his accession his first act had been to strangle his brother. He was proud of his victories and he boasted that after defeating Austria he would march into France, and feed his horses at the altar of St. Peter's.

He was lord of Constantinople in all but name; his lands extended up to the city walls; his judges were installed in several of its courts and from two minarets in the city muezzins called the Turks to prayer. Manuel, the present Emperor of Constantinople, paid him tribute for possession of the city. Venice and Genoa treated with him, as its future master. To the Turks Constantinople with its gardens and marble palaces was the city of promise—Istamboul.

The march of Islam up from Mecca had gone around the imperial city, which was still protected by its lofty walls and the war galleys of the European powers. But Bayazid was about ready to take possession—had, in fact, prepared to besiege it—when the call to a crusade resounded through Europe. It was to be a crusade against the Turks. Sigismund of Hungary, being most menaced by the approach of the Thunder, was its sponsor, and Philip of Burgundy was its advocate, for reasons of his own.

For a time there was quiet in the various kingdoms. The issues of the day, the Great Schism, the Hundred Years' War, the disputes of the Imperial Diets, the yearning of the commoners for property rights after the ordeal of the Black Death—all these were more or less in stalemate, and the barons gave ear to the call of the Church.

The intermittently mad king of France lent his support to the sane but apprehensive king of Hungary. From England and the Netherlands came volunteers. The muster-roll of these later-day crusaders sounds like the genealogy of all Europe. The Bastard of Savoy, the Master of the Prussian Knights, Frederick of Hohenzollern, the grand master of Rhodes—knights of St. John, electors, burgraves and palatines. The strongest forces came from France. Among them were scions of the houses of Bar and Artois, Burgundy and St. Pol. And the marshal, the admiral and the Constable of France—all under the orders of John Valois, Count of Nevers.[1]

[1] Son of Philip of Burgundy and grandson of the King of France. His birth alone gave him command of the expedition, as he was a youth without military experience or the qualifications of leadership.

Some twenty thousand chevaliers, including their squires and men-at-arms, rode to the west and joined the host of Sigismund, nearly a hundred thousand in all. They seem to have been well supplied with women and wine. So great was the multitude that the chevaliers boasted that if the sky were to fall they would hold it up by their spears.

The chevaliers themselves—the French, English and German knights—seem to have had only a hazy idea as to what lay before them. They believed that the Sultan of the Turks—they did not know his name —was rallying all Islam, including Egypt, Persia and Media, to oppose them; that he was lurking beyond Constantinople, and their only anxiety was that they should come up with him before he fled. After that they would press on to Jerusalem.

Sigismund of Hungary, somewhat wiser, assured them that "There would be no going away without the battle." As, indeed, there was not.

Moving down the Danube at ease, they were joined by Venetian galleys that came up the river. Matters went very well indeed. The Turkish outposts surrendered, and the crusaders massacred numbers of the people of the country, not realizing or caring that these were Serbians and Christians. They encamped in a fair country, to besiege Nicopolis, and here they heard that Bayazid with a formidable army was approaching rapidly.

At first they were incredulous. But Sigismund convinced them of the truth. The battle line was drawn up, and Sigismund—who knew the strength of the Turks—urged the chevaliers to form in the rear and let his sturdy infantry, the Hungarians, Wallachians and Croats, bear the shock of the Moslem attack.

This enraged the nobles, and the dispute grew violent when Bayazid's skirmishers appeared. It seemed to the French and Germans that Sigismund was tricking them into idleness while he himself gleaned the glory of the day. Finally Philip of Artois, High Constable of France, cried out:

"The king of Hungary would have the honor of the day. Whoever agrees with him, I shall not. We have the advance guard and the first battle belongs to us." Whereupon he gave command to lift his banner. "Forward, in the name of God and Saint George!"

In a mass the other lords followed him, with their squadrons of mailed riders—after first massacring their Turkish and Serbian prisoners. Streamers fluttering from their lance tips, shields erect, their heavy barded chargers thundering into a gallop, the chivalry of Europe charged. Princes, knights and men-at-arms, they scattered the skirmishers, forced their way up a long slope, cut to pieces the ranks of foot archers they found there, and reformed to assail the regiments of *sipahis* who now appeared.

They smashed through the *sipahis*, the Turkish light cavalry, and broke them, and pressed on again. It was a very gallant charge and it lost the battle.

These first three lines had been no more than Bayazid's advance. When they gained the next ridge the wearied chevaliers found themselves confronted by the flower of the Turkish army, sixty thousand strong— by the white turbans of the *janissaries* and the armored regiments of cavalry drawn up in a half-circle about them. Without wasting men in a counter charge the Turks began to shoot down the horses of the Christian knights with their arrows. Dismounted, hindered by their heavy armor, some of the crusaders fought on grimly—others turned and fled before their horses went down.

But with the forces of the Turks closing up around them and their own allies outdistanced, most of the chevaliers threw down their arms.

Meanwhile Sigismund had kept his part of the army intact. He had pushed forward some distance to follow up the mad career of the horsemen, but he was unable to support them. Whether he hung back through fear, or whether the reckless charge of the chevaliers put them beyond aid, is an open question that was hotly debated in Europe thereafter.

It is certain that the rout of the chevaliers lost the battle beyond hope. The rush of exhausted and bloodied fugitives with the Turks at their heels shook the courage of the infantry. On the wings, the Wallachians drew away to save themselves. Sigismund's Hungarians and the Elector's Bavarians made a valiant stand, but Sigismund himself and his nobles were soon galloping down to the river to seek refuge on the Venetian galleys.

As for the captive chevaliers, Bayazid was not the man to spare them, after their massacre of prisoners, and the losses he had suffered at their hands. Froissart, their chronicler, says dolefully:

"Then they were all brought before him naked in their shyrtes, and he behelde them a lytell and then turned fro them warde and made a sygne that they shulde be all slayne and so they were brought through the sarazyns that had redy naked swordes in their handes, and so slayne and hewen all to peces without mercy."

Ten thousand of them were dealt with in this way. Bayazid was persuaded by his nobles to hold twenty-four of the Christian peers for ransom, among them the ill-fated Count of Nevers, and Boucicaut, of France.

Two hundred thousand pieces of gold were required by the Turks for the ransom of this grandson of the king of France and his companions. And this sum, moderate in the eyes of the Turks, strained the exchequers of Europe. Eventually it was paid, and the surviving captives freed. Froissart tells us that Bayazid addressed to them a farewell message, bidding them muster new hosts and prepare to face him again:

"For I am able to do dedes of armes, and redy to conquere further into crystendom. These hygh wordes the Erle of Nevers understode well, and so dyd his company; they thought on it after as long as they lyved."

But only the gallant Boucicaut, now marshal of France, came back to try conclusion with the Turks. So ended ingloriously the last crusade, and the mourning of the European courts was equaled by the despair of Constantinople that had seen aid so near at hand and now believed itself doomed.

Meanwhile—the battle of Nicopolis was in 1396—Bayazid invested Constantinople and occupied himself with adding Greece to his empire. Momentarily the arrival of Boucicaut with five hundred knights and some galleys heartened the Christians of Constantinople.

It will be recalled that the Asia half of the Turks' dominions was separated from the European provinces by water. At this time the fleets of Venice and Genoa could have struck a blow at the Turks and probably saved the city. All they needed to do was to occupy the straits. But this they did not do.

Venice and Genoa were fighting for the trade of Asia, and to cripple each other. Bayazid, an astute diplomat, negotiated with both, and held out to both the bait of the Asia trade. They vied with each other in making gifts to the Sultan, and a new appeal from the Pope for an effort to save Constantinople went unheeded. The surviving lords of Europe were occupied in civil war again.

We are now confronted by one of the strangest spectacles of history. The city of the Cæsars, once mistress of the world, defended by several hundred adventurous knights and the mercenaries of the Greek nobles, so poverty stricken and so hungry in the midst of its great edifices that Boucicaut's voyagers had to go out and capture Turkish galleys to feed themselves, and were paid not at all. Manuel, its Emperor, departed on a tour of Europe to try to raise men and money for its defense. His entourage was so miserably clad that an Italian noble took pity on him and outfitted him more in keeping with his exalted rank.

From court to court this descendant of the Cæsars went, and was received with all ceremony and accorded endless sympathy but no aid at all. The crusading spirit had died in that last mad charge of chivalry, and the European monarchs were occupied with trade and the political alignments of the day. The Church might issue proclamations and the solitary Emperor might appear in person to plead, in vain.

While Manuel grew heart-sick and the men of Constantinople began to let themselves down over the walls to go to the Turks for food, and even Boucicaut abandoned the city, and the Emperor's nephew in Constantinople was drawing up terms for the surrender of Constantinople to Bayazid—for the second time the beleaguered city was granted a respite.

Unexpectedly out of the east the Tatars appeared,

and struck at Sivas and passed on. Bayazid suspended the siege to hasten into Asia.

Then every Turkish soldier in Europe was called to arms and ferried across the water. And the lord of Constantinople made a treaty to surrender the city if Bayazid should overcome Timur.

CHAPTER XXIX

TIMUR MEETS THE THUNDER

EARLY THIS SUMMER of the year 1402 the conqueror of eastern Europe mustered his strength to meet the conqueror of Asia. The veteran regiments of Kossova and Nicopolis were mobilized at the reigning city of the Othman Turks—Brusa, near the sea of Marmora. There the armies of Anatolia joined them, and twenty thousand mailed cavalry under Peter Lazarus, king of Serbia. The chronicle says of these that they were so covered with steel that only their eyes could be seen. Thither came Greeks and Wallachian infantry to serve their new master, the Sultan. The host may have been anywhere from 120,000 to 250,000 in numbers.

It was accustomed to a lifetime of victory. The *sipahis* and *janissaries* were always under arms. Its discipline was rigid, and its obedience to Bayazid slavelike. As for Sultan Bayazid he was utterly confident, and he feasted hugely while he waited.

Timur was on the march, and this pleased the Turks. Their main strength lay in the infantry, and the Turkish infantry was always best in a defensive action. The greater part of Asia Minor was broken, wooded country, ideal for them. Only one road ran west from Sivas, and upon this road they expected to meet Timur.

Slowly Bayazid moved his host east, as far as Angora. Here he established his main camp and pushed on, crossing the river Halys and entering the hilly country beyond. His outposts brought him word that the Tatars were at Sivas, some sixty miles ahead of him.

Bayazid halted his advance, placed his regiments on favorable ground, and waited.

He waited three days—a week. His scouts brought in people from Sivas with disconcerting tidings. Only the usual Tatar garrison was in that city. Timur and his army had departed long since, going toward the Turks.

But Timur was not between Sivas and the Turkish camp. The scouts galloped through all the hills, and returned, unable to find a trace of the Tatars. They had vanished somewhither, taking their elephants with them.

The situation was something of a novelty to the Turks. They were quartered in battle formation in the wastes of broken country in the heart of the great bend of the Halys that rises beyond Sivas and sweeps far south, turning north again almost within sight of Angora and emptying its waters into the Black sea. Bayazid waited where he was, determined not to move until he had definite news of the Tatars.

At dawn of the eighth day he heard from them. A regiment of scouts commanded by one of Timur's amirs galloped in upon the outposts of his far right wing, made prisoners and departed again. The Turks were certain now that Timur was to the south of them, and thither they moved accordingly. In two days they reached the river, but found no Tatars. Bayazid sent out cavalry columns of his own across the river under command of his son Suleiman, an able leader.

Almost at once Suleiman returned with information. Timur had evaded the Turks entirely and was now marching rapidly toward Angora, behind them.

Startled out of his apathy, the Sultan crossed the river and set out upon the path his enemies had made, toward his own base.

What Timur had done was amusingly simple. When he had studied the hilly country west of Sivas, and found it unsuitable for his cavalry, he had turned off to the south and marched along the valley of the Halys, keeping the river between himself and the Turks. So he was moving around the outer bend of the river, while Bayazid waited in the center.

At that season the crops were ripe for gathering, and the grazing was good for the horses. He had detached a column under one of the high amirs to establish contact with the Turks, and now—after the brush with Suleiman's force—he was quartered in the village of Kuch Hissar, lecturing his grandsons and officers upon the subject of strategy.

"There are," he told them, "two courses to follow now. We can wait here, refresh the horses, and stand against the Turks. Or we can push on into their country, laying it waste and compelling them to follow. Their army is mostly infantry, and marching will tire them."

And after a moment's pause, he added, "That is what we will do."

From this village Timur's routine of march changed. He left a strong rearguard in the village, and dispatched ahead a cavalry division under two amirs, with details of infantry that were to dig wells on the sites selected for the daily camps, while the horsemen of the advance gathered in the grain in readiness for the main body.

The Tatars found the country more open here— they had turned away from the river—and the water supply sufficient. Moreover—and this was really ideal —they learned that Bayazid's main camp was near Angora in their path. So Timur hastened his marches, covering the hundred miles to Angora in three days.

He put on his armor, which he seldom did in these later years, and rode around the city to inspect it. The Turks within prepared to defend it, and Timur ordered an assault—going off himself to look at Bayazid's base camp, deserted now by the followers the Turks had left there.

Angora lay in the center of a wide plain, and Timur decided that the position Bayazid had picked out was as good as any other. So his Tatars made their quarters in the tents of the Turks. At the order of their Amir, they dammed up the small river that flows into Angora, changing its course to run behind their new position.

The only other water available to the oncoming Turks was a spring, and this Timur ordered destroyed, and the water polluted. Before his men could make any impression on the walls of Angora, his scouts reported that Bayazid was approaching, twelve miles away.

Timur abandoned the attempt to take the city—even ordering some Tatars down from a bastion they had stormed. That night he intrenched his camp, and kept fires burning bright. His cavalry patrolled the plain. But the Turks did not come up until morning.

They had marched rapidly for a week, with little water, and less grain, along the devastated swathe left by the Tatars; they were weary and suffering from thirst, and the heat of the plain. They found the Tatars installed in their own base, with ample supplies. Worst of all, there was no water to be had anywhere except behind the Tatar line. They had only one alternative and that was to attack Timur.

Bayazid was forced to do what he least desired—to launch his inferior cavalry against the masses of horsemen from Central Asia. His men went into battle weakened by thirst. He had been outmaneuvered and finally led back to Angora as if on a string. And the battle was lost before the first sword flashed in the sun.

At ten o'clock in the morning under a burning sun, the Turks moved forward with the stubborn courage that has so often proved invincible. The front of the two armies extended for more than fifteen miles over the plain, one wing of the Tatars resting upon the small river, the other—invisible in the distance—upon a fortified height. The chronicle adds that the Turks came on with a thunder of drums and a clamor of cymbals while the squadrons of Tatars waited in a great silence.

Timur did not mount his horse until the last moment. The battle for the present was in the hands of his generals. He had with him no more than forty troops of cavalry, upon a ridge with the infantry, in the rear of the massed horsemen. Prince Muhammad, his grandson, commanded the center, with the host of Samarkand and eighty regiments with colonels from most of Asia. Here too were the elephants in their armor of painted leather—more for moral effect, it seems, than for any tactical purpose.

Upon the far right of the Tatars, Suleiman, Bayazid's son, launched a cavalry charge, leading himself the horsemen of Asia Minor. They were met by a devastating fire of arrows and flaming naphtha—horses and men going down in masses under the rising curtain of dust and smoke.

While the Turks were in disorder, the first line of the Tatar right charged, and Nur ad-Din, the ablest of Timur's amirs, followed with the main body of that wing.

In the first hour the advance of the Turks was checked, and the Tatars took the offensive. Nur ad-

Din broke up Suleiman's wing so thoroughly that some divisions of the Turks withdrew from the field. A contingent of Tatars from Asia Minor, impressed into service by Bayazid, discovered that their own lords were with Timur, and took advantage of the confusion to desert the Turks.

When Nur ad-Din had things well in hand upon the right, the left wing of the Tatar cavalry advanced in three waves, breaking through the Turkish skirmishers, and overthrowing the poorly mounted Turkish cavalry at this point. They went so far that Timur could no longer see them.

It was then that Prince Muhammad galloped back to his grandfather, and dismounted. Throwing himself on his knees he begged permission to advance with the Tatar center upon the masses of Bayazid's infantry. This consent Timur would not give.

Instead he ordered Muhammad to take the Samarkand corps and a division of the *bahaturs*—the picked men of the Tatars—and go at once to support the left wing that had overreached itself.

So the favorite grandson of the old conqueror lifted his red standard, and galloped off, followed by the flower of Timur's army. And at a gallop he struck into the most serious fighting of the day—where the mailed Serbian cavalry, caught motionless by the Tatars, struggled for life, and the groups of stalwart European infantry held every hillock. Here fell King Peter of Serbia and here the gallant Muhammad was so injured that he had to dismount. But Bayazid's right wing was crumpled up.

Bayazid was left with the mass of his infantry, without intrenchment of any kind, while the Tatar horsemen closed in upon the right and left. Then Timur took command of the Tatar center and advanced.

The splendid Othmanli infantry—the *corps d'élite*, the *janissaries*—had not struck a blow. They were predoomed, their situation hopeless, their emperor helpless before the maneuvering of the great chess player of Asia. Regiments in the rear fled while the way to safety was still open. Others, broken by successive charges, took their stand wherever they found any rising ground. Through them moved the armored elephants, liquid fire descending from the castles on the giant beasts. In a wrack of dust and din, on that suntortured plain, the weary Turks died. Even many who fled, fell dead from exhaustion.

Bayazid, with a thousand of his *janissaries*, drove the Tatar horsemen from a hill and fought there grimly throughout the afternoon, taking an ax himself and standing with his men. As one battalion of the Old Guard held its ground on the field of Waterloo when Napoleon's army had become a rout of fugitives, these household soldiers of the Sultan died weapon in hand.

Late in the afternoon Bayazid took to horse and with a few mounted followers tried to escape through the Tatars. He was pursued, his companions shot down and his own horse brought to earth with arrows. Then he was bound and escorted back to Timur's pavilion at the hour of sunset.

Legend has it that Timur was then playing chess with Shah Rukh. When he saw the bearded Turk, still majestic in calamity, he rose and went to the entrance. A smile lighted his dark face.

"It is ill," cried Bayazid, who lacked neither pride nor courage, "to mock one whom God hath afflicted."

"I smiled," Timur answered slowly, "that God should have given the mastery of the world to a lame man like me, and a blind man like thee." And he added gravely: "It is well known what would have been my fate and the fate of my men, if thou hadst prevailed over us."

To this Bayazid made no response. Timur ordered that his bonds should be taken off, and seated him at his side within the pavilion. It pleased the aged conqueror to have the great Sultan a prisoner under his hand, and he treated Bayazid courteously.[1] The captive asked that search be made for his sons, and Timur commanded that this should be done. One of them, Musa, was brought in a prisoner, and given a robe of honor and seated by his father. Another, who died in the battle, was never found. The rest had escaped.

Timur's divisions had been sent to pursue the remnants of the Turks in all directions as far as the sea. After Nur ad-Din captured Brusa, the reigning city of the Othmans, he sent back to his Amir the personal treasure of the Sultan, and Bayazid's women slaves who were both numerous and beautiful. The chronicle relates that the Tatars found them skilled in music and dancing. And the Tatar troopers returned to Timur's headquarters with all manner of spoil. The customary feast was held, adorned this time by European wines and women.

To this feast Bayazid was invited and came perforce. He was seated near Timur, and the old Tatar commanded that his imperial regalia—part of the loot of Brusa—be brought to him. Perforce the dour Turk put on the jeweled turban and took in his hand the gold mace that had been the symbol of his conquests.

---

[1] The well-known story that Bayazid was put into a cage and carried around like an animal is found in Marlowe's "Tamburlaine the Great." It rests upon no greater contemporary authority than Ibn Arabshah's verse, "The son of Osman fell into a hunter's snare and was confined like a bird in a cage." Herbert Adams Gibbons explains that it was probably a barred litter; but Bayazid fell sick soon after his capture and undoubtedly had to be carried in a litter. Timur sent physicians to treat him, and seems to have acted toward him with courtesy except in compelling him to be present at the festival after the victory.

Thus attired, he was offered his own wines and the drugs to which he had been accustomed. But he tasted nothing. Before his eyes his fairest women, stripped of their clothing, waited on the conquerors.

He saw among them his favorite, the Despina, sister of the dead Peter of Serbia—a Christian girl to whom he had been so devoted that he had not compelled her to turn Muhammadan.

He had to sit impassive and voiceless while through the clouds of incense smoke passed the white figures of the women he had held in his arms—that he had chosen as fancy impelled him from a dozen captive people. Among them were dark-haired Armenians, and golden Circassians, the heavier beauties of Russia and clear-eyed Greeks. These women had not, before now, been seen outside the harem, the sanctuary.

Upon Bayazid were the eyes of the lords of Asia, curious, mocking and intolerant. Bayazid had reason then to reflect upon the letters he had written a year ago to the lord of these Tatars. His fierce pride hid the rage that gripped him like a fever. But he could not eat.

Was Timur merely indifferent—curious perhaps to see Bayazid attired in the robes of state? Did he really think he was honoring his distinguished prisoner? Or was this feast a subtle mockery? No one knew, and the Sultan, it seems, was past caring. The Tatar war drums roared in his ears, and the wild pipes whined, while the minstrels of the steppes made a song of their victory.

Still Bayazid gripped his golden mace, his massive body shaken with agony. But when the Tatars ordered in his own *bayaderes,* his singing girls, and bade them sing the love songs of the Turks, Bayazid's will gave way. Rising, he made a gesture toward the entrance.

They let him go, then. Two Tatar officers sprang up and caught his arms, and led him through the feasters, his turbaned head sunk on his chest.

Later, Timur ordered the Despina to be sent in to Bayazid with the message that he was returning to the Sultan his favorite wife.

So passed the Thunder. His strength sapped by debauchery and the ordeal of battle, his pride broken, he died a few months later.

CHAPTER XXX

AT THE GATES OF EUROPE

So UTTERLY HAD THE TURKS BEEN CRUSHED that no second battle took place. Angora yielded—Brusa and Nicea were carried by the rush of the Tatar pursuit. Down to the sea on all sides of the peninsula of Asia Minor the fleeing Turks thronged, princes, pashas and officers at the head of the fugitives. Fishing boats and pleasure barges carried crowds of them to the islands. Even the galleys of the Greeks and Genoese aided the wrack of the Sultan's host to cross into Europe.

What induced the Christians to help their former oppressors to safety is not clear. Perhaps they were paid a price—perhaps it was the old policy of the Greeks, to ingratiate themselves with all powers. Their agents had pledged Timur aid with money and ships if he advanced against the Sultan, and their double dealing enraged the old Tatar, especially when they refused to ferry over his divisions after the Turks.

In a month there was not an armed Turk in Asia. On the other hand, there was not a Tatar in Europe. The horsemen from Samarkand rode down to the shore and looked across at the gold domes of Constantinople. They galloped over the long-buried ruins of Troy where Helen once held court. Later they discovered the citadel of the Knights of St. John at Smyrna. It was winter then, a season of heavy rains, but Timur, hearing that Smyrna had withstood Bayazid's siege for six years, went to look at it.

The Christian knights in the fortress—which was upon a height at the edge of the bay—refused to surrender and Timur invested the place, building wooden platforms out over the water, and covering his miners with a barrage of arrows and naphtha bombs. He also started building a mole to close the narrow entrance of the bay. Two weeks of this was enough for the Europeans and they fought their way down from the height to their galleys, before the way to the sea could be blocked. Some three thousand of them escaped to the ships, beating off with swords and oars the wretched townspeople who tried to follow them. The next day a relieving fleet appeared from Rhodes.

When the galleys of the knights came in close to the shore the Tatars now quartered in the citadel greeted them in ghastly fashion. The head of a slain crusader was placed in one of the catapults and shot into the nearest galley. The Christian fleet drew off and the Tatars abandoned Smyrna, leaving behind them as a monument two pyramids of heads.

In the evacuation of Asia Minor the two much-hunted princes, Kara Yussuf and Sultan Ahmed fled by different paths. The lord of Bagdad took refuge at the Mamluk court in Egypt, while the Turkoman khan chose the Arabian desert. The desert proved to be safer than the court. Egypt, open now to invasion by the Tatars, hastened to send its submission, and an offer of tribute and Timur's name was read in the public prayers. The unfortunate Ahmed was chained and thrown into prison.

The monarchs of Europe were in a mixed state of mind—vastly curious, and astonished, somewhat gratified and more than a little fearful. Such an upheaval at their threshold bewildered them. Where the Turks had been lords for a century, a Tatar conqueror had appeared, out of the depths of the east. Bayazid and his armies had vanished, quite.

Henry IV of England wrote to Timur congratulating him as one sportsman to another on his victory. Charles VI, *Dei gratia rex francorum*, remembered the message John of Sultaniah had brought from the Tatars, and summoned the bishop to an audience, entrusting to him letters and gifts for Timur.

The wandering Emperor, Manuel, hastened back rejoicing to his city of Constantinople, from which he sent his submission and an offer to pay tribute to Timur. The destitute heir of the Cæsars had found a patron greater than any European king. Across the Golden Horn, the Genoese flew Timur's standard from the towers of Pera.

But it remained for the Spaniards to establish actual contact with the lord of Tatary. A little while ago Henry III of Castile had sent two military observers to the east, to report upon the plans and powers of the Turks. These two knights Pelayo de Sotomayor and Fernando de Palazuelos wandered through Asia Minor and ended up in Timur's army in time to watch the battle of Angora. Timur gave them an audience, and made them gifts of two Christian women that he had sorted out of Bayazid's captives—the chronicle records them as Angelina, daughter of John, Count of Hungary (a celebrated beauty), and Maria, a Greek. With the Spaniards, Timur sent an envoy of his own.

To return the courtesy, Don Henry dispatched three ambassadors to escort this "Tartarian knight" back to his lord, Timur. The leader of the ambassadors was Henry's chamberlain, the good Ruy de Gonzalez de Clavijo.

With his companions and Timur's officer, Clavijo set forth in a carrack from the port of Saint Mary, in May

1403. But when he reached Constantinople he learned
that the Tatars were gone. In obedience to his orders
he departed after them. And his search led him on to
Samarkand.

Timur had made no effort to enter Europe. The
way over the straits was closed to him, but he was
capable of marching around the Black sea—in fact, he
had visited the Crimea not many years ago. An incen-
tive, however, was lacking. His men longed to return
to Samarkand. And Bayazid's cities had yielded great
wealth—among other things the silver gates of Brusa
adorned with the figures of the Saints, Peter and Paul,
and the Byzantine library that had fallen into the hands
of the Sultan. All this Timur took away with him.

For a while he busied himself with politics, arrang-
ing tribute payments, appointing new governors of the
Turkish provinces, receiving embassies. Meanwhile
Bayazid died, and Timur was pondering another conquest.

And at this time he suffered a loss as unexpected as
grievous. Officers came to tell him that Prince Muhammad who had never recovered from the injuries
received at Angora, was dying. Timur set out at once
to go to his grandson, and ordered the most skillful of
the Arab physicians to attend him. But when he
reached Muhammad's camp, he found the young prince
speechless, and the end at hand. It was then that
Timur ordered the great drum to sound the muster and
the regiments to be collected for the march back to
Samarkand.

In turn he had lost Jahangir, his first-born, and Omar
Shaikh. Miran Shah had proved himself an unworthy
son, and in Shah Rukh—now past the prime of life—
there was apparent a mildness and indifference to war.

Timur's favorite of these last years had been his courageous grandson, Prince Muhammad, the idol of the army.

The body of the youth who had died in the hour of victory was embalmed and carried back by the divisions that had followed him from Samarkand, their gay coloring changed to somber black. To the wailing grief of Khan Zadé, the mother of Muhammad, Timur listened unmoved; but when he noticed Muhammad's infant sons among those who had come out of Tabriz to receive the cortège, sorrow weighed upon him and he remained some days solitary in his pavilion.

It seemed to the Tatar conqueror, brooding as aged men do upon the past, that some power greater than his own will had taken from him in turn all those who could best serve him. The great amirs of his early conquests were in their tombs—Saif ad-Din the righteous, Jaku Barlas the faithful, and this son of his first-born. Even the devoted Ak Boga, who had risen to the government of Herat, and had contributed sons of his own to the army, was dead.

In their places he saw now Nur ad-Din and Shah Malik, brilliant leaders in war, but incapable of handling the reins of civil government. And always the imams of the Church thronged about him with their prayers and prophecies and condolences for the dead that he carried with him back to Samarkand. His sleep was troubled by strange dreams. Visions of long dead Khans who had led the hordes across the desert to Cathay.

Even when he ordered Bagdad and the ruined cities built up again, these fancies lingered in his brain. When he gave to Shah Rukh the government of Khorassan, and India to Muhammad's brother, he meditated upon the Gobi and the tales he had heard when he was a youth, hunting deer about the Green City.

And out of these dreams he had formed a plan. He would lead the army into the Gobi; he would break through the great wall that guarded Cathay, and overcome the last power in the world that could oppose him.

He said nothing of this to his officers. Perforce he had to hold the army in winter quarters at Tabriz, where he threw himself into the work of bringing order out of the wrack of the campaigns. With the coming of the first grass he was on the march east to Samarkand with the army and the great court.

In August he was back in his city, quartered in the garden called Heart's Delight. He rode past the new cathedral and reproached the architect because the inner gallery had not been made larger. He sat in judgment upon the ministers who had governed in his absence, hanging some and rewarding others. A fever of energy seemed to animate his aged body. He planned a new tomb for Prince Muhammad, with a dome of gold and white marble, and under the lash of his will a new garden palace rose—built of black and white stone and ebony and ivory, supported by silver pillars.

He was working against time. His sight had failed steadily in the last two years; his eyelids had fallen so that he looked as if he were asleep. He was sixty-nine years old, and he knew that his life was near its end.

"For two moons," he commanded, "there will be festival. Let no man say to another, 'Why have ye done this?'"

To Samarkand, to this festival of the conqueror came ambassadors from twenty kingdoms, among them dark faced envoys of the Mongols of the Gobi—who had been driven out of Cathay. With them Timur had long talks.

And he found time to greet Ruy de Clavijo, chamberlain of the king of Spain, who had followed him hither from Constantinople. This interview the good knight gives in his own words.

"On Monday the 8th of September the ambassadors [1] departed from the garden where they had been lodged, and went to the city of Samarkand. When they arrived they dismounted and entered a garden of a palace, where two knights came to them and said they were to give up the presents they had brought. So the ambassadors placed the presents in the arms of the men who were to carry them respectfully before the lord, and the ambassador from the Sultan did the same.

"The entrance to this garden was very high and broad, and beautifully adorned with glazed tiles, in blue and gold. At the gate were many porters with maces in their hands. The ambassadors came to six elephants, with wooden castles on their backs, and men in the castles.

"Then the ambassadors were grasped by the arm pits and led forward, and the envoy that Lord Timur had sent to the king of Castile was with them, and the Tatars who saw him laughed at him because he was dressed in the costume of Castile.

"The ambassadors were conducted to an aged knight who was seated in an ante-room, and they bowed reverentially before him. They were then brought before some small boys, grandsons of the lord. Here the letter that they carried from the king to Lord Timur was

---

[1] Clavijo speaks of himself and his companions as the ambassadors, and calls Timur the lord. The Sultan mentioned here is the Sultan of Egypt. This account is taken, slightly condensed, from the narrative translated by Clements Markham and published by the Hakluyt Society.

demanded, and they presented it to one of the boys who took it, and carried it within, to the lord who desired that the ambassadors be brought before him.

"Lord Timur was seated in a portal, in front of the entrance of a beautiful palace, and he was sitting on the ground. Before him there was a fountain where red apples floated, and which threw up the water very high. The lord was seated cross-legged on silken embroidered carpets among round pillows. He wore a robe of silk with a high white hat on his head—on the top of the hat a spinal ruby with pearls and precious stones round it.

"As soon as the ambassadors saw the lord, they made a reverential bow, placing the knee on the ground and crossing the arms on the breast; then they went forward and made another; and then a third, remaining with their knees on the ground.

"The lord ordered them to rise and come forward; and the knights who had held them until then let them go. The princes who stood by the lord, among them Nur ad-Din, then took the ambassadors by the arms and led them before the lord that he might see them better —for, being so old, his eyesight was bad.

"He did not give them his hand to kiss, for that is not the custom; but he asked after the king, saying, 'How is my son the king? Is he in good health?'

"Then he turned to the knights seated around him, among them a son of Toktamish the former emperor of Tatary, and several of the blood of the late emperor of Samarkand [2] and said, 'Behold, here are the ambassadors sent by my son the king of Spain who is the

---

[2] The Jat Khan, driven out by Timur. Clavijo gained a pretty accurate idea of events in Asia. He was the only western European to visit Samarkand before the nineteenth century, and by then great palaces that Timur had meant to endure for ages were ruined for the most part by weather and earthquakes.

greatest king of the Franks and lives at the end of the world.'

"So saying, he took the letter from the hand of his grandson and opened it, declaring that he would hear it presently. The ambassadors were taken to a chamber on the right of the place where the lord sat, and the princes who held them by the arms made them take their places below an ambassador whom the emperor of Cathay had sent to Lord Timur.

"When the lord saw the ambassadors seated below the envoy from Cathay, he ordered that they should be seated above him, and he below them, saying that they were from the king of Spain his son and friend, and the envoy of Cathay was from a thief and a bad man."

CHAPTER XXXI

THE WHITE WORLD

THE OLD CONQUEROR had built his Utopia—an encampment, a city and a garden in one. And in it he feasted magnificently. In these two months, when the dim sun of autumn sank closer to the blue ridges of the mountains Samarkand must have seemed a city visited by the genii.

It seemed so to the wondering Clavijo, who beheld courts covered with flowers and ripe fruit, and litters moving through the streets flaming with precious stones, within them singing girls, escorted by lute players and tigers and goats with golden horns that were not beasts but other fair girls thus attired by the skinners of Samarkand. He wandered through a castle higher than the mosque towers—built of crimson cloth by the weavers. He saw elephants fight, and Tatar princes arrive from India and the Gobi, bringing their gifts to Timur.

"No one," he said, "could describe it, without gazing and walking everywhere with slow steps."

And then, abruptly, the ambassadors were dismissed, the carnival ended.

Timur summoned before him the council of princes and amirs. "We have conquered," he told them, "all of Asia except Cathay. We have overthrown such mighty kings that our deeds will be remembered always. You have been my companions in many wars, and never has victory failed you. To overthrow the pagans of Cathay not much strength or power will be needed, and thither you shall march with me."

So he harangued them, his mind made up, his deep voice vibrant with purpose. This was to be his last campaign—to cross the home-land of his ancestors and the great wall of Cathay. And they, who had rested no more than three months, cried out to lift the standards.

Little more was needed—so great a multitude of warriors was gathered at Samarkand. Two hundred thousand moved off in different corps to cantonments along the road. It was the beginning of winter, and they would have to wait out the snows on the roof of the world; but Timur would not delay for the spring.

He sent Prince Khalil with the right wing of the army to the north, and went himself with the center that Muhammad had commanded. They moved out with great trains that were like a wooden city, because they had to take their supplies with them, and Timur had seen to it that they did not lack.

They crossed the river of Samarkand, and Timur turned in the saddle toward the city, but said nothing. He could no longer see the domes and the spires of the minarets.

It was then November, and bitter cold. When they passed through the open gorge that was known thereafter as the Gates of Tamerlane, snow began to fall. The winds from the northern steppes swept the plain, and, numbed by a blizzard, they went into camp.

When they moved out again, it was into a world white with snow. Streams were ice coated, the roads heavy with drifts. Some men and horses died, but Timur would not turn back.

Nor would he go into winter quarters where Khalil had quartered his men in huts to wait out the cold, at the Stone City. The aged conqueror explained that he would go on to Otrar, the citadel of the far northern

PERSIAN SWORDSMEN CASTING HEADS OF THEIR ENE-
MIES AT THE FEET OF THEIR PRINCE. TIMUR, IN
PUTTING AN END TO THE DYNASTY OF THE MUZAF-
FARS, BROUGHT TO A CLOSE A LONG PERIOD OF
ANARCHY, DURING WHICH ONE PERSIAN SHAH
BOASTED THAT HE HAD PUT TO DEATH MORE THAN
EIGHTY CAPTIVES WITH HIS OWN HAND.

"THE PAGEANTRY OF MONARCHY." THE COURT OF AU-
RANGZEB, DESCENDANT OF TIMUR, AND LAST OF THE
GREAT MOGHULS TO ENJOY THE FULL POWER OF
EMPEROR. THIS EUROPEAN ENGRAVING, INSPIRED
LARGELY BY TRAVELERS' TALES, REFLECTS CHRISTEN-
DOM'S IDEA OF ASIATIC POMP AS LATE AS 1699.

IN THE TOMB OF THE AMIR. TIMUR'S BODY
LIES UNDER THE DARK CENOTAPH. *From a
Painting by Verestchagin.*

frontier, and he ordered his grandson to catch up with the main body as soon as the roads were open.

They themselves had to lay felts on the snow at the beginning of a march and trample down the surface until the wagons and camels—a black line crawling through the white plain—could move forward. They found the ice three feet thick on the river Syr, and they crossed over on the ice.

Then the winter set in, with its merciless battering. Sleet, rain, wind and snow—the pale glare of a low sun upon ice. They did not plunge ahead as they had done years ago in going to meet the Golden Horde. A few miles a day they forged on, toward Otrar and the great north road to Cathay.

Slowly the standards moved into the mountain passes, through dark ravines that seemed to sink deeper below the summits, veiled in mist. Slowly as a laden animal, they felt their way through the passes and came out on the northern plain, and saw before them the walls of Otrar—shelter for the winter.

Here Timur could rest. He planned to go forward with the first warmth of spring.

And as he had ordered, the army took the road again in March 1405. The standards were lifted and the great drum roared, the regiments were drawn up on the plain for review. The lords of divisions assembled their musicians for the nightly salutation to the Amir, while the pipes shrilled and the drums echoed the thudding hoofs.

But it was a salutation to the dead.

Timur had died at Otrar. In obedience to his will, the host marched again toward the great north road. His white horse, saddled, was in its post under the imperial standard. But no one was in the saddle.

The chronicle has left us a glimpse of Timur's last scene. Outside the wooden walls of the castle, amirs and officers of all ranks stood in the snow. Within the halls sat the great empress Sarai Mulkh Khanum attended by her women. She had made the journey from Samarkand when tidings of Timur's illness reached the imperial city.

Outside the entrance of Timur's chamber stood bearded imams, leaders of the Church, reciting sonorously the verses of the Koran.

"By the sun in noonday brightness, by the moon when she followeth him in the night that enshroudeth him—"

So had they stood for weeks, the chorus of their prayer unceasing, and unavailing. The chief of the physicians, Moulana of Tabriz, had said: "There is no help. It is the day appointed."

Lying outstretched on his cushions, his lined face gray, in the white mass of his hair, Timur gave his final directions to the high amirs. "Keep your swords valiantly in hand. Keep agreement among ye, for in disorder there is ruin. Do not turn aside from the march to Cathay."

Charcoal braziers burned near his head, and his voice was no more than a whisper.

"Do not rend your garments and run to and fro like madmen because I have left you. That will breed disorder."

Summoning Nur ad-Din and Shah Malik to his side, he raised his voice. "I appoint Pir Muhammad, the son of Jahangir as my successor. He must reside at Samarkand and have in his hands absolute authority over the army and civil affairs. I command you to devote your lives to him, and support him. He must rule the distant provinces of the world as well as Samarkand, and unless you obey him utterly, there will be conflict."

One after the other the high amirs and lords took oath to carry out his will. They urged, however, that Timur send for his other grandsons to hear in person his commands.

He spoke then with a trace of the old impatience of hesitation and delay.

"This is the last audience. God will have it so."

After a while he said as if to himself, "I would like nothing, except to see Shah Rukh again. But that is—impossible."

It was, perhaps, the only time he had uttered that word. The iron spirit that had cleaved its way through life, accepted the end of life without protest.

Some of the amirs were weeping and the low wailing of the women could be heard. Into the chamber advanced the servants of the Church. *"God is one. There is no God except the One—"*

Afterword

WHAT CAME OF THE ATTEMPT

THE HAND THAT HAD WELDED AN EMPIRE out of fragments could do no more; the will that had built an imperial city could no longer urge on the Tatars.

The lords of Tatary had lost more than an emperor. Timur had raised them to incredible power; he had guided them, and had held in his hands all the reins of government. Under him they had become masters of nearly half the world. Most of them were sons of the men who had served him, and many were grandsons. For fifty years they had known no other will than Timur's.

Then, too, the army and the city had been populated with other races. Here were Mongols of the Golden Horde, Turks, and Persians—Afghans and Syrians. Not yet were they welded firmly into a new people.

So great was their respect for Timur and their grief at his death that the army and the city thought only of carrying out his commands. If his successor, Pir Muhammad, had not been absent in India—and it is a weary way from Otrar to India and back to Samarkand —if Shah Rukh, his ablest son, had not been intent on his own government of Khorassan, and if the great amirs had not tried, in blind obedience, to go on with the march to China, the empire might have been held together.

But no man was able to take up the reins Timur had let fall. The great amirs at Otrar did their best. They held a solemn council—decided not to announce Timur's death publicly, but to elect one of his younger grandsons to command of the army and trust that the Chinese would never believe that Timur was dead if the army appeared at the great wall. They seemed to be sure of their ability to conquer China.

The body of the dead conqueror was sent back with Ulugh Beg, the eldest son of Shah Rukh and a strong escort, to where the empresses waited to receive it. Couriers were dispatched to Pir Muhammad, with the utmost speed. Tidings of the event were, of necessity, sent to the governors of the distant provinces and the princes of the family.

But almost at once the march of the main body of the army was halted. Word reached it that the lords of the right wing had vowed fidelity to Khalil, Miran Shah's son, and planned to seat him on the throne of Samarkand. At the same time the commander of the left wing disbanded his troops and hastened back to Samarkand.

In this crisis the great amirs, Nur ad-Din and his fellows, held another council. They could not keep on toward China, leaving a division of authority behind them. They turned back, and caught up, by forced marches, with the funeral cortège at the Syr.

They found the gates of Samarkand barred against them—although they had with them the great empress Sarai Mulkh Khanum, and Timur's casket and the standard and the great drum. The governor of the city had pledged himself to Khalil—wrote to the amirs explaining that it was necessary to have some one on the throne until Pir Muhammad could arrive.

But it was the youthful Khalil, the lover of Shadi Mulkh, who arrived, with a strong following of nobles gained by the influence of Khan Zadé, who had planned this long ago. The people of the city knew not what to think. Timur had died beyond the frontier; they had not heard his last commands. Khalil was seated on the throne—acknowledged emperor.

Bitter was the letter the veteran Nur ad-Din sent to the new court:

"Our hearts are torn with grief, for the most powerful of emperors, the soul of the world, is dead; and already ignorant youths whom he raised from the lowest state to the highest honors have become traitors to him. Forgetting the obligations they owe him, they have disobeyed his orders and violated their oaths. How can we dissemble our grief at so terrible a misfortune? An emperor, who has made the kings of the earth to serve at his gate, and has indeed earned the name of conqueror, no sooner leaves us than his will is set aside. Slaves have become the enemies of their benefactor. Where is their faith? If rocks had hearts they would mourn. Why are not stones rained down from Heaven to punish these ungrateful wretches?

"As for us, God willing, we shall not forget our master's wishes; we shall carry out his will, and obey the young princes his grandchildren."

Again the amirs consulted together, and in the end they agreed upon one thing. They went to the pavilion where the standard stood, and ordered the great kettle-drum broken. They did not want Timur's drum that had roared out the tidings of victory to them so often to be sounded in honor of any other man.

Khalil's first act was to marry in public the courtesan Shadi Mulkh with whom he was infatuated.

A man too young to rule with authority, intoxicated with the wealth under his hands, and dominated by the beautiful Persian—he plunged from one feast into another, composed poems to his new empress, and gave away the treasures of Samarkand. For a while his splendor and thoughtless squandering earned him both favor and followers. But he dismissed the older officers for men of his choice, Persians, courtiers, what not. And Shadi Mulkh, who had been saved from death by the empress dowager, now thought only of humiliating Sarai Khanum. A mad carnival reigned in the gardens of Samarkand. Precious stones were scattered on the earth and left for any who wished to gather up again. Wine flowed in the fountains.

Khalil exulted and Shadi Mulkh had her revenge, and between them they brought on civil war.

In time Pir Muhammad came up from India and was defeated by Khalil's army. Changes followed swiftly. With the portion of the army that had remained faithful to them, the great amirs descended on Samarkand and overcame the new emperor, sending him into guarded captivity and exposing Shadi Mulkh to public shame.

With Timur, the empire had died. There was no longer any hope of holding it together.

Stirred out of his indifference by increasing calamity, the mighty Shah Rukh appeared at last from Khorassan, and captured the city. Thereafter Beyond the River remained in his hands, and he bestowed Samarkand, looted of much of its treasure, upon Ulugh Beg, his son. Between them they kept intact the core of the empire, from India to Mesopotamia.

They were men of peace, patrons of the arts—heirs of that other side of Timur's strange nature that built things up again after his fury had destroyed. They shunned war, yet they were wise enough to defend themselves, with the help of the veteran soldiers who gathered in their courts. Their cities were islands of refuge in the chaos of dismemberment.

Under Shah Rukh and Ulugh Beg began an era of splendor. New buildings rose on the *registan*, the painters and the poets of Persia flourished under their protection. Shah Rukh was the Augustus, and Ulugh Beg the Marcus Aurelius of the dynasty. Ulugh Beg— a rare astronomer, geographer and poet—built the great observatory at Samarkand, and plunged into a study of the sciences. They are known as the Timurids —probably, with the Ming dynasty of contemporary China, the most enlightened monarchs of their day.

Their genius fulfilled half of Timur's ambition, for Samarkand was now in reality the Rome of Asia. But it was isolated. The continental avenues of trade had been broken by the struggles that followed Timur's death; once more—from 1405 to the age of the sea penetration by Portugal, and then England—the mass of Asia was separated from Europe. No Marco Polo visited Samarkand. It was, more than Lhassa, a forbidden city. Not until the middle of the nineteenth century did a Russian army advance that far, and scientists rush in eagerly, to search among other things for the Byzantine library that Timur carried back from Brusa. They searched in vain.

Time and frost and a burning sun and earthquakes had reduced the *registan* and the Bibi Khanum quarter to ruins. The walls that Timur had meant to be indestructible were falling year by year. Even to-day no tourists and very few travelers reach the public square that Lord Curzon has called the noblest in the world. Yet time has given to the ruins the imperishable beauty of the past.

The literature of this Augustan age of the Tatars has, for the most part, not been translated, and so is not fully known. But the great grandsons of Shah Rukh and Ulugh Beg created new glory of their own. They went down, out of Samarkand into India and there founded the dynasty known to us as the great Moghuls.

Like the advent of Genghis Khan, the westward march of Timur changed the political scheme of things, and affected the destinies of Europe.

He opened again the transcontinental trade routes, which had been blocked for a hundred years; he made Tabriz, within reach of the Europeans, the center of the commerce of the near-east, instead of the remoter Bagdad; the upheaval after his death caused the great Asia trade to dwindle, and this was one of the reasons why Columbus and Vasco da Gama set out to open a new road over the sea to far Asia.

The Golden Horde was crushed, and the way opened for the Russians to make themselves a free people. The Muzaffars were exterminated in Persia, and two centuries later under Shah Abbas, Persia became itself a notable empire. The Othman Turks were broken and scattered, but so impotent was Europe to free itself from their adhesion that they regained their power and took Constantinople in 1453.

For the rest, the Mamluk Sultan promptly forgot his oath of allegiance. That strange pair, Kara Yussuf and Sultan Ahmed hastened back to Mesopotamia to quarrel anew.

In the north, the Mongol and Tatar elements of the army under Nur ad-Din and other amirs retired to the steppes and frontier citadels where their descendants to-day—the Kirghiz and Kalmuk Tatars, so called— graze their sheep and horses by the ruins of the towers that Timur built. His death caused the helmeted men, the warriors of Turan, to separate in this fashion from the turbaned men of the south, the cultured peoples of Iran.

As for the Church of Islam, it never recovered. With the passing of Timur the dream of a universal kalifate ended. The leaders of Islam had sought to build up their power upon the Tatar's conquests. But they discovered that Timur's wars had shattered the foundation of Islam. Timur had never shaped his plans to the pressure of the imams, and in the end it is clear that he cared little for them.

The new empire of Persia was schismatic—always at odds with the orthodox Othman Turks. Timur's descendants, the Moghuls of India, were, like himself, Muhammadans in name but tolerant of other religions. The kalif of Cairo was no more than a shadow of the Commander of the Faithful who feasted in Bagdad aforetime. Probably no human power can ever unite the Muhammadans of the various nations into one political unit.

No man since Timur has attempted to dominate the world. He accomplished all that Alexander was able to do—Alexander of Macedon who followed on the heels of Cyrus the Great, as the Tatar conqueror followed Genghis Khan. And he was the last of the great conquerors. It is not likely that any human being will win such power by the sword again.

Throughout Asia to-day, if you go there, you will be told that three men conquered the world—Iskander (Alexander) and Genghis Khan and Timur.

And if you go to Samarkand you will notice a great dome rising above a grove of trees near the citadel. The dome is still blue in spots, and the sun gleams upon its fragments of turquoise tiles. The masonry of the walls is pitted with bullets fired by Russian rifles, and all the arches but one are down in ruins.

In the vestibule you will find three aged mullahs sitting on a carpet and, if you wish, one of them will rise and light a candle and lead you to the inner chamber where the light coming through the carved alabaster embrasures is dim.

Within a lattice work of stone, there are two cenotaphs, one white and one greenish black. The white tombstone covers the body of Mir Sayyid, a servant of Islam, who was Timur's friend. The dark stone above it, the mullah will explain, is jade and it was sent to the tomb by a Mongolian princess. Under it Timur's body lies.

If you ask the mullah in the tattered robe and the white turban who Timur was, he will reflect, while the candle flickers in his thin fingers. And very probably he will say,

"*Tura,* I do not know. He lived before my birth, and before the birth of my father. It was a long time ago. But, verily, he was *The* Lord."

Part Four: Notes

I

THE WISE MEN AT THE BATTLE

TIMUR was almost constantly on the march and usually took part of his court with him to a campaign. Arabshah says that he was in the habit of having books read to him in the evenings, especially histories. Even in the hard campaign against the Golden Horde, one of his princesses accompanied him. During the invasion of India there was a good deal of uncertainty and moodiness in the army when they were about to face the power of Mahmoud of Delhi, and the elephants. Sherif ad-Din says:

"The soldiers were not greatly disturbed about the Indian army, but as they had never seen elephants before, they imagined that the arrow and the saber had no effect on these animals, and that in battle they would toss both horse and horseman into the air. When the posts were appointed, for the officers and lords, Timur asked the men of learning where they would prefer to remain during the battle.

"Several of these educated men, who had heard of the elephants, answered at once: 'If it please our Lord, we choose to be near the ladies.' "

Timur was aware of this dread in the army and made careful preparations to meet the elephants. A ditch was dug along the center of the line, and a rampart,

strengthened with shields, built behind it.   Stakes were
driven into the ground and great, three-pronged hooks
fastened to the heads of the stakes.   Buffaloes were
lined up under the stakes, bound together by the necks,
and brambles and hay bundled into their horns, in
readiness to be set on fire.   But these defenses were not
needed.

II

BOWS, IN THE EAST AND WEST

IT IS A QUITE GENERAL SUPPOSITION that the horse
archer of Asia used a light bow that proved ineffec-
tive against the heavy armor of Europeans. As a matter of fact the Turks, Tatars and Mongols made use
of both the short and long bow.

In the time of Timur and the earlier day of Genghis
Khan the horsemen usually carried both—the long bow
for destructive fire on foot, the shorter weapon for use
in a charge and in fighting from the saddle at close
quarters. The bow was their favorite arm and the
Mongols, for instance, never discarded it unless compelled to in a press of men and horses. The contemporary chronicles of Europe bear witness to the devastating fire of the Asiatics, stating that great numbers
of the Christian men and horses were slain before the
"battle" began.

The Tatars were equipped with arrows of varied
lengths and weights, and different kinds of heads—
some designed for piercing armor, and some for arrow
grenades and flaming naphtha. An idea of the length
and weight of the Tatar bow can be gained from the
illustration on page 40. The writer has seen among
the test bows used by candidates for the Peking guards
—Manchus of one to two centuries ago—bows of
twelve "strengths" or about 156 pounds pull. These
were over five feet in length and very heavy.

The longest shot on record seems to have been made
by a member of the Turkish embassy in England, in

1795. This was either 467 or 482 yards. A few years ago a modern archer nearly equaled it, but he used a Turkish bow in his attempt.

A decided superiority in fire—portable mangonels and catapults being carried on pack animals by both Mongols and Timur's army—an inflexible discipline, and lifelong familiarity with battle tactics combined with the genius of their leaders gave the Mongols and Tatars such advantage over the motley and ill-led armies of thirteenth and fourteenth century Europe that the record of their encounters is one of almost continuous disaster for Europe. The spirit of the Christian man-at-arms was excellent, but he was accustomed to go to battle as if to a general tournament— to march at ease to the scene of conflict, to make camp and prepare at leisure, and to abide by the issue of an hour's hand-to-hand fighting. Such things as artillery preparation, night attacks, and pursuit that destroyed all elements of an army filled him with superstitious dread. He died on the field or in futile flight usually without having had a chance to wield his sword or pike. His leaders were ignorant of strategy, and sometimes— as in the case of King Bela of Hungary in 1241, and Duke Witold of Lithuania in 1399—saw that the issue was lost and abandoned their men to save their lives.

From the ghastly defeat of the Russians in 1221 by the marshals of Genghis Khan, and the downfall of Louis of France before the Mamluks of Egypt, to the overthrow of the European chivalry by Bayazid at Nicopolis, the arms of Asia prevailed. There were exceptions—the minor successes of the Catalans, professional soldiers under experienced leaders, around Constantinople in 1309, and the defeat of the Arabs in Spain.

The most effective arm of the Europeans during

these centuries of disaster was the cross-bow, which the Mongols and Tatars treated with respect. Except in sieges and in the hands of the Venetians and Genoese it played only a small part in the struggle. The long bow was not used at the time of the early crusades, and reached its great effectiveness in the hands of the English in the Crécy-Agincourt period, from 1300 to 1450.

The writer has been asked how the English archer of this time compared with the Tatar mounted bowman. He can only point out that they never met in ranged battle, and we can only conjecture what the result of such a meeting would have been. The English long bow had a range as great as the Tatar—destructive from two to three hundred yards—and the English yeoman could shoot his arrows as swiftly. Timur's men were not equipped with the elaborate plate armor of the French chivalry, and one may add that they would certainly never have charged the front of the English as foolishly as the knights of France.

Outside of individual valor and their skill as bowmen, the English were no better qualified to meet the Tatars than the Teutonic knights or the Knights of St. John. Against fire preparation and attack upon the wings and rear, the Black Prince would have been as helpless as his European cousins.

III

THE FLAME THROWERS

THAT TIMUR'S ARMY made use of flame projectors of various kinds is clear. But the contemporary accounts give no description of the weapons themselves, and in translation only "fire pots" appear.

We know that the Chinese, centuries before Timur's day, made use of gunpowder in war. It is not generally understood that the Chinese were familiar with the detonating effect of gunpowder. There are several references to this. A Chinese annalist says of the siege of Kaifong in 1232 by the Mongols:

"As the Mongols had dug themselves pits under the earth where they were sheltered from missiles, we decided to bind with iron the machines called *chin-tien-lei* (a kind of fire projector) and lowered them into the places where the Mongol sappers were; they exploded and blew into pieces men and shields."

The Mongols made some use of these Chinese inventions and Genghis Khan in his invasion of the west in 1220 had with him a corps of Chinese artillerymen and machines called *ho pao*—fire projectors. Timur's Tatars were familiar with these. And also with the uses to which the Arabs and Persians put naphtha.

During the crusades the Arabs made use of various inventions—a fire mace, with a glass ball for a head, filled with naphtha. A fuse leading to this was lighted and the mace thrown at an enemy or broken over his armor, the flaming naphtha running down his body. Their trebuchets and mangonæ cast heavy shells of clay filled with naphtha or Greek fire. These were used in sieges.

A grim story is told of one siege, where the crusaders had built wooden towers over against the walls. The Arab machines cast against these towers a number of shells that broke and soaked everything with a liquid, but caused no damage. The Christians mocked the efforts of the besieged, who continued to soak down the wooden towers, until a flaming torch was tossed out, and men and towers went up in fire. The liquid was naphtha.[1]

[1] For fuller details, consult John Hewitt, *Ancient Armour*, and Captain Favé and M. Reinaud, *Le feu grégeois*.

IV

ANGORA

IN JUSTICE to the memory of a great soldier, it must be pointed out that European accounts of Timur's victory at Angora have been, in the past, very prejudiced. They were taken mainly from Othman Turkish and Greek accounts, seldom from sources and almost never from Tatar sources. The standard version is Von Hammer's, edited by Prof. Creasy, author of *The Fifteen Decisive Battles of the World*. In its essential point it is as follows:

"Timour's secret agents were sent to the Ottoman camp and urged, on the numerous soldiers of Tartar race who served there that they ought not to fight against Timour, who was the true chief of all Tartar warriors. . . . Bajazet [1] advanced with about 120,000 men against the far superior forces of Timour which were posted near Sivas. The Mongol emperor manœuvered so as to ensure that the battle should take place on ground advantageous for cavalry and on which he could avail himself most fully of his numerical superiority. By an able forced march through Kaisyraiah and Kirschehr he evaded Bajazet and reached the city and plain of Angora. As he had expected the Ottoman sultan hurried to the rescue of Angora. . . . Notwithstanding the immense preponderance of numbers which he possessed, the Mongol sovereign ob-

[1] Hammer wrote Bajazet for Bayazid. The Turkish lettering is much the same, but the word is Bai-zid. He speaks of Timur, as many do, as a Mongol ruler.

served all military precautions . . . Bajazet . . .
seemed to have lost all the generalship which he usually exhibited. . . . He camped first to the north of
Timour's position; and then, to show his contempt for
his enemy, he marched his whole army away to the
high grounds in the neighborhood, and employed them
in a grand hunting. Unfortunately the districts in
which Bajazet made this, his last chase, were destitute
of water. . . . Five thousand of the Ottoman soldiers
perished with thirst and fatigue. After this imperial
folly Bajazet marched back to his enemy, but he found
that the camp which he had left was now occupied by
the Tartars, and that the only stream of water to which
the Ottoman army could gain access, had been turned
and filled up by Timour's orders.

"Bajazet was thus obliged to seek a battle. The
Mongol army is said to have exceeded 800,000 men,
and it certainly was far more numerous than that led
by Bajazet, who could not have brought more than
100,000 men into the field; and not only in numbers
but in equipment, in zeal, and in the skill with which
they were directed, the superiority was on the side of
the Mongols."

Von Hammer and Creasy add that some of the Ottoman princes of Asia followed the Tatars over to
Timur's side, and that only the Serbians and *janissaries* made effective resistance to the fierce and frequent charges of the Mongol cavalry.

Lane-Poole, in his *Turkey*, follows the above version
closely, adding this observation:

"On the one side were men thirsty and exhausted,
inferior in numbers, and discontented with their leader:
on the other, a vast host, strongly posted, splendidly

generalled, neglecting no precaution of war, and possessing every advantage of numbers, discipline and physical condition . . . The valour of the Janissaries and the Serbs could avail little against Timur's numbers, and the end was utter route."

As to the battle itself, Lane-Poole quotes quaint old Knolles who wrote in 1603.

This spectacle of the Turkish army disbanded to go hunting in barren country, under the eyes of the Tatars drawn up for battle, owes its origin to the Turkish historians of a later day, whose object was to explain the overthrow of their sultan. It is supported by no contemporary evidence, and common sense alone would indicate that if Bayazid had been insane enough to attempt it, Timur would never have stood by as a spectator to await his return. That men like Von Hammer, Creasy and Lane-Poole accept the story is amazing.

As to Bayazid's desertion by his Tatar allies, there is no record on the Tatar side that Timur intrigued with the offending chieftains. There is an account of several tribes of Black Tatars who drifted into Asia Minor and were enrolled in the Turkish army. These presumably were in Bayazid's host and went over to the Tatars during the battle. Their numbers were small, and Timur seems not to have held communication with them until after the conflict, when he forced them to go back with him to Samarkand.

As to Timur's host of 800,000, it never existed. An army of that size could not have lived off the country in Asia Minor, much less maneuvered as Timur's did— and the Othman accounts are clear that Bayazid saw nothing of the Tatar troops until they had gone past him. Furthermore there is no evidence that Timur ever assembled more than 200,000 men at any one place. The Tatar records only mention numbers occasionally—72,000 men in the later campaign in Persia, 90,000 that went into India, 200,000 mustered for the last campaign into China.

Timur only advanced into Asia Minor after four years of almost constant war; he left some forces at Samarkand—after Prince Muhammad joined him—and was forced to guard his communications over a vast territory. Another army was at Tabriz, and several divisions in Syria. The list of the various amirs and commanders at the battle of Angora would indicate a strength of from 80,000 to 160,000.

Apparently Bayazid's army was the more numerous. It is doubtful if Timur would have accepted a defensive position in the beginning unless this had been the case. Knolles says that the Turks advanced in a half-moon formation, which—if true—would indicate that their wings overlapped the Tatar line.

Herbert Adams Gibbons says, "Bayezid would have weathered the Tartar storm, had he been the same man he was at Nicopolis. In facing a Tartar invasion, the advantage was all on Bayezid's side. He failed because his mental and physical faculties, which rivalled, if they did not surpass, those of any man of his age, had become impaired by a life of debauchery."

Had Bayazid been the victor at Angora, and had Constantinople fallen to him as it must, thereafter, he would have appeared in the pages of history as the dominant figure of the fifteenth century—a Napoleon of the early ages. It is clear that he was completely outgeneraled by the Tatar, then nearly seventy years of age, and in the heart of the Turkish empire, more than two thousand miles from Samarkand. In the

Tatar accounts, Angora appears as a minor battle of only passing importance, and Bayazid as a general inferior to Toktamish.

Clavijo, an impartial witness, tells the story in his own way: [2]

"When the Turk knew that Lord Timour was in his territory he marched with his army to a strong castle called Angora. As soon as Lord Timour heard of this sagacious movement of the Turk, he left the road by which he was marching, and led his army over a high mountain. When the Turk, therefore, found that Timour had left the road, he thought that he had fled, and marched after him as fast as he could.

"Lord Timour, after marching through the mountains for eight days, returned to the plain and came to the castle of Angora, where the Turk had left all his baggage, and he pillaged it. When the Turk heard this, he came back as fast as he could and when he arrived, his men were tired.

"Lord Timour had made this movement to throw his enemy into disorder; and they fought and the Turk was taken prisoner."

[2] He heard of it from the two Spanish envoys who were present. For additional details, consult *The History of the Ottoman Turks* by Professor Creasy; *Turkey*, by Stanley Lane-Poole; *The Foundation of the Ottoman Empire*, by Herbert Adams Gibbons—also Clavijo, Sherif ad-Din and Arabshah.

DUKE WITOLD AND THE TATARS

LESS THAN THREE YEARS after the chivalry of western Europe had gone down before Bayazid at Nicopolis, the host of eastern Europe encountered the Tatars in a curious way. This was in 1399.

Mad Witold,[1] Duke of Lithuania, had allied himself with the king of Poland, and had launched forth into southern Russia, capturing Kiev and Smolensk. This brought him into contact with the Tatars, after Timur's last battle with Toktamish. To Witold and his Christian host Toktamish fled for refuge. Meanwhile Timur had withdrawn from Russia.

Two Tatar chieftains who had helped him against Toktamish and had resided some years at his court now took possession of the Volga and the steppes. They were Idiku of the Nogai clan and his protégé, Timur Kutluk Khan. It occurred to them to send to Witold's court a request that Toktamish be surrendered to them. And Witold, who was a cousin of the Polish king and father-in-law of the Grand Prince of Moscow, became fired with the idea of leading a crusade against the Tatar Khan.

Judging from the Polish annals, Witold thought that he was going against the great Timur of Samarkand. At all events, mustering his Lithuanian nobles, and Polish allies, and a contingent of five hundred Teutonic Knights of the Cross, he set out.

"Why dost thou march against me?" Timur Kutluk

[1] "Vitut (Witold) was no doubt the most powerful monarch in Europe" —Sir Henry Howorth.

sent a message of remonstrance. "Never have I invaded your land."

"God hath appointed me master of the world," Witold responded. "This choice is open to thee: be my son and vassal, or my slave." He also demanded, it seems, that Timur Kutluk should stamp the Lithuanian arms upon the Tatar coins.

The Tatar Khan demurred, although he sent gifts to the Christian duke when the two hosts were in sight of each other in the plains. He delayed until his older ally, Idiku, arrived with the Nogais. And Idiku would have nothing of the Christian's terms. He asked for a conference with Witold and the two leaders met at a small river.

"Prince," said Idiku, who was not without a sense of humor, "our Khan has rightly recognized thee as his father, since thou art the elder. But as thou art younger than I, recognize me and put my picture on the coins of Lithuania."

Witold returned to his quarters in a rage, and would not heed the warning of the palatine of Cracow that he must be cautious. The vainglorious Lithuanian knights taunted the lord of Cracow: "If thou fearest death, do not stand in our way, who seek glory."

The Lithuanians and Witold prevailed and the host advanced on the Tatars. The Christians were furnished with some cannon or hand-guns, and expected to break up the Tatar array with these new weapons. But the clumsy firearms had no effect on the rapidly shifting Tatar horsemen who fought in open order. And the close-packed mass of Witold's men was thrown into confusion when Timur Kutluk attacked them in the rear. The confusion became a route and Witold fled headlong with the survivors of the Lithuanian nobles who had boasted before the battle, leaving two-thirds of his host dead upon the field—among the slain the brave palatine of Cracow, and the princes of Smolensk and Galicia. The pursuit was terrible, and lasted as far as the Dnieper. Kiev paid tribute to the Tatars, and the Tatars did not turn back until they had ravaged Witold's country as far as Poland.

Ignored by the general historians, this battle caused changes in the progress of Europe. The defeat of the Poles and Lithuanians eliminated the greatest foe of the Russians, who feared them more than the Tatars. And Witold recoiled upon Prussia and the Teutonic Knights, breaking—with the king of Poland—their power forever.

THE TWO MASTERS OF WAR

OF TIMUR, Sir Percy Sykes says this: "No Asiatic conqueror in historical times has performed such feats of arms as these, and consequently none is entitled to the fame of Tamerlane. His achievements seemed almost to border on the superhuman."

Timur, in common with Genghis Khan, had that strange genius for war that made them appear supermen. Much as we admire the campaigns of a Cæsar, the exploits of a Hannibal, or the inspired strategy of a Napoleon, upon reflection it is becoming clear that these two conquerors from Asia are, with Alexander, the masters of war upon the stage of the world. Their feats of arms may have been duplicated by others in miniature, but never upon the earth as a whole.

Genghis Khan remains to-day a good deal of a mystery, and there is much in Timur that we cannot understand. Did Genghis Khan have a profound plan for the conquest of the world, or was he an inspired barbarian? We only know that he was wise, with a wisdom that proved terrible to the world we live in. And we can measure Timur's mighty achievement and ponder it, and still search in vain for the secret of his success.

Alexander we understand; he was the son of Philip of Macedon, heir to a mighty army, and in his conquest he swept without check over the area opened by the Persian empire that preceded him and which he overthrew. But between us and these two warriors of Asia there is the veil of distance and the strangeness of another world.

Some things we can say with assurance. Like Alexander they had immense endurance and a driving energy that would check at nothing. There the similarity ceases. Genghis Khan was patient, Timur impetuous; the great Mongol directed his campaigns from his headquarters, after his early years, but the lord of Samarkand could usually be found upon the scene of action. The nomad of the Gobi shared his responsibility among ministers and generals; the Tatar leader accepted all responsibilities himself.

Was this policy? Or was Genghis Khan better served? It would seem so. His Chinese ministers, and those four sons of war, Subotai, Chepé Noyon, Bayan and Muhuli, were more than able to carry on a campaign themselves. After his death they—the survivors of them—enlarged the empire. Saif ad-Din, Jaku Barlas, Shaikh Ali Bahatur, and the rest never accomplished such results for Timur.

The Mongols of the thirteenth century had a natural aptitude for leadership in war, and a bee-like coherence that made coöperation perfect between them; the Tatar soldiers of the fifteenth century, like Hannibal's, were only partially welded together. Without Timur's presence they lost half their efficiency. The Mongols could maneuver in widely separated army corps; in the face of a powerful enemy, Timur always moved with a single army.

Genghis Khan had rare skill in the organization and the movement of men; he planned a campaign to its remotest details and discussed it for weeks with his marshals before setting out; a master strategist, he avoided battle when unnecessary, and moved directly to the annihilation of the center of resistance, and the death of the opposing leader. Terror and secrecy surrounded his movements and behind him he left a hideous toll of dead.

The paralysis of fear inspired by the approach of the Mongols is almost beyond our conception. It is said that in one captured town a single Mongol warrior gathered together some twenty captives preparatory to putting them to death. Then he found that he had forgotten to bring his sword with him, and he ordered the twenty to wait there until he could find it and bring it back. They did so—all but one. He was the man who told about it.

Timur's Tatars were different. The case of Ak Boga charging two score Persians by himself is not a solitary incident. His men believed themselves invincible; his almost transcendental ability seemed to them to be fate itself.

Timur was as careful in preparation as Genghis Khan, but he was not so consummate a strategist as the Mongol. Genghis Khan avoided difficulties, where Timur met them and overcame them. The Mongol would never have galloped ahead of his army into Bagdad with only a few hundred men, or have climbed alone to the wall of Karshi.

In China, Genghis Khan first laid waste entire provinces, to maneuver through the chaos thus created. Timur would allow an enemy to concentrate and then advance to give battle, and he was always victorious in later life. Like Napoleon, he marched prepared for all contingencies, and relied on his own ability to do the right thing at the right time to break the power of an enemy. No problem seemed to disconcert him.

We do not know how Genghis Khan developed such strategic insight, or how he perfected such a military organization in his desert. And Timur's secret of victory still remains a riddle.

VII

THE SUDDEN APPEARANCE of Timur at the threshold of Europe and his equally abrupt vanishing with all his pomp and power kindled the imagination of the European poets. Tamerlane, or Tamberlain, became a legend—a fantasy shaped out of the garbled stories of the Greeks and the Turks.

We find some early references to Tamerlane, the enemy of Bajazet, as the sixteenth-century Germans called the Othmanli Sultan. In contemporary history he emerges as the grand Cham of Tartary, descended from—an echo of Herodotus—the Scythian shepherds. All of which is not so ridiculous as some later histories. But for a long time Timur, in the minds of the European writers, was associated only with the Turks, and vaguely with the conquest of "Natolia," and victories over the "Soldans of Egypt, Jerusalem and Babylon."

Christopher Marlowe, in the early Elizabethan age, knew no more about him than this. He saw in Tamerlane an irresistible power, and all the grandeur of the unknown east. And he put this imagery into resounding rhetoric—the first play to be written in English verse. His "Tamburlaine the Great" is built up out of imagination, its foundation no more than the annals of the ancient Græco-Persian world.[1]

[1] We may search the play in vain for any authentic detail, or even a real personage—barring Timur and Bayazid—in the cast of characters. There is only one name with a true oriental ring to it, "Usumcasane." Bergeron's *Traicte des Sarasins*, 1635, mentions an Usumcassan who served Timur, apparently a Turkoman of the White Sheep. Marlowe

Tamburlaine appears upon the scene in the now-famous coach and kings:

> Holla, ye pamper'd jades of Asia!
> What, can ye draw but twenty miles a-day
> And have so proud a chariot at your heels,
> And such a coachman as great Tamburlaine,
> But from Asphaltis, where I conquer'd you,
> To Byron here, where thus I honour you?

This play, written in 1586, is immortal, but only by reason of the fire and energy of the English poet. Tamburlaine resembles Timur only in his unbreakable will power and love of magnificence—and that is because Marlowe himself loved both power and magnificence. It is evident that he had not seen the Spanish publication of Clavijo's journal, which appeared in 1582 with some slight additional accounts of Timur.

But from that time Timur is a more frequent figure, much distorted, in the European histories. Leunclavius mentions him in 1588, and Perondinus in 1600. Jean de Bek published the mythical account of an unknown Alhazen (Al Hussayn?) in 1595. Good Richard Knolles incorporates him within the voluminous annals of the Turks, published in 1603. Many of these early accounts are collected in *Purchas, his Pilgrimes*, 1625. Magnon, in 1647, wrote his quaint *Le Grand Tamerlan et Bajazet*. In 1634 appeared Pierre Bergeron's collection of *Voyages en Tartarie* with a good deal of rather accurate information about the Tatars and Muhammadan peoples. This was the beginning of real knowledge, increased shortly by the translation

does mention the kings of Amasia and Soria, probably Syria. Amasia and Syria were real provinces but lacked rulers. An Uzun Hassan was chief of the White Sheep Turkomans and married a Greek princess, but he lived two generations after Timur.

of Ahmed Arabshah's history by Vattier, published at
Paris in 1658.

We find a reflection of this legendary Tamerlane in
Milton's Satan—the great trumpets summoning the
armed host to battle, the upraised standards, the mar-
shaled battalions of the powers of darkness at the gates
of paradise, and all the contemporary imagery of oriental splendor. For a long time Tamerlane figured in
European literature as the typical oriental despot, to
be joined later on by the concept of the great Moghul,
and—during the Voltaire era in France by the image
of the Chinese Emperor. He took the niche once occupied by the "Grand Kaan of Tatary" who owed his
prestige to Marco Polo. All this had very little to
do with real history and real men.

Not until Petis de la Croix translated Sherif ad-Din's
long chronicle, "The Book of the Victories of Lord
Timur the Splendid," early in the eighteenth century,
was more accurate knowledge available.

Poe's poem, which deals in reality with human love,
reveals no more of Tamerlane than

> The pageantry of monarchy
> And the deep trumpet-thunder's roar
> . . . telling
> Of human battle . . .

VIII

MONGOL

THE WORD MONGOL is applied to so many things by non-Asiatic writers that it is necessary to look back at the beginning of things to understand what it means.

In the beginning it was *mong-ku, or mung-ku*—which meant either the brave people, or the silver people. They were descended from the Tungusi, one of the aboriginal tribes of elder Siberia; and from the ancient Turks. Except that they conquered China, they had no relation to the Chinese of their day.

They were nomads, tall and hardy, illiterate, living upon their herds and hunting and following the grass—desert dwellers, in the plateaus of the Gobi and the tundras of the north. They were the Scythians of Herodotus, cousins of the Huns and Alans who migrated westward, to the sorrow of Europe. They were horsemen then and the remnants of them are horsemen to-day.

The Chinese called them, long ago, the *Hiung-nu,* and various kinds of devils, and built the great wall to keep them out. Just as Alexander a little earlier—so legend has it—built the *portæ Caspiæ* to keep these nomads out of his empire. They were the riders of high Asia, the breeding ground of conquerors. These horse-riding, flesh-eating, milk-drinking nomads were called Scythians by Herodotus, Huns by the later Romans, and *Hiung-nu* by the Chinese. All these words were used to describe a race.

Hiung-nu meant the mass of the nomads—we cannot very well say confederacy, because they were almost always at war. Now, at the time of Genghis Khan, 1162 A.D., this mass was composed of a score of nations. Such as—from east to west—the ancestors of Manchus, the Tatars, Mongols, Karaits, Jalairs and Uigurs. Genghis Khan, the chieftain of the Mongols, overcame the others and created out of them the heart of the Mongol empire.

Genghis Khan was the founder of the empire; his Mongols were his immediate followers; the massed nomads were his first conquered peoples. With them he overcame and entered China. With them and the Chinese he overcame the Turks of Central Asia, and *then* a large part of the rest of the world.

So the word Mongol to-day means one of two things—a resident of the great Mongol empire of the twelfth and thirteenth centuries, or a descendant of the original Mongol people. In this last sense the word is used in this book.[1]

[1] For a fuller discussion, consult *A Thousand Years of the Tartars*, by E. H. Parker; *The Ancient History of China*, by Friedrich Hirth; the *Histoire généalogique des Tartars* of Abulghazi Bahadur Khan; the *Cambridge Medieval History*, Vol. IV.

IX

TATAR

THE WORD TATAR has been even more mixed up
with other things than the word Mongol. In the
beginning it was the name of a small nomad people
living east of the Mongols proper, and very much like
them. Whether the word originated in the name of
an early chieftain Tatur, or in the Chinese term *T'a T'a*
we do not know.[1]

But the Tatars were the clan or nation nearest the
Chinese and so it happened that the Chinese spoke of
the rest of the nomads also as Tatars, or rather as
Ta-ta-erh. The name stuck; the mass of the Chinese
use it to-day. It stuck so fast that Europeans have used
it persistently for all of the nomads, in spite of the
fact that the first Europeans to visit the nomad empire,
in the thirteenth century, were warned by the Mongols
not to use the word Tatar in speaking of them, since
the Tatars were one of the peoples they had conquered.
The Norman of twelfth-century Britain did not relish
being called a Saxon.

Being conquered by the Mongols, the Tatars to all
general purposes vanished, after 1200 A.D. They
were merged into the mass of the armed men of the
empire.

[1] There is a tendency among scholars to-day to restore the word to its
old form Tartar. The argument is that the Mongol word *tar* means something, and repeated for emphasis, is *tar-tar*. And that the Chinese who
cannot assimilate an "r" write it and speak it as *T'a-t'a-erh*. Early European travelers all wrote it as Tartar. On the other hand, the Arab and
Persian historians did not, and modern Tatars do not usually pronounce
it so. The root *tar* means wanderer or riser-up. It may be related to the
root *tir* or *tur* which appears in Turan, and Tur-ki, but this is doubtful.

Now in the mind of the Asiatic a thing is more important than its name. To European historians Genghis Khan was the emperor of the Mongols—to his own subjects he was Kha Khan of the world, the Great King. It was not good form to mention him by name. His empire was what he possessed—the name did not matter. The Mongols and Tatars proper did not write at that time; they had foreign secretaries and the written language was different from the spoken. In their communications to Europe, these secretaries have written down the names and titles of the Great Khans as (1) a blank, (2) the representative of Heaven upon earth, (3) the ruler of the world, or the emperor of all men. The word Mongol was almost never used. Marco Polo came back with the word Tartar, and Tartary.

Apart from this, and by circumstances unknown to us, the Russians who had the first and most lasting contact with the nomad conquerors, of their own accord adopted the word Tatar, and stuck to it. Howorth suggests that Tatars may have formed the advance guard of the first Mongol controlled army to invade Russia. From contact with Russia, the Europeans adopted the word, and also knew China as *Khitai*—Cathay. Cathay was dropped after a while, but the nomad peoples who moved out into the world under the Mongols are still called Tatars, and it is too late to change.

The Barlas clan, Timur's ancestors, had nothing whatever to do with the original Tatars who hunted around Buyar Lake, and elsewhere. The Barlas men were more what we call ancient Turk than anything else.

But we have no better name for them than Tatar. Sherif ad-Din uses the word, as do Mir-Kwand and

Kwand-Amir. So does Abul Ghazi. Other Persian and Arab writers of a later day name them Tatars and Turks. Among modern scholars, Sir Henry Howorth accepts Tatar as the best alternative; Edward G. Browne does likewise. For reasons of their own, Léon Cahun and Arminius Vambery are emphatic that only Turk is correct.

In this book Tatar is used, not in a racial or historical sense, but as a better word than the others, to describe Timur's people. After all, it is the thing that matters, not the word. The Jats and the Golden Horde are described as Mongols because they were still ruled by the direct descendants of the Mongol Khans.[2]

[2] For additional details, consult Howorth, Vol. II; *The Turks of Central Asia,* by M. A. Czaplicka; *The Mohammadan Dynasties* by Stanley Lane-Poole; *La Lutte des Civilisations et des Langues dans l'Asie centrale,* by P. Kuznietzoff; and the discussion of the words Turk and Tatar by S. W. Koelle in J. R. A. S., New Series, Vol. XIV.

X

TURK

THE WORD TURK has been the football of linguists, ethnologists and historians, and archeologists— and the Pan-Turkish politicians for many weary years. One can no longer see the football for the dust.

The legends of a she wolf and a "Turk, son of Japhet" and a vanished empire enjoying a high culture, especially in working metals and horse trading in Central Asia long ago, are interesting but not entirely convincing—although there is said to be a movement on foot to replace the crescent of Constantinople with a golden wolf's head. It seems that before the fifth century of our era nothing was known of the Turks.

Thereafter, a clan, breaking away from the mass of the *Hiung-nu* settled under the Golden mountains between China and the Gobi. Its families were called Assena, but sometimes *Turk*—which meant helmet— because they resided near a dome-shaped hill, or because they wore helmets. The Chinese, it is said, called them *Tou-kie*, because the Chinese could not pronounce the "r." But *Tou-kie* apparently used to mean insolent dogs, and still means foreign dogs as many of us can testify. It does not seem quite clear whether the Chinese heard the word spoken by the Assena nomads, or whether they were calling the nomads names.

At any rate, drawing largely from the Chinese annals, European scholars have given to most of the other great clans kindred to the Assena (Turks) the racial designation of Turks. In the eastern part of the mass, the Uigurs and Jalairs are so christened, and in the

286

west our friends who later formed the nucleus of the Golden Horde—Karluks, Kankali, Kara Kalpak, Kipchak—Snow Dwellers, High Carts, Black Hats, and Desert Men.

They have been so christened because they spoke the same—or nearly the same—language. And this language is now called Turkish. But it is not the Turkish of Constantinople. In the beginning some of its dialects were very similar to Mongol.

So the European men of letters have taken the name—what they have accepted as the name—of one small tribe to designate a number of great clans. One is reminded of that early Lithuanian prince who turned Christian and summoned his people to be baptized, by groups. One group he christened Peter, another Paul.

At all events, there were the Turks, off in the back door of China, meat eaters, silk wearers, milk drinkers, their valiant men of war called *bagaturs*, their princesses *khatuns*, their chieftains *kha khans*. They had horn bows, and whistling arrows, coats of mail, and a *vugh-tugh*, which is a wolf's head standard—a golden wolf's head, emblem of the *lin kha khan*, the wolf chieftain. Only a king could have such a standard, and only he the right of beating kettledrums five times a day. We recognize the ancestors of Timur.

This was about the seventh century, when the Mongols were still wearers of skins, both fish and animal, and filthy eaters. They were still dwellers in the Sibir—the north, our Siberia. What happened next was complicated. These great clans who had little in common except a similarity in the language that we call Turkish (which, by the way, seemed to be written down only in some form of dog-Sanscrit and Syriac, at that time) moved away for various reasons mostly having to do with war.

And they moved west and they scattered, widely. Upon the vast expanse of Central Asia empires merged together and parted, under a kind of theoretical Chinese overlordship, and the harrying of the newly-great Arabs. The so-called Turks, of course, were pagans. The Uigurs and Karluks and Black Cathayans all had their day, and then came the Mongols of Genghis Khan and scattered them some more, and then gathered most of them in the Mongol Horde.

All these clans had kept their own names, although the names tended to vary as they merged and parted company. Some, like the Kirghiz and the Karait survive to-day. The Barlas clan was in all the fighting, and it ended up in Beyond the River. There is a legend that one of its chiefs was the *karachar* or commander-in-chief of one of the mighty Mongol princes.

At this time—after the death of Genghis Khan and before the birth of Timur—these clans christened Turks by the men of letters and called Tatars by their neighbors of that day, were nominally Mongols *pro tem.* But like the clans of Scotland they stuck to their family names. They learned to write in different letterings, and a lot of them were converted, to some degree, into Muhammadans. Others, Buddhists. They emerged into the pages of history in various countries, and nearly always caused trouble. Timur rounded up most of them.

It does seem as if there never was a Turkish empire or even a nation of Turks. The Othmanlis—pronounced also Osmanlis, and often written Ottomans—were wandering Turkomans, who were not descended from the reigning clans. They conquered and intermarried with part of Europe and most of the near east; their language was largely compounded of Arabic and Persian. They were never Turks.

Good William of Tyre, the chronicler of the crusades, came very close to the heart of the riddle when he said that the word Turk meant a lord, and Turkoman meant a vagabond.

The situation of the Othmanlis was rather absurd. They were called Turks by the Europeans, and so in time they were forced to accept the name, to some extent. The Turkey of our histories was not Turkey to its present occupants. It was, until this decade, *Osmanli vilayeti*, the country of the Othmans.[1]

[1] For additional discussion, consult Léon Cahun, E. H. Parker, Abul Ghazi Bahadur Khan. Also, Arminius Vambéry, *Das Turkenvolk*; E. Chavannes, *Les Tou-kiue occidentaux*; Herbert Adams Gibbons, *The Foundation of the Ottoman Empire*.

XI

THE OLD MAN OF THE MOUNTAIN

WHEN HE WAS PASSING THROUGH PERSIA, Messer Marco Polo heard the various stories related about the followers of Hassan ibn Saba who were known as Assassins. There is more truth than fancy in his account, and it is worth looking at.[1]

"The Old Man was called in their language Aloadin. He had caused a certain valley between two mountains to be enclosed, and had turned it into a garden, the largest and most beautiful that ever was seen, filled with every variety of fruit. In it were erected pavilions and palaces the most elegant that can be imagined, all covered with gilding and exquisite painting.

"And there were runnels too, flowing freely with wine and milk and honey and water; and numbers of ladies and of the most beautiful damsels in the world, who could play on all manner of instruments and sing most sweetly, and danced in a manner that was charming to behold. For the Old Man desired to make his people believe that this was actually Paradise.

"So he had fashioned it after the description Mahommet gave of his Paradise, to wit, that it should be a beautiful garden running with conduits of wine and milk and honey and water, and full of lovely women

[1] The Old Man of the Mountain is literally the meaning of Shaikh al Jabal—the lords of mountain strongholds who gained their power by threat of the assassin's dagger. In the account of an unknown Jesuit who knew the east, they are described as '*Execrandos et fugiendos nomine Assassinos . . . salutem et vitam hominis paruipendunt.*" Marco Polo's story is quoted from the Yule-Cordier edition of the immortal Venetian.

for the delectation of its inmates. And sure enough the Saracens of those parts believed that it *was* Paradise.

"Now, no man was allowed to enter the Garden save those whom he intended to be his Ashishin. There was a Fortress at the entrance to the Garden, strong enough to resist all the world, and there was no other way to get in. He kept at his court a number of the youths of the country, from 12 to 20 years of age, such as had a taste for soldiering, and to these he used to tell tales about Paradise, just as Mahommet had been wont to do, and they believed in him just as the Saracens believe in Mahommet. Then he would introduce them into his garden, some four or six, or ten at a time, having first made them drink a certain potion which cast them into a deep sleep, and then causing them to be lifted and carried in. So when they awoke they found themselves in the Garden.

"When therefore they awoke and found themselves in a place so charming, they deemed that it was Paradise in very truth. And the ladies and damsels dallied with them to their heart's content, so that they had what young men would have; and with their own good will, they never would have quitted the place.

"Now this Prince whom we call the Old One kept his court in grand and noble style, and made those simple hill folks about him believe firmly that he was a great prophet. And when he wanted one of his Ashishin [2] to send on any mission, he would cause that potion whereof I spoke to be given to one of the youths in the garden and then had him carried into his palace.

"So when the young man awoke, he found himself in the Castle and no longer in that Paradise; whereat

---

[2] Hashish eaters. Apparently this is the origin of the word Assassin, which was brought back by the crusaders, as appears in the acount of the Jesuit, written about 1320.

he was not over well pleased. He was then conducted to the Old Man's presence, and bowed before him with great veneration as believing himself to be in the presence of a true Prophet. The Prince would then ask whence he came, and he would reply that he came from Paradise! and that it was exactly such as Mahommet had described it in the Law. This of course gave the others who stood by and who had not been admitted, the greatest desire to enter therein.

"So when the Old Man would have any Prince slain, he would say to such a youth: 'Go thou and slay So and So; and when thou returnest my Angels shall bear thee into Paradise. And shouldst thou die, natheless even so will I send my Angels to carry thee back into Paradise.' So he caused them to believe; and thus there was no order of his that they would not affront any peril to execute, for the great desire they had to get back into that Paradise of his. And in this manner the Old One got his people to murder any one whom he desired to get rid of. Thus, too, the great dread that he inspired all Princes withal, made them become his tributaries in order that he might abide at peace and amity with them." [3]

[3] The list of Asiatic dignitaries killed by the Assassins is long indeed. It included a Kalif of Egypt, and princes of Aleppo, Damascus and Mosul —also Raymond, Count of Tripoli, and Conrad of Montserrat. The last being attributed for a long time to the hand of King Richard. The Assassins made the mistake of killing a Mongol prince and most of their strongholds were demolished by the Mongols. Timur completed the work. For further particulars consult the Yule-Cordier Marco Polo, the travels of Odoric, the chronicle of Joinville. Also Quatremère's translation of Rashid ad-Din's history of the Mongols of Persia.

XII

THE GREAT AND NOBLE CITY OF TABRIZ

IT NEEDS, perhaps, an effort of imagination to realize the true size of such a metropolis of Asia. To-day Tabriz is no more than a ruinous and drowsy town, tucked between Armenia and the Caspian—its name more obscure than that of its neighbor Mosul which is mentioned in dispatches by virtue of a controversy over oil rights.

In Timur's day Tabriz—sometimes written Tauriz by the early Europeans—was an *entrepôt* of the world's trade, where the great Khorassan road joined the southern route to Bagdad, Persia and the gulf. Looking at it through the eyes of men who visited it in that age, we find the following:

Marco Polo says, about the year 1270, "Tauris is a great and noble city . . . having such a good position that trade is brought here from Bagdad, India and the hot regions. In it there are Armenians, Nestorians, Jacobites, Georgians, Persians, and finally natives of the city themselves who are worshippers of Muhammad."

Turning to the Venetian archives, we find that in 1341 the Genoese had a factory there, with a council of twenty-four merchants—the word factory here meaning rather a warehouse station than a manufacturing plant.

Rashid ad-Din, a celebrated Persian historian living about 1300, says: "At Tabriz there were gathered under the eyes of the Emperor of Islam (Ghazan, the Il-Khan) philosophers, astronomers, scholars, historians—of all religions, of all sects. And people of Cathay, of India and Kashmir, of Tibet, of the Uigur and other Turkish nations, Arabs and Franks (Europeans)."

From Ibn Sayyid and Mustawfi we learn that with its suburbs it was 25,000 paces around the outer wall, that its public buildings—mosques, academies and hospitals—were faced with glazed tile and often made of marble and limestone. It had 200,000 houses besides the inns and *sarais* for travelers, which means a population of about a million and a quarter. We hear that 40,000 may have died in a single earthquake.

Ibn Batuta mentions that even the sellers of musk and ambergris had separate markets, and that when he walked through the bazaar of the jewelers his eyes were dazzled by the precious stones that richly dressed slaves offered to the Tatar ladies.

Of the priest-voyagers, the good Jourdain de Sévérac says, in 1320, "*Thauris quod est civitas permaxima . . . ibi habemus ecclesiam satis pulchram et bene mille personas conversas ad fidem nostram.*"

And Fra Oderic, writing at almost the same time: "This city, I tell you, is the finest in the world, for trade. Every article is found here in abundance. It is so marvellous that you would scarcely believe everything unless you saw it. . . . The Christians of this place say that the revenue it pays to its emperor is greater than the revenue all of France pays to its king."

As late as the seventeenth century the explorer Chardin estimated its population—which had steadily decreased—at 552,000.

It was larger than Samarkand, which measured, without the suburbs, some 10,000 paces around the walls. Clavijo says there were about 150,000 people in the Ark of Samarkand, by which he means the *arak* or citadel alone.

XIII

CLAVIJO AT TABRIZ

CLAVIJO, the chamberlain of the King of Castile, passed through Tabriz, and gave a full description of it. This is one of the few clear accounts of a city under Timur's rule—the Tatar conqueror first entered Tabriz fifteen years before Clavijo's visit.

And Clavijo's description is important, not only in revealing how one of the great cities of Asia impressed a European, but in showing that Timur was capable of preserving and improving a captured metropolis. European histories have mentioned in particular the burning of more than one building whose stones remain intact to-day without evidence of fire. Terrible as was the navoc wrought in his invasions, it will be recalled that he retained unharmed the cities that submitted without resistance. In nearly every case he ordered the public buildings spared—the mosques, academies, water systems and schools and tombs. And in the majority of cases, he ordered the ruined places to be rebuilt. So we often find Asiatic travelers giving descriptions of cities populous and apparently little the worse for war, after his death, while these same places are presented to us in European histories as no more than charred ruins.

There is a reason for this misunderstanding. European narrators were most familiar with the provinces most remote from Samarkand—southern Russia, western Asia Minor, the coast of Syria, the extreme south of Persia, and India. Timur had little interest in repairing damages here. Instead he carried off whatever was most valuable to Samarkand. It was part of his policy to leave the frontiers a waste and build up within the empire. And this was the foundation of the splendor of the Shah Rukh's empire, in Persia and Samarkand, and what is now Afghanistan. It resulted in the golden age of Persian architecture, over the two thousand miles from Ghazni to Tabriz—which is about the length of Europe proper. And this may be termed the area of Timur's building. Except for Tabriz it was an area almost unknown to the Europeans for centuries.[1]

Clavijo says:

"From the hills on the right a great river descends to the city, and is divided into many channels which flow through the streets. The streets are well ordered, with very large buildings with many doors within which are shops guarded by officers. Here they sell many things—cloth, silk, cotton and other stuffs—and this city has a great trade.

"In one place there are men who sell certain scents and coloring for women, and hither come the women to paint and anoint themselves. These women go about covered with a white sheet, a horse-hair net hanging over their eyes.

"The grand edifices are ornamented very skilfully

[1] In this volume no attempt has been made, consciously, to ignore the cruel side of Timur's character, or the destruction he wrought. He has been presented to us so often in the past as an architect only of pyramids of skulls, and as a barbarian destroyer, that an effort must be made to realize what the man actually was. One noted historian of to-day characterizes him briefly as "more terrible than Genghis Khan"—at the same time that orientalists are making known to us the high culture prevailing among the Timurids.

To take an opposite case, Harun ar-Rashid, thanks to the "Arabian Nights," has impressed us as a most benevolent monarch; but the annals of Asia reveal him as not less cruel and destructive than Timur, upon a smaller scale. Muir says, "The witchery of oriental romance has cast an adventitious glow about the name of Harun al Rashid."

with mosaics and blue and gold work made in Greece. They say that these great works were made by very rich men, who were jealous of each other, and each strove to erect the most wonderful work and in this way they spent their wealth. Among these buildings is a great house, which was surrounded by a wall, very beautiful and rich, in which there are a multitude of chambers and apartments; and they say this house was built by Sultan Owais with the treasure that was paid him by the Sultan of Babylon.

"The city of Tabriz is very rich by reason of the great quantity of merchandise that passes through it every day. They say in former days it was more populous; but even now there are more than two hundred thousand inhabited houses. There are also many market places in which they sell very clean and well-dressed meat, cooked in a variety of ways, and plenty of fruit.

"In the streets and squares of this city there are many fountains, and in summer they fill them with pieces of ice, and put brass and copper jugs near them, so that the people can come and drink. The magistrate of Tabriz, called the *Darogah*² received the ambassadors very honorably.

"Here are many rich and beautiful mosques, and the finest baths that, I believe, can be seen in the whole world. When the ambassadors wished to depart, horses were provided for themselves and their retinue. From this place the ruler of the country had horses in readiness, that those who are coming to him might travel night and day, in relays, and thus the post is arranged all along the road as far as the city of Samarkand."

² The civil governor.

XIV

THE AMIR'S PAVILION

CLAVIJO gives an excellent description of one of Timur's tent palaces—he calls it a great and lofty pavilion:

"It was a hundred paces broad, and had four corners and the ceiling was round, like a vault. It was pitched upon twelve poles, each as large around as a man's chest, and each painted gold and blue and other colors. When they pitched the tent, they used wheels like those of a cart, which were turned by men and they have ropes fixed in various directions to assist them.

"From the vault of the ceiling of the pavilion silken cloths descended, making an arch from side to side. Outside this square pavilion there were porticoes, and from it at least five hundred red cords were stretched. Inside there was a crimson carpet embroidered with gold threads. In the four corners were the figures of four eagles with their wings closed. The outside of the pavilion was covered with silk stripes, black, white and yellow.

"At each corner was a high pole with a copper ball and the figure of a crescent, and on the top of the pavilion there was a tower of silken cloths, with turrets and an entrance door.

"This pavilion was so large and high that from a distance it looked like a castle, and it was a very wonderful thing to see and possessed more beauty than it is possible to describe."

THE GREAT DOME

BEFORE TIMUR'S LIFETIME the domes of Persian
architecture were of the pointed variety and did
not swell outward from the base. Timur's earlier buildings showed no change from this plan. But both the
Bibi Khanum and his own tomb, the Gur Amir, have
the majestic swelling dome that appeared later in the
buildings of the Moghul era in India and much later
in Russia, where it was exaggerated to a great degree.

K. A. C. Cresswell, in *The History and Evolution of
the Dome in Persia*, maintains that no such domes could
have been seen by Timur in his invasion of India, because the tombs of northern India did not have this
feature of design. The only one in existence was on
the great Umayyad mosque in Damascus, and it was
built of wood—and burned in the fire that destroyed
the city. It was immense and majestic, towering over
the plain, and for at least a month Timur camped where
he could see it.

"Timur cannot fail to have been impressed, keenly
appreciating architecture as he did, with this great building, in his day one of the wonders of medieval Islam.
He was much more likely to have some of its most
striking features reproduced for him at Samarkand
than he was to copy a tope in India. There is ample
evidence that Timur greatly appreciated architecture.
He was impressed by the Juma Musjid at Old Delhi,
and took a model of it home. He admired the Kutb

Minar and carried off workmen to construct a similar one in Samarkand, which intention, however, was never carried out."

Mr. Cresswell explains that the measurements of the Bibi Khanum dome and the one destroyed at Damascus are similar—that the Bibi Khanum tomb was the first building completed after Timur's return from Damascus—it had been in construction for two or three years. And that there can be little doubt that Timur copied it from the only example known, at Damascus.

Ibn Batuta says of it, "From whatever direction you approach the city you see this dome, above everything, as if suspended in the air." [1]

This bulbed dome, preserved by Timur's fancy, and rebuilt by the enormous resources at his disposal, was carried out in the splendid buildings of his children. It was transported to India by the Moghuls, his descendants, appearing there for the first time in the mausoleum of Humayun, and eventually in that masterpiece, the Taj Mahal.

[1] Journal of the Royal Asiatic Society, 1914.

XVI

THE PYRAMIDS OF SKULLS

IN EUROPEAN HISTORY the towers of the heads of enemies slain by the Tatar conqueror have been always associated with the name of Timur. They were terrible, and grimly picturesque, and so they appear in the pages of most histories. But Timur cannot be judged by the milder civilization of to-day.

Turning back to his own time, we find that the Maliks of Herat and other princes erected such monuments of victory. They differed from Timur's only in being smaller.

The same is true of the massacres. It must be remembered that the Tatar conqueror lived where mercy was usually looked upon as a sign of weakness. We find the European princes of his day little more inclined to mercy—the Black Prince made a shambles of Limoges, and Charles of Burgundy killed like a wolf among sheep at Dinant. At Agincourt the English killed French prisoners in order to be rid of them for the final phase of the battle; at Nicopolis, the English, German and French crusaders massacred the Serbian and Turkish prisoners before the battle. The massacres ordered by Timur differed only in being on a vaster scale.

Colonel Sykes explains that the massacres ordered by Timur were due to imperative military necessity. While this is doubtful, it is clear that the Lord of Samarkand was more tolerant than most of the rulers of his day. A story is told that in every siege his tent was hung with white banners the first day, to indicate to the people within the city that they might surrender and be spared; with red the second day, to show that if they surrendered now their leaders must die; with black thereafter, to warn them to look for nothing but burial. This story has no good authority to support it, but is typical of the man.

In the case of Herat, it was treated leniently in the first siege, and with terrible rigor in the second. Bagdad got off with a ransom the first time, and was destroyed the second. We read that Urganj was made into a mass of ruins, but farther on we learn that it was built up again.

If Timur had been possessed by the ferocity of a Genghis Khan, no second siege would have been needed. But he was pitiless in subduing revolt.

His own followers did not find him cruel; his enemies found him remorseless. The historians of Asia comment on the splendor of his achievements rather than upon his cruelty—with the exception of Arabshah, who hated him. Timur squandered the lives of others, but he was reckless of his own.

XVII

FEW MEN IN HISTORY have been so hated and so loved as the Lord of Samarkand. The two chroniclers who lived at his court present him as a demon, and as a matchless hero.

Ibn Arabshah calls him a merciless slayer, a master trickster, and a very devil of malignity.

Sherif ad-Din says: "Courage raised him to be the supreme Emperor of Tartary, and subjected all Asia to him, from the frontiers of China to those of Greece . . . he governed the state himself, without availing himself of a minister; he succeeded in all his enterprises. To every one he was generous and courteous, except to those who did not obey him—he punished them with the utmost rigor. He loved justice, and no one who played the tyrant in his dominion went unpunished; he esteemed learning and learned men. He labored constantly to aid the fine arts. He was utterly courageous in planning, and carrying out a plan. To those who served him, he was kind."

Of modern commentators, Sir Percy Sykes and Léon Cahun hold to Sherif ad-Din's view, as does Arminius Vambéry. Edward G. Browne quotes this opinion from Sir John Malcolm:

"Such a leader as Timour must have been idolized by his soldiers . . . he was careless of the opinion of other classes in the community. The object of this monarch was fame as a conqueror; and a noble city was laid in ashes, or the inhabitants of a province massacred on a cold calculation that a dreadful impression would be made which would facilitate the purposes of his ambition. . . . Timour, though one of the greatest of warriors, was one of the worst of monarchs. He was able, brave and generous; but ambitious, cruel and oppressive. He considered the happiness of every human being as a feather in the scale . . . against his personal glory. The vast fabric of his power had no foundation, it was upheld by his individual fame and the moment that he died, his empire dissolved. Some fragments of it were seized by his children; but it was in India alone that they retained dominion for any length of time. In that country we yet perceive a faint and expiring trace of the former splendor of the Moghul dynasty; we view in him the gradual decline of human greatness, and wonder at the state to which a few centuries have reduced the lineal descendants of the great Timour." [1]

[1] Malcolm wrote while a puppet emperor was still on the throne of India. He, like Browne, was chiefly interested in Persia, and naturally judged Timur only in the light of a conqueror. In the present volume an attempt has been made to show the mighty Timur from the viewpoint of his own people, not through the eyes of captives who hated him, or through the historians of Europe, Persia and India.

XVIII

TIMUR AND THE CHURCH

IT IS SELF-EVIDENT that the Tatar conqueror was not a devout Muhammadan, but a man who followed his own ideas. We cannot be sure of his true feeling about religion. But it has been said so often that he was a Muhammadan animated by zeal for the glorification of Islam, that it is necessary to consider the evidence. And his own deeds are the clearest evidence we can have.

He never accepted an Islamic sur-name, which was customary with devout believers, as, for example, with Harun ar-Rashid—Aaron the Blessed—such a name as Nur ad-Din, Light of the Faith. Nor did he so name his sons. Jahangir is the World Gripper, and Shah Rukh, the Soul of a King. Only in his grandsons, whom he did *not* name, appear the Islamic titles—Pir Muhammad, etc.

He never shaved his head, wore a turban, or clad himself in the dress ordained by the Church. He and his Tatars were called half-Muhammadans by their neighbors, and often heretics and pagans. The true leaders of Islam were the Kalif in Egypt and the orthodox Sultan of the Othmanlis. These emphatically looked upon Timur as a pagan, a barbarian (which he was not) and an enemy to be dreaded. The Tatars were newly converted, and they were soldiers before they were churchmen.

Timur tried to establish friendly relations with the Christian princes of Europe. This the Turks refused to do, at that time. And in his communications he did not style himself a monarch of Islam, which is almost invariably the case with Muhammadan rulers. He paid no attention to the various holy cities, Meshed, Mecca, and Jerusalem, although he did make a habit of visiting shrines on his line of march, whether from policy or inclination.

The fact that he complied with the routine of the church and spared the buildings of the church from demolition, and built mosques of his own fancy means very little. As in the Europe of that day, the routine of daily life conformed to the rules of the church. Most of the public buildings were mosques, tombs, academies, and it would have been sacrilege to destroy them; most of Timur's soldiers were devout Muhammadans and he shaped his conduct to their opinion.

In two instances he massacred the Christian element when he spared the Muhammadan of a garrison that had held out against him and this would have been significant, but for the fact that these particular Christians had been the cause of heavy loss among the Tatars and he made an example of them. On the other hand, at least three times—near Moscow, and Constantinople, and southern India, he could have earned for himself the title of Ghazi—Conqueror for Faith—by turning aside long enough to make war on a Christian or Hindu people. He did not do so. The Christian Georgians were in his path, and he trampled on them. Smyrna was a stronghold of Asia Minor and he advanced upon it to reduce it accordingly.

Evidence is clear that there were colonies of Jews, Nestorian Christians, Malakites, and so forth in Samarkand and Tabriz, and their churches also. At least once he made use of a Christian bishop as envoy. But the most decisive point is brought out by his Muhammadan panegyrists, who did everything possible to make him out a devout believer. Some of them maintain that he was a Sunnite (orthodox) and some that he was an Alyite (schismatic). He himself wrote only, "I, Timur, servant of God."

Bibliography

I

THE SOURCES

IN THE LATER PART OF HIS REIGN Timur ordered his men of letters to keep a daily record of events, and anecdotes.[1] The greater part of them were written, apparently, in Uigur and in Persian.

To a writer of Bagdad named Nizam-i-Shams, who joined his court at the end of 1400, Timur entrusted these records, with the order that Nizam-i-Shams should write from this material a history of his reign in a simple style, without ostentation. Nizam's work was finished a year before the death of the conqueror and presented to Timur entitled *Zafar Nama*—Book of Victory. It was in Persian, and only one copy is known to-day, still untranslated, in the British Museum.

A distinguished Persian, Ali of Yazd, sur-named Sherif ad-Din, who had traveled about with the Tatar

[1] Browne 183, Bouvat 20, Blochet 88. Sherif ad-Din states that Timur always kept secretaries with him to note down events, and that officers and lords who had been present at any happening were expected to give an account of it, and all these were collected. And Timur—"eut la patience de les arranger lui même, apres quoi il les fit verifier en sa presence de la maniere suivante. Un lecteur lisoit un de ces memoires; et lorsqu'il en étoit sur quelque fait important, ou quelque action remarquable, il s'arretoit, les temoins oculaires faisoient leur rapport, et verifioient les circonstances du fait, les rapportant telles qu'ils les avoient vues; alors l'Empereur examinoit lui-même la verité du fait, et ayant bien confronté ce que les temoins rapportoient avec le contenu des memoires, il dictoit aux secretaires la maniere dont ils devoient l'inserer dans le corps de l'ouvrage, et se le faisoit relire ensuite, pour voir s'il étoit tel qu'on ne pût y rien trouver, ajouter, ni à diminuer." *Histoire de Timur-Bcc*, preface of the author.

conqueror and had been present at several of his later battles, wrote a second history. It was also in Persian, and it was also called the *Zafar Nama*. Sherif ad-Din practically rewrote Nizam's history, with all its detail, apparently, and added to it his own observations, bringing in the events following Timur's death. Sherif ad-Din lived at Shah Rukh's court, wrote under his patronage; his history is marred by fulsome praise of every act of Timur, and by a style that is hideously ornate. It gives, however, a wealth of detail of Timur's reign. It was completed in 1425, and was translated into French by Pétis de la Croix, *L'Histoire du Timur-bec connu sous le nom du gran Tamerlan*, Paris, 1722—and from the French into English—*The History of Timur-Bec, Known by the Name of Tamerlain the Great, Emperor of the Moguls and Tatars*, London, 1723.

Before this, appeared the *Asahot Tavarikh* or "Exact Chronicle" of a certain Muhammad ibn Fazallah Musavi, in 1412-1414. Then the *Zubditot Tavarikh* or "Excellent Chronicle" of Hafiz Abru, who accompanied Timur on his last campaigns, and wrote, in 1423-1424, by order of one of Timur's grandsons. This is a very large compilation, written in a clear style; but it has not yet been edited or translated.

Then came the work of Ahmed ibn Arabshah, a former secretary of Sultan Ahmed, who was carried off to Samarkand. His *Adjab al-Makdur fi Nawab Timur*, is bitterly hostile to the Tatar, and at times is pure satire. The style is concise and clear, and the work is valuable for its details of the last campaigns, its appraisal of Timur's character, and especially its description of Samarkand after the death of the conqueror. It is available in a Latin translation, *Ahmedis Arabsiadæ Vitæ*, by Samuel Manger, Leovardiæ, 1767-1772, and in a rather indifferent French version, *Histoire du Gran*

Tamerlan avec la suite de son histoire, by Pierre Vattier, Paris, 1658.

Upon these four works subsequent histories by Asiatic scholars were based in large part. Among these the best-known are the *Ruzata-Safa* of Mir Khwand, who died in 1498, and the *Habiba Siyar* of his grandson Khwand Amir, 1525. The last gives much fresh and valuable information about Timur, especially the dealings with Egypt and Syria. It is summarized in *La Bibliothéque orientale* of D'Herbelot, 1780.

In Timur's case one of the greatest puzzles of oriental research has arisen. That is, the "Memoirs" and "Institutes" that were believed to be his own. Early in the seventeenth century a certain Abu Talib al-Hussayni came forward in India with a long work in Persian, which he claimed to be Timur's memoirs and notes written by his own hand. The text proved to be clear and apparently without question authentic. And its authenticity has been debated for about a hundred and fifty years.

Briefly the arguments in favor of it are: that its substance proves its authenticity; that its discoverer would have no motive in writing himself such a long work and attributing it to Timur; that it is, or was, accepted by Asiatic scholars. That it is written in a terse and beautifully clear style, unlike anything ever set down by a Persian, or by any other Asiatic writer of history.

The arguments against it are: that contemporaneous writers—Nizam, Sherif ad-Din and the rest—make no mention of it; that—granting it could have remained hidden for two centuries after Timur's death—its discoverer never produced the original from which the Persian translation was made.

This *Mulfuzat* and *Tuzukat-i-Timuri* were brought

to Europe in a manuscript copy. In 1783 text and translation were published—*Institutes Political and Military written originally in the Mogul Language by the Great Timour, improperly called Tamerlane*—by Major Davy and Joseph White. In 1787 Professor Langlès published a French translation.

The *Mulfuzat Timury, or Autobiographical Memoirs of the Moghul Emperor Timur, written in the Jagtay Turky Language, turned into Persian by Abu Talib Hussyny* was published by Major Charles Stewart, London, 1830.

Until the last of the nineteenth century their authenticity was generally accepted. Arminius Vambéry and Léon Cahun do not question them. Scholars of the last decade do not accept the Memoirs; Rieu rejects them, and Browne and Bouvat question them.

No new evidence for or against has turned up, but it seems improbable that Timur wrote such a work with his own hand, and extremely improbable that if he did so Sherif ad-Din and the others would not have known about it, and said something about it. Two of the three arguments in support of Abu Talib's document are answered by the fact that he wrote in the reign of Shah Jahan, a descendant of Timur, who valued such a work —and in the matter of style, the Memoirs probably imitated the splendid Memoirs of Babar, the first of the Moghuls and Shah Jahan's ancestor.

The third argument, that the Memoirs prove their own worth, is not yet satisfactorily answered. The answer may lie in the original material gathered by Timur's secretaries and turned over in part to Nizam. And this is probably lost beyond recovery.[2]

---

[2] The present writer has compared the *Mulfuzat* with Babar's Memoirs in the Erskine-Leyden translation, and has found the style almost identical in some incidents. Some things, however, in the *Mulfuzat* are puzzling if we are to accept them as the concoction of a panegyrist who lived two

centuries later : (1) certain incidents are repeated elsewhere by the author, who did not seem to realize he was saying over the same thing—this would seem to indicate that he was translating or working from material not of his own making : (2) it is stated frankly that Timur was not a *tura,* or descendant of the reigning Mongols—a fact that Sherif ad-Din glosses over—and it is difficult to understand why a panegyrist would put this in a history to be presented to one of Timur's descendants.

In this volume, the data of the *Mulfuzat* has not been accepted as coming from Timur. Some of the incidents have been set down as apparently authentic.

II

EUROPEAN SOURCES AND TRAVELERS

BERGERON, PIERRE. *Relation des voyages en Tartarie Plus un traicté des Tartares, de leur origine, mœurs, religion, conquestes, Empire, Chams, Hordes. Avec vn abrégé de l'histoire des Sarasins.* Paris, 1634.

(Remarkably good for its day—unfortunately, excessively rare. The present writer values highly the copy in his collection, which includes more than half the titles given in this bibliography.)

CLAVIJO, RUY GONZALEZ DE. Narrative of the Embassy of Ruy Gonzalez de Clavijo to the Court of Timour, at Samarkand, A.D. 1403-6. Translated by Clements R. Markham. Hakluyt Society, 1859.

(The invaluable story of the Spanish chamberlain who journeyed to Timur's court at the end of his reign.)

CONTARINI. Travels to Tana and Persia, by Josafa Barbaro and Ambrogio Contarini—Hakluyt Society, 1873.

DE SACY, SILVESTRE. *Mémoire sur une correspondance inédite de Tamerlan avec Charles VI—Mémoires de l'Académie des Inscriptions et Belles-Lettres, Tome Sixième.* Paris, 1822.

(An analysis of the letters that passed between Timur and the French king. De Sacy believes Timur's letter was written before the battle of Angora.)

FROISSART. *Chroniques.* Paris, 1835.

(A detailed account of the crusade against the Turks.)

314

HAITHON, JOHN. *Les Fleurs des histoires de la terre d'orient compillées par frère Hayton . . . cousin du Roy Darménie.* Translated by Nicholas Salcon. Paris, 1475.

(A valuable summary of the affairs in the east at that time.)

Historia Tartarorum. In MSS., Leyden.

PERONDINO, PIETRO. *Magni Tamerlanis Scytharum imperatoris vita.* Florence, 1553.

PODESTA, BAPTISTA. *De gestis Tamerlanis.*

(This, like the above, is an early European viewpoint, with extracts from the Turkish sources. Of little value.)

RIEU, C. P. H. Catalogue of Persian Mss. in British Museum. London, 1879-83.

(The Persian sources and the "Memoirs" discussed.)

SCHILTBERGER, JOHANNES. *Gefangenschaft in der Turckey.* Frankfort, 1557. Published by Hakluyt Society, 1879—The Bondage and Travels of Johann Schiltberger.

(The crudely told story of a young German who was taken prisoner at the battle of Nicopolis, and served Timur's son, and the Tatar Khan Idiku.)

SEADEDDIN. *Tajul-Tavarikh.* Translated by Kollar, *Seaddini annales Turcici usque ad Murad.* Vienna, 1755.

SÉVÉRAC, JOURDAIN CATALANI. *Mirabilia Descripta sequitur de Magno Tartaro.* Translated by Cordier, *Les Merveilles de L'Asie.* Paris, 1925.

TURNER, T. HUDSON. Unpublished Notices of the Times of Edward I and of his Relations with the Moghul Sovereigns of Persia. Arch. Journ. VIII. London, 1851.

III

SECONDARY ASIATIC SOURCES

ABULGHAZI BAHADUR KHAN. *Historia Mongolorum et Tatarorum nunc primum tatarice edita.* Kazan, 1825.

(A chronicle of the Tatar Khans of the Caspian region, written two centuries after the death of Timur by an Uzbek Khan.)

BABAR. Memoirs, translated by Leyden and Erskine. London, 1826.

(These autobiographical memoirs of the first of the so-called great Moghuls, Timur's descendant, refer occasionally to Timur's works but are important in showing Samarkand and the golden age of literature that came after the great conqueror.)

HAIDAR, MIRZA. *Tarikh-i-Rashidi.* Edited by N. Elias, translated by E. Dennison Ross. London, 1895.

(A history of his own people, written by a Mongol Khan of the Chagatai or Jat branch. A beautiful translation.)

IBN BATUTA. Travels, translated by Defrémery and Sanguinetti. Paris, 1853.

(Batuta passed through Persia and Beyond the River, at the time of Timur's birth.)

IBN KHALDOUN. By Baron de Slane. Journal Asiatique, IV Serie, III.

(An account of the meeting at Damascus between Timur and this celebrated historian of Egypt.)

KHWAND AMIR. *Histoire des khans moguls de la Transoxiana.* Defrémery. Paris, 1853.

MEYNARD, BARBIER DE, *Extraits de la Chronique Persane D'Herat*. Journal Asiatique, V Serie, XVII. (The chronicle of the Maliks of Herat.)

MIR AL CHIR NEVAII. *Extraits et traduction.* Journal Asiatique, V Serie, VII.

IV

GENERAL HISTORIES

BOUVAT, LUCIEN. *L'Empire Mongol* (2 ème phase).
Paris, 1927.
(A résumé of the Mongol empire after Genghis
Khan.)

CAHUN, LÉON. *Introduction a l'histoire de l'Asie:
Turcs et Mongols, des origines à 1405.* Paris,
1896.
(The chapter devoted to Timur is marred by harping
upon the Turks. The viewpoint of a brilliant scholar.)

DE GUIGNES. *Histoire générale des Huns des Turcs
des Mogols.* Paris, 1756.
(An exhaustive work in its day.)

FERISHTA. A History of the Rise of the Mahomme-
dan Power in India till the year 1612 A.D.
Translated by J. Briggs. Calcutta, 1910.
(A full account of the dynasties in India.)

GIBBONS, HERBERT ADAMS. The Foundation of the
Ottoman Empire. New York, 1916.
(A good modern account of the Othmans and Baya-
zid.)

HAMMER-PURGSTALL, J. VON. *Geschichte des Osman-
ischen Reiches.* Vienna, 1835.
Geschichte der Goldenen Horde. Buda, 1840.
(Important works on the Turks and the Khans of
the Golden Horde based largely on the Othman and
Byzantine chronicles.)

318

HOWORTH, SIR HENRY. History of the Mongols. London, 1876-88.

(A full account of the Khans of the Golden Horde in Vol. II, and of the Muzaffars and Sultan Ahmed in Vol. III.)

LANE-POOLE, STANLEY. The Mohammedan Dynasties. London, 1894.

(Genealogical tables, following Howorth largely where the Tatars are concerned.)

LEVCHINE, ALEXIS DE. *Description des Hordes et des Steppes des Kirghiz-Kazaks.* Traduite du russe par M. Ferry de Pigny. Paris, 1841.

MAKRISI. *Histoire des Sultans Mamlouks de l'Egypte.* Translated by M. Quatremère. Paris, 1837.

MALCOLM, SIR JOHN. History of Persia. London, 1829.

(One of the best appreciations of Timur's character.)

MUIR, SIR WILLIAM. The Caliphate: Its Rise, Decline and Fall. London, 1892.

(The Arab powers before Timur's day.)

PRICE. Chronological Retrospect. London, 1811-1821.

(Vol. III, Part I gives an abstract of Timur's campaigns.)

RAMBAUD, ALFRED. *Histoire de la Russie.* Paris, 1914.

(Excellent in its account of the relations of the grand princes with Lithuania and Poland.)

SKRINE, and DENNISON ROSS. The Heart of Asia, a History of Russian Turkestan and the Central Asian Khanates from the earliest times. London, 1899.

(A good summary of the political changes in Central Asia.)

SYKES, LIEUT. COL. P. M. A History of Persia. London, 1915.

(A good modern sketch of Timur,[1] his military feats, and an appreciation of the architecture of his day.)

VAMBÉRY, ARMINIUS. History of Bokhara, from the earliest period down to the present. London, 1873.

(The two chapters devoted to Amir Timur are uneven—careless and yet colored with real understanding.)

WEIL, GUSTAV. *Geschichte der chalifen.* Mannheim. 1846-1862.

WOLFF. *Geschichte der Mongolen.* Breslau, 1872.

1 The histories of this group have very little to say about Timur. Only Malcolm and Vambéry discuss him with some detail,

V

SAMARKAND AND ARCHEOLOGY

BLANC, E. *Antiquités de Samarkande. Revue des Deux Mondes,* 1893.

Mausolée de Tamerlan a Samarkande. Académie des Inscriptions et Belles-Lettres, 1896, pp. 272-303.

CRESSWELL, K. A. C. The History and Evolution of the Dome in Persia. Journal R. A. S., 1914.

CROZIER. *Les Monuments du Samarkande de l'époque des Timourides.* Paris, 1891.

CURTIS, WILLIAM ELEROY. Turkestan: "The Heart of Asia." New York, 1911.

KHANIKOFF, N. DE. *Samarkand. Bull. de la Soc. de Geog.* 1896, V Série, T. XVII.

LECLERQ, JULES. *Les Monuments de Samarcande. Soc. Roy. Belge de Geog. Bull.* XIII, 1890, VI, pp. 613-32.

LE STRANGE, GUY. The Lands of the Eastern Caliphate—Mesopotamia and Central Asia from the Moslem Conquest to the Time of Timur. Cambridge, 1905.

(An exceedingly valuable work, giving a description of the cities, roads and trade of all but the northern portion of Timur's empire. Taken from Asiatic sources, Batuta, Mustawfi, Abul Fida, etc.)

MORDOWTZEFF, D. In the capital of Tamerlan. Picturesque Russia, 1901, I.[1] (In Russian.)

---

[1] The author is fortunate in having entrusted to him some of the MS. notes of Daniel Mordowtzeff, unpublished as yet.

RADLOFF, W. W. Ancient architectural remains in Samarkand. Mem. I. R. G. S. 1880 VI. (In Russian.)

SCHUYLER, EUGENE. Turkistan, Notes of a Journey in Russian Turkistan, Khokand, Bukhara and Kuldja. New York, 1876.

    (In addition to the description of the ruins, Prof. Schuyler launches upon a lively criticism of Vambéry's history.)

VI

MISCELLANEOUS

BEAZLEY, CHARLES RAYMOND. The Dawn of Modern
Geography. London, 1897-1906.
(Contains notices of the fourteenth and fifteenth
century travelers into Asia, and a slight account of the
cities.)

BELL, M. S. The Great Central Asian Trade Route
from Peking to Kashgar. Proc. R. G. S. 1890.

BLOCHET, E. *Introduction à l'histoire des Mongols
de Fadl Allah Rashid ed-Din*. Leyden, 1910.
(Details of the correspondence between Timur and
the Ming dynasty.)

BRETSCHNEIDER, E. Notes on the medieval geography
and history of Central and Western Asia. Journal
of the North China Branch R. A. S.

BROWNE, EDWARD G. A History of Persian Literature under Tartar Dominion (A.D. 1265-1502).
Cambridge, 1920.
(An exceedingly valuable work, giving the contrast
between the Persians and the Tatars. A brief discussion of Timur.)

CAHUN, LÉON. *Formation territoriale de l'Asie.
Timur et le Second Empire Mongol*. (*L'Histoire
Générale*—E. Lavisse and A. Rambaud.)

CZAPLICKA, M. A. The Turks in Central Asia. Oxford, 1918.
(A very full bibliography.)

DUBEUX, LOUIS. *Tartarie*. Paris, 1840.

ENCYCLOPÆDIA BRITANNICA, eleventh edition. (Ar-

ticles on Mongols, Golden Horde, Turks, Samarkand, Henry IV of England, Bagdad, Moscow.)

HELLWALD, FREDERICK VON. The Russians in Central Asia. A critical examination down to the
present time of the geography and history of Central Asia. (Translated by Theodore Wirgman.)
London, 1874.

HOLDEN, EDWARD S. The Mogul Emperors of Hin-
dustan. New York, 1895.

MANOUCHI. The History of Tamerlane the Great,
Emperor of the Mogols and Tartars. With an
Account of his Court. London, 1722.
(Of little value.)

MARGAT. *Histoire de Tamerlan, Empereur des Mo-
gols et Conquérant de L'Asie.* Paris, 1739.
(A well meant attempt to combine the works of
Arabshah and Sherif ad-Din.)

NÈVE, FELIX. *Exposé des guerres de Tamerlan et de
Schah-Rokh dans l'Asie centrale.* Bruxelles,
1860.
(Important in that it is based on Thomas of Mez-
doph.)

POPOWSKI. The Rival Powers in Central Asia. London, 1893.

RICKMERS, W. RICKMER. The Duab of Turkestan.
Cambridge, 1913.
(The physiography of Timur's country.)

STEIN, SIR MARCUS. Serindia. Oxford, 1921.
(Archeology of Central Asia and Western China.)

YULE, SIR HENRY. Cathay and the Way Thither.
Hakluyt Soc. 2nd Series, Nos. 33, 37, 38, 41.
(Important discussion of early travelers, and routes.)

ZIMINE, L. Details of the death of Timur. (Proto-
cols and Communications of the Archeological Society of Turkestan, VIII year.)

(Special bibliographies: The Persian sources are discussed in Bouvat. The early history of the Turks and Tatars, and the archeology of Samarkand, in Czaplicka. The Othman campaign and the situation in Europe, in Gibbons. For maps, Le Strange is most valuable. Howorth, Vol. I contains a general map of the period before Timur. Mirza Haidar an excellent map of Central Asia at that time.)

VII

PICTORIAL SOURCES

BLOCHET, E. *Peintures de manuscrits arabes, persans et turcs de la Bibliothèque Nationale.* Paris.

(A collection rich in sidelights on medieval customs in Persia and Turkey.)

MARTIN, F. R. Painting and Painters of Persia, India and Turkey. London, 1912.

(The age of Timur and his successors is portrayed in its plates which reproduce miniatures by the Persian and Indian masters.)

SCHULZ, PH. WALTER. *Die Persische-islamische Miniaturmalerei.* Leipzig, 1914.

(A survey of the costume and manners of the times more extensive, if possible, than Martin's monumental work.)

SYKES, LIEUT. COL. P. M. A History of Persia. London, 1915.

(Contains reproductions of Verestchagin's paintings of Timur's tomb, exterior and interior, and of views of Samarkand.)

WETZEL, H. E. Persian and Indian Paintings in the Museum of Fine Arts, Boston. "Art in America," Vol. 3. New York, 1915.

(Interesting comment on Mongolian and early Persian art.)

Index

A

Abbas, Shah, 257
Abdullah, 81
Abul Ghazi Bahadur Khan, 282, note; 285; 289, note
Acre (see Akka)
Adrianople, 140
Afghanistan, 59
Agincourt, 301
Ahmed the Jalair, Sultan of Bagdad, 150, 177 et seq., 197, 209, 210, 214, 218, 257
  captured, 239
  fear of Tamerlane, 182-183
  flight, 179 et seq.
  in Cairo, 180-181
  reinstalled in Bagdad, 181 et seq.
Aintab, 212
Ak Boga, 242, 277
  at White Castle, 173
  bravery, 169-170
  rewarded, 174
Akka, 214
Ak Sarai, 105, 146
Alans, 115
Al Burz, 143
Aleppo, 212, 214
Alexander, 105, 159, 258
  war genius, 275 et seq.
Ali Bahatur, Shaikh, 94, 95, 99, 102, 135, 146, 152, 276
  and Khitai Bahatur, 96-97
Ali Beg, 56
Ali of Zazd (see Sherif ad-Din)
Aljai Khatun Agha (first wife of Tamerlane), 36, 49, 50, 53, 59, 61, 62, 68, 105, 109, 192
  appearance, 37

Aljai Khatun Agha (Cont.)
  character, 54
  death, 73
  imprisoned, 56
  marriage, 37 et seq.
  Tamerlane's love for, 39, 57
Almalyk, 67, 94, 113, 120, 145, 163
  Christian mission, 112
Aly Bey, 124
Amasia, 279, note
Amu River, 20, 41, 50, 63, 66, 80, 81, 98, 102, 164
Anatolia, 228
Ancient Armour, John Hewitt, 266
Ancient History of China, The, Friedrich Hirth, 282, note
Angelina (daughter of John of Hungary), 240
Angora, 228, 229, 230
  accounts of battle, 267 et seq.
  conquered, 238
Arabs, 160, 263
  admired by Barlas Clan, 25
Arabshah, Ibn, 260; 271, note; 302
  description of Tamerlane, 168-169
  on Tamerlane's character, 303
Aral Sea, 51, 76, 98, 108, 145
Araxes River, 219
Arctic Ocean, 131
Armenia, 293
Armenians, 113
Armor, 25
Army, importance, 165
Artois, house of, 221
Asia, characteristics of people, 158-159

THE ● END